WITHDRAWN

Poverty

and

Inequality

in

Latin America

Poverty

and

Inequality

in

Latin America

*The Impact of Adjustment
and Recovery in the 1980s*

Samuel A. Morley

The Johns Hopkins University Press

Baltimore and London

© 1995 The Johns Hopkins University Press
All rights reserved. Published 1995
Printed in the United States of America on acid-free paper
04 03 02 01 00 99 98 97 96 95   5 4 3 2 1

The Johns Hopkins University Press
2715 North Charles Street
Baltimore, Maryland 21218-4319
The Johns Hopkins Press Ltd., London

Library of Congress Cataloging-in-Publication Data will be found at the end of this book.
A catalog record for this book is available from the British Library.

ISBN 0-8018-5064-9

Contents

Preface

Even before the severe adjustments of the 1980s, Latin America had the most inequitable income distribution and the highest level of poverty relative to its income of any area in the world. The questions that I wanted to address in this study were: What would the 1980s adjustment mean for the poor? or, Who would bear the cost of the adjustment? For the poor in Latin America the key facts were that unskilled workers had almost no job security, social safety nets were virtually nonexistent, and many countries had authoritarian regimes unlikely to be sensitive to worker pressure for higher wages. At the outset, adjustment meant a contraction in the economy to correct the balance of payments deficit. That was bound to hurt the poor. But to make matters worse, at least in the short run, adjustment over the decade grew to include downsizing the government and increased reliance on price signals and the market. That meant selling off overstaffed state enterprises, raising energy and transport prices to market levels, and reducing other subsidies that favored the poor. All of this was bound to exacerbate the impact of the adjustment on the poor.

In many ways the results were every bit as bad as pessimists had feared. Output per capita fell by over 10 percent, the real value of the minimum wage fell by over 25 percent, and the numbers of poor people rose by almost 50 percent. But what is surprising is that out of this convulsive decade emerged a fairly widespread consensus on a growth strategy for the future and a way of dealing with the poverty question. The growth strategy relies on the private sector more than the government, on exports more that import substitution, on foreign capital to augment national saving and entrepreneurship, on social investments in education and health rather than antipoverty welfare or subsidy programs, and on democracy rather than authoritarianism. Most of the countries in the region have implemented a significant part of this general program.

Now, as a recovery gets under way, what should we expect to happen to poverty and the distribution of income if the Latin nations stick to this broad growth strategy? This is a crucial question, for in a very real sense the whole model of capitalist development in an open democratic political regime is on trial in Latin America. In the long run, can private enterprise and the market deliver enough benefits to the general public and to the poor to justify the sacrifices that were made to put it in place? Do the benefits come fast enough to maintain the political support for the tough measures that were taken? Are there ways that the model can or should be modified to make growth more beneficial to the poor?

To answer these questions one needs to know why there is so much poverty in the first place. My hypothesis is that most poverty results from an excess supply of unskilled labor forced to work at a wage too low to support a family at an income above the poverty line. Since no government is able to guarantee both a high minimum wage and full employment, the labor market clears at a very low wage for the unskilled. In this view, Latin America has a lot of poverty, mainly because it has an oversupply of unskilled and undereducated labor. There are three possible solutions for this sort of poverty: rapid growth, education, and welfare. The first increases the demand for unskilled labor. The second reduces the supply of unskilled labor. Either sooner or later will raise the wage. The third simply transfers money from the government to augment the market wage. That will eliminate poverty temporarily for as long as the country can afford to continue the transfers.

The general consensus is that temporary poverty alleviation through income transfers or subsidies is not a viable long-run strategy for poverty reduction, because most countries are not wealthy enough to afford it. Instead they have to rely primarily on a macroeconomic strategy that produces steady sustainable growth complemented by a major effort to improve the level and quality of human capital. It should be possible to do more, but these two things should come first. Among the other things that can and that should be done to make growth more beneficial to the poor is to make as much of that growth as possible come out of sectors and regions where production is labor intensive or which employ a relatively high proportion of the poor.

There is some reason for optimism that such a strategy will work. By 1989, if not before, many countries in the region completed their balance of payments adjustment and began a fairly vigorous recovery. Wherever that has happened there has been a significant decline in poverty. Growth increased the demand for labor and permitted a significant increase in the income of the unskilled. But as recent events in Mexico and Argentina have shown, this recovery is fragile. Many countries like Mexico and Bolivia never reached a satisfactory rate of growth despite their reforms. Others like Venezuela, Paraguay, and Uruguay are again mired in recession after a short burst of growth in the early 1990s.

In the long run the challenge for the region is going to be to find a strategy that will generate sufficient employment for the new and more skilled entrants coming into the labor force, along with the foreign exchange necessary to produce an adequate growth rate. Bloated government employment and high protection of the internal market are strategies that have failed in the past. In the future, countries are going to have to concentrate on expanding the production of competitive traded goods. At the same time they will need to develop innovative strategies to improve and increase education and to incorporate in some way those left behind by the macroeconomic growth strategy. How easy all this will be for each country is going to depend on its natural resource base, the policy of its government, the skill level of its labor force, and the patience of its electorate.

Many people in the academic world, the region, and in Washington helped make this study possible. But I would particularly like to thank Jere Behrman, Al Berry, Eliana Cardoso, Al Fishlow, Catherine Gwin, Emmanuel Jimenez, Nora Lustig, Ricardo Moran, Martin Ravallion, and George Psacharopoulos for their suggestions on previous drafts of this paper. I owe a special debt to Carola Alvarez Foxley, Haeduck Lee, George Psacharopoulos, and Bill Wood for the work they did in assembling and analyzing the basic household surveys on which much of this study is based. At the Inter-American Development Bank I would especially like to thank Nohra Rey de Marulanda and Louis Emmerij—Nohra for the encouragement and facilities she gave me during the year I spent as a visiting fellow in her department, and Louis for giving me the time and freedom to finish the manuscript. Needless to say the views expressed here do not necessarily represent those of the Inter-American Development Bank. What I have said in the pages that follow and any errors that remain are my own responsibility. Note that portions of this work draw from my earlier study, *Poverty and Inequality in Latin America: Past Evidence, Future Prospects,* published by the Overseas Development Council in 1994.

Poverty

and

Inequality

in

Latin America

Introduction

For all Latin American countries, the 1980s were a period of unprecedented adjustment. They came into the decade after a long period of easy credit, which enabled most of them to roll up large external debts and big current account deficits. Then, in August 1982, Mexico announced a moratorium on debt service. Suddenly, capital inflows stopped, and these highly indebted countries were forced to stop new borrowing and make a start on debt repayment. Seldom have a group of countries made so wrenching a change as these did. In 1980 the average trade deficit was around 4 percent of gross domestic product (GDP). Nine years later, despite severe trade shocks in most countries, the average deficit had been turned into a 4.6 percent surplus. Thus, aggregate demand was reduced by almost 10 percent relative to aggregate supply, an impressive adjustment by any standard.

But the cost of this adjustment was high. Most countries faithfully applied the orthodox medicine of real devaluation and fiscal deficit reduction. There was a contractionary recession in every country. The fortunate cases were those where the adjustment was successfully completed in a relatively short period, allowing a resumption of growth after 1985. For the region as a whole, per capita income fell by 11 percent over the decade. Only two of the continent's twenty countries (Chile and Colombia) had a higher per capita income in 1990 than they had in 1980. Nothing like this lengthy and almost universal decline in living standards had ever been observed before in Latin America.

Conditions varied across countries, but on average by 1982, when the debt crisis started in earnest, the total outstanding debt had risen to 54 percent of GDP and 384 percent of exports (Kuczynski, 1988, p. 33). Voluntary new lending by multinational banks ceased. That meant that the heavily indebted countries were forced not only to eliminate their trade deficits but also to turn them into large surpluses to sustain interest and amortization payments on the debts they had contracted—in most cases, unwisely. They had to find a way to reduce domestic consumption and capital formation by 5–10 percent of GDP. At the same time, they had to change the structure of the economy so that it would produce more goods to sell, either abroad, to pay the interest bills that had come due, or to their own citizens, in place of goods formerly imported.

To make this change, the orthodox remedy called for two basic policy interventions, both of which are painful and difficult. First, the government had to reduce domestic demand so as to eliminate the excess of absorption over production. That implied reducing government spending, raising taxes, and squeezing credit, none of which could be expected to be any easier politically in Latin America than anywhere else. Second, it had to devalue the exchange rate to make the production of tradable goods (exports or import substitutes) more profitable. Long experience with real devaluation elsewhere has shown that it is usually accompanied by rising inflation rates and falling real wages.

On the positive side, theory tells us that, because real devaluation increases the profitability of tradable goods, it should lead to an expansion of production, which should help offset the effects of fiscal and monetary contraction on aggregate demand. This is exactly what happened in Southeast Asia during the 1980s, when it faced a debt crisis similar in size to Latin America's. But changing the structure of the economy so that it could produce more traded goods turned out to be particularly difficult for most Latin American countries. In some cases, the difficulty lay in the type of goods they exported. For oil producers like Mexico and Venezuela, sales were controlled by quota rather than price. For natural resource exporters like Guatemala and Honduras, falling external demand appears to have offset whatever advantage their exporters could have gained from real devaluation. In other cases, domestic manufacturing was too overprotected to be competitive, even with a sharp rise in the real exchange rate.

As a result, the reduction in aggregate demand needed to eliminate the trade deficit caused a prolonged recession in most countries. Ideally, a boom in the production of exports and import substitutes could have offset this contraction in domestic demand, but that did not happen in most countries. Instead, the adjustment to eliminate balance of payments deficits brought recession, falling real wages, and rising unemployment.

While the benefits of the orthodox stabilization program may have been clear to economists, the sacrifices they entailed could have been expected to cause severe political difficulties for any sitting government. Governments that ask such sacrifices of their citizens often lose their mandates. In 1980 the bulk of the countries in Latin America were under military regimes (Brazil, Chile, Argentina, Uruguay, Paraguay, Guatemala, Panama, and Honduras). Most observers expected such regimes to have an easier time making hard economic choices and extracting sacrifices from their citizens than the more representative governments of places like Costa Rica, Venezuela, Colombia, or Mexico. That expectation turned out to be completely wrong; by 1990 all the military regimes were gone, swept away by the desires of people for more open government. What followed was not necessarily fully functioning democracies, and in several cases, such as Peru, there was a reversion to a more autocratic regime. Nonetheless, what the Latin American experience teaches is that the legitimacy conferred on an elected government by its method of selection gives it a basis to demand sacrifice, in contrast to a military regime, whose only legitimacy is its supposed ability to make incomes grow. When these latter governments were unable to do that, they lost whatever implicit support they had, relinquishing power virtually without a shot being fired.

As to poverty and inequality, the main themes of this study, Latin America has always had a high level of both relative to its income. The typical Latin American growth strategy did nothing to alter this situation. In the big economies like Brazil, Mexico, and Argentina, growth was led by modern, high-wage, high-profit sectors. Since the educational level of the average Latin American worker was low, the mass of labor was poorly positioned to take advantage of such a growth strategy. As a result, income inequality widened as these economies grew. Some benefits did trickle down to the poor, but it took very high rates of growth to make that happen, rates that were impossible to maintain after 1980.

In 1969 a World Bank study estimated that 11 percent of the population of Latin America was below the poverty line of $50 per year of income

($191 in 1992 dollars)—about the same degree of poverty as in Taiwan, a country that then had only three-fifths the average income of Latin America (Chenery et al., 1974, p. 12). Rapid growth during the 1970s did not change the relative situation. In 1985 a new study by the World Bank, using a poverty line of $375 per year (equivalent to $490 in 1992 dollars), estimated that 19 percent of the Latin population was living in poverty (World Bank, 1990b, p. 29).[1] That was about the same level as in China, whose average income was less than one-fifth that in Latin America. The incidence of poverty was higher in Latin America than in Indonesia, even though income was four times higher in Latin America as in Indonesia.

Thus, as the eighties began, Latin America had a large burden of foreign debt, a serious imbalance between domestic demand and production, a relatively small and unresponsive traded goods sector, and a very large number of poor people relative to the average level of per capital income. This book is the story of what happened during the decade. Recently available household surveys establish what happened to poverty and inequality and isolate the main factors that determine changes in poverty. The experiences of several countries are then compared to see why the adjustment process was more benign in some than in others and why some countries were better able to protect their poor than others. The question is then asked, was that due to differences in policy, in initial conditions, or in economic structure? That is, did some countries do better because of the policies they followed, because their initial debt levels were lower, or because of the products they produced?

Chapter 1 presents an overview of trends in macroeconomic variables in the main countries. Chapter 2 shows changes in poverty level and distribution of income and relates this to changes in such nonincome social indicators as education and infant mortality. Despite the downturn in income during the 1980s, most countries continued to make progress in the social areas of education and health. Chapter 3 documents this fact and describes the emergency employment programs that were enacted to provide jobs and maintain the family incomes of the unemployed poor.

The following two chapters are case studies of four countries, two (Argentina and Venezuela) in which poverty increased dramatically and two (Colombia and Costa Rica) in which it declined. This comparison helps shed light on the fundamental question of why the experiences of these four countries are so different, even though they all went through a fairly significant balance of payments adjustment. Those characteristics of economic structure, initial conditions, and government policy that appear to be related to differences in adjustment are highlighted.

In chapter 6 a broader sample of time-series evidence is used to investigate the link between macroconditions, economic structure, and poverty. Observations made over the decade in a large number of countries show convincingly how important level of economic activity is: poverty and inequality are strongly procyclical, rising in recessions and falling during recoveries. Other variables more directly tied to government policy, such as minimum wage and inflation rate, are important too, but none has such a clear and pronounced effect on poverty as economic growth.

The adjustments of the 1980s were of two kinds and happened in two stages. The first adjustment was an emergency effort to resolve the balance of payments crisis of 1982 through massive devaluations and domestic recession. The second stage was a structural reform designed to change the development paradigm of the region. The main reform elements were the streamlining and downsizing of the state, the privatization of government enterprise, the elimination of price controls and government subsidies, and trade liberalization through the reduction of tariff and nontariff protection of domestic industry.[2] These reforms came in the second half of the decade in most countries and are still in the process of being implemented. In chapter 7 the story is carried forward into the 1990s, to look both at the effects of recovery in those countries where data is available and at the effects of second-stage structural reforms in those countries that first adopted them.

The fact that poverty is so strongly linked with growth means that the poor paid a high price for the balance of payments adjustment. This adjustment cost a whole decade of growth—indeed, it set average per capita income back to the level of 1970. This does not mean that the poor could have escaped the effects of overborrowing, nor can one say what would have happened to the poor had there not been an adjustment. But the insistence by the commercial banks and their backers that the interest be fully paid was a major reason for the severity and length of the adjustment.

Ironically, out of this externally imposed necessity, these countries were forced to change their development paradigm. They had to accept their dependence on the international economy and to learn that, for better or worse, they were embedded in a worldwide trading and financial system, from whose rigid rules there was no easy escape. They also learned to view skeptically both government and state enterprises as agents for development. They came to accept that government enterprises were more likely to be corrupt and inefficient and to run at a deficit than they were to make a positive contribution to the economy. Both their own experience and international pressure forced countries to embark on new growth strategies based on exports and the private sector.

Most Latin American countries learned their lessons well and began to build a basis for growth and development. Whether that growth will be sustainable, whether it will be more equitable than in the past, and whether it will compensate the poor for the losses they suffered in the 1980s are questions that cannot be answered yet.

Chapter One

A Comparison of Macroeconomic Performance and Policy

The 1980s were a development disaster for Latin America. No country escaped the wave of retrenchment that swept over the continent. Overall GDP per capita fell by 10 percent. Only Chile and Colombia managed to increase per capita income, and that just barely.

One can distinguish several distinct stages in the reaction to the crisis. At first, governments were primarily concerned with the balance of payments deficit, which most of them addressed by large real devaluations, contractions in the government deficit—mainly through reduced government investment—and a contractionary monetary policy. This first stage of the adjustment process resulted in severe recessions in the early to middle 1980s and by 1994 had been pretty much completed.

In the second stage of the adjustment, the focus shifted from emergency balance of payments measures to broader structural reforms. These reforms came in the second half of the decade in most countries and by 1994 were still being implemented. The details of what happened to production in the fifteen largest economies in the region are shown in table 1-1. El Salvador and Nicaragua are excluded because their civil wars so distorted the economic pictures in those two countries. Likewise, the Caribbean islands are excluded because economic conditions in these countries were so different from those in the continental countries and because very little information was available on their poverty level and income distribution.

Table 1-1. Gross Domestic Product per Capita, Fifteen Latin American Countries, 1980–1993 (1988 U.S. dollars)

Country	1980	1981	1982	1983	1984	1985	1986	1987	1988	1989	1990	1991	1992	1993
Argentina	4,709	4,369	4,170	4,267	4,286	3,947	4,181	4,231	4,100	3,794	3,755	4,046	4,347	4,552
Bolivia	1,199	1,182	1,105	1,031	1,001	969	922	924	928	934	947	974	976	982
Brazil	2,385	2,225	2,185	2,058	2,118	2,235	2,362	2,394	2,346	2,377	2,233	2,215	2,158	2,229
Chile	2,339	2,447	2,105	2,014	2,095	2,104	2,178	2,270	2,395	2,589	2,614	2,726	2,940	3,056
Colombia	1,253	1,253	1,240	1,236	1,256	1,275	1,332	1,376	1,410	1,430	1,457	1,459	1,486	1,537
Costa Rica	1,789	1,698	1,530	1,525	1,598	1,565	1,603	1,630	1,634	1,675	1,688	1,682	1,763	1,822
Ecuador	1,403	1,421	1,401	1,308	1,316	1,334	1,336	1,253	1,320	1,293	1,298	1,328	1,346	1,337
Guatemala	1,109	1,086	1,018	965	942	910	886	891	900	909	910	916	933	943
Honduras	861	855	811	780	786	797	780	802	816	822	798	798	818	825
Mexico	2,421	2,568	2,480	2,308	2,336	2,347	2,199	2,190	2,172	2,203	2,256	2,291	2,307	2,262
Panama	2,314	2,357	2,421	2,371	2,320	2,378	2,411	2,415	1,998	1,953	2,008	2,145	2,283	2,381
Paraguay	1,560	1,641	1,572	1,476	1,476	1,489	1,441	1,461	1,511	1,554	1,557	1,549	1,532	1,546
Peru	1,877	1,925	1,878	1,584	1,617	1,608	1,752	1,890	1,685	1,436	1,339	1,349	1,287	1,350
Uruguay	2,864	2,899	2,606	2,434	2,385	2,406	2,596	2,787	2,768	2,789	2,791	2,860	3,059	3,078
Venezuela	4,048	3,915	3,840	3,548	3,373	3,357	3,472	3,540	3,670	3,275	3,400	3,655	3,850	3,715

Source: IADB, Economic and Social Data Base.

It is clear from table 1.1 that the fall in income over the decade was not constant and that there was a good deal of variation in the experience of the various countries. The list below shows the years of recession (defined as falling per capita GDP) for the countries in table 1-1:

- —Argentina: 1981–82, 1985, 1988–89
- —Bolivia: 1980–86
- —Brazil: 1981–83, 1987–89
- —Chile: 1973–75, 1982–83
- —Colombia: 1981–83
- —Costa Rica: 1980–83
- —Ecuador: 1982–83, 1987–89
- —Guatemala: 1981–86
- —Honduras: 1980–86
- —Mexico: 1982–83, 1986–88
- —Panama: 1983–84, 1988–89
- —Paraguay: 1982–86
- —Peru: 1982–83, 1985, 1988–89
- —Uruguay: 1982–84
- —Venezuela: 1981–85, 1989

Every country in the sample, including those that had positive growth during the eighties, had a period of contraction in the beginning of the decade, the period when they were first hit by the crisis. Most were heavily indebted, many faced a sharp decline in their terms of trade, and all were confronted by an almost complete halt in capital inflows. Since most were running trade deficits financed by foreign capital when the crisis began, they were very suddenly confronted with the necessity of eliminating those deficits. Those with heavy foreign debt obligations had the additional burden of finding the resources to service their debts.

In the short run, these factors forced every economy into recession. The fortunate were Chile, Colombia, Costa Rica, and Uruguay, where the contraction was short. The unfortunate were Guatemala, where the adjustment lasted most of the decade; and Argentina, Brazil, and Venezuela, where the adjustment process was interrupted by a short-term recovery before it achieved the necessary contraction in fiscal and balance of payments deficits—resulting in two recessions over the decade. These countries could not sustain their recoveries in the face of continuing deficits particularly in government accounts. Ranked by growth over the decade, Colombia, Chile, Paraguay, Uruguay, Brazil, and Costa Rica lead the list; those with slowest growth were Peru, Argentina, Bolivia, Venezuela, and Guatemala. Except for Brazil, all of the first group had relatively short adjustments, whereas all of the second group suffered through either long and continuous adjustments or stop-and-go cycles.

WHY GROWTH RATES DIFFERED

Many factors explain this difference in performance. The countries differed in amount of debt they carried into the adjustment. Movements in the terms of trade, which measure the price of exports relative to the price of imports, also varied between countries, with the oil exporters (Venezuela, Mexico, and Ecuador) doing the poorest. Also, some countries specialized in exports for which demand was stagnant, which could have made it difficult to generate foreign exchange to meet debt payments. And of course, some countries may have used a more successful adjustment strategy than others. The indicators in table 1-2 show these factors.

If one compares countries by their interest burden and subsequent growth performance, it seems fairly clear that their economic performance was not closely related to the burden they started with. One expects a negative relation between debt burden and subsequent growth rate, and that is borne out for Colombia, Argentina, Bolivia, and Mexico. But it leaves unexplained many other cases. How for example did Chile, Brazil, and Costa Rica do so well in spite of their high debt burdens? And why did Venezuela and Guatemala do so poorly in spite of their relatively small debt?

One possible answer is terms of trade. Clearly, the oil economies—Mexico, Ecuador, and Venezuela—suffered a tremendous decline. That helps to explain the poor growth performance of Venezuela and makes one appreciate how well Mexico and Ecuador did to limit the decline in their per capita incomes to 10 percent over the decade, despite their heavy debt burdens and falling oil prices. Terms of trade may also have had something to do with the relative growth records of Argentina, Uruguay, and Paraguay, since the latter two rose while the former fell quite sharply. But it makes one wonder even more about Peru and Panama, both of which had severe collapses despite only average interest burdens and a rise in their terms of trade; the problems in these two countries must have resulted from internal conditions rather than external conditions. Nor

Table 1-2.   Macroeconomic Indicators, Fifteen Latin American Countries, 1980s

Country	1980 Ratio of Interest to Exports	1989 Terms of Trade (1980 = 100)	1989 Exports[1] (1980 = 100)	1989 GDP[2] per Capita (1980 = 100)	Trade Deficit as Percent of GDP (constant US$)	
					1980	1989
Argentina	.22	80	119	74	−6.9	+10.9
Bolivia	.25	93	84	83	+5.4	+3.1
Brazil	.34	91	172	102	−2.3	+7.3
Chile	.19	100	161	110	−6.7	+2.0
Colombia	.12	89	138	109	−3.2	+3.3
Costa Rica	.18	91	154	94	−6.4	+4.5
Ecuador	.18	63	100	94	−10.1	+4.5
Guatemala	.05	85	82	82	−0.3	−2.7
Honduras	.11	91	116	90	−3.1	+0.9
Mexico	.30	54	158	90	−2.3	+7.7
Panama	.15	135	108	83	−3.3[3]	+7.6
Paraguay	.13	134	258	100	−3.7	−4.0
Peru	.18	106	98	77	−4.0[4]	+9.3
Uruguay	.11	114	131	95	−6.1	+2.2
Venezuela	.08	62	70	78	−8.2	+13.0

Source: IADB, Economic and Social Progress Report 1991; ECLAC, various years, Statistical Yearbook.
Note: Since the latest household survey data for most countries are from 1989, 1989 data relative to 1980 data are shown. The patterns for the entire decade would not differ significantly.
[1] Exports of goods and nonfactor services are in current dollars.
[2] GDP is in 1988 dollars. An index in constant local currency would not change the rankings.
[3] In current dollars.
[4] 1981.

does the terms of trade factor really explain why Guatemala, Honduras, and Bolivia were unable to grow.

A variable that does seem closely linked with income growth is the export sector; there is a striking positive correlation between the growth rate of exports and per capita income. Of the top seven countries in the income growth group, six also rank high in exports.[1] Of the five countries lowest in income growth, four are lowest in export performance as well.

There are two possible reasons for the positive relation between export and income growth. One, exports supplement internal demand at a time of general contraction; two, foreign exchange production permits a higher level of imports and income. To test these notions, a calculation was made of the growth of import capacity, defined as change in exports plus capital inflows less interest payments. The finding is that this measure is not highly correlated with growth performance. For example, two of the five countries highest in increases in import capacity were Guatemala and Bolivia, yet they had among the worst growth records. Conversely, two fast-growing countries, Colombia and Uruguay, had a very slow growth in import capacity.

Thus, the significance of exports does not primarily lie in the foreign exchange it makes available; rather, it probably stands as a proxy for the ability of a country to make the required structural adjustment in production of traded goods in response to real devaluation and to contraction in domestic demand. Countries that transferred production into traded goods and that were competitive enough to expand exports to replace shrinking domestic demand had relatively short recessions and high growth. Of course, no country's growth record matched that of earlier decades, but the gaps were larger for countries with slow export growth.

When the debt crisis hit Latin America in 1982, most Latin countries were running very large trade deficits, which meant that they were using foreign savings to finance an excess of domestic consumption and investment over domestic production. When capital inflows stopped, those excesses had to be eliminated. Worse, if the countries were to service their debts, their trade deficits had to be turned into surpluses.

In 1980 the average Latin American country was running a trade deficit of 4 percent of GDP. Nine years later, that average had been turned into a 4.6 percent trade surplus, which implies that, on average, domestic demand was reduced by almost 9 percent relative to domestic production. But the reductions must actually have been greater than that, because production itself declined by 10 percent. Most of these repayments were not made willingly; intransigent foreign lenders, particularly banks, forced them to service their loans. Most countries had, at one time or another, to ask for rescheduling or outright debt relief. In most cases, they did not get much relief until the Brady Plan in 1989. Instead, they were forced to generate large trade surpluses, typically produced by recession and a reduction in imports rather than by a large expansion in exports. It is no accident that Argentina, Peru, Venezuela, and Panama were among the countries with the largest shifts in trade balance; these are the countries that were in the deepest recession in 1989.

By definition, if a country is to eliminate a trade deficit, it must reduce either its consumption or its investment. From the growth perspective, it is better if this is done by reducing consumption rather than investment.

Reducing investment as an adjustment strategy makes sense if the need to adjust is for the short run only. If it is not, the lower level of capital formation will reduce long-term growth. Adjustment in Latin America was not a short-run phenomenon, and it should therefore have been accomplished by reducing consumption. However, this was not what Latin America did. With very few exceptions, those countries that reduced their trade deficits did it at the expense of investment rather than consumption. Gross investment as a share of GDP fell during the 1980s in every one of the countries in the sample. For the continent as a whole, the decline in the investment ratio was 7 percentage points, with the largest drops concentrated in the biggest economies. It is easy to understand why this strategy was chosen: investment is import-intensive, so reducing it is a quick and easy way to reduce the import bill. Furthermore, investment does not immediately affect living standards, unlike consumption. The alternatives of cutting government spending or raising taxes to shrink private consumption would both have incurred heavy political costs. Nonetheless, the long-run implications of this strategy are somber: these countries essentially borrowed from the future of their own citizens to repay their external obligations.

Brazil, Mexico, and Colombia, whose foreign debt in the 1970s financed the creation of export capacity, adjusted more easily than those whose debt financed either consumption or capital flight. But in all cases, the general shrinkage of capital formation presaged slower growth, even supposing that the immediate debt crisis was resolved, as it now appears to be in most countries.

REAL WAGES AND THE REAL EXCHANGE RATE

A key feature of any adjustment program to correct a balance of payments deficit is a real devaluation, defined as an increase in the relative price of traded goods. A real devaluation does two things, both of which are crucial to improving the balance of payments. First, it makes the production of tradable goods, that is, exports and import substitutes, more profitable. Second, it pushes consumers to switch purchases to lower-priced, nontraded goods, thus improving the trade balance.

In practice, political pressure may keep a government from enacting real devaluations for a sustained period. For a real devaluation, a government devalues the nominal exchange rate; at the same time, it must reduce aggregate demand, because, if it doesn't, there will be a strong tendency for the prices for home goods to rise enough to completely offset the nominal devaluation. One can imagine how this might happen. The nominal devaluation creates upward pressure on nominal wages because it raises the price of all traded consumer goods. If demand has not been reduced by some contractionary government policy, there will be excess demand in the nontraded goods sector because of shifting by both consumers and producers. This permits sellers of nontraded goods to raise their prices and meet the wage demands of their workers, bringing the real exchange rate back to its initial level. Here, devaluation simply triggers a self-defeating cycle of inflation. This was exactly the sequence that was expected, particularly in countries with a strong labor movement, which could resist downward pressure on real wages.

The tough actions required to produce a real devaluation cannot be expected to have much political support, because they require contraction and pressure on real wages. Governments, particularly those that are democratically elected, might not be expected to maintain that pressure. Such fears turned out to be unfounded. Despite labor pressure, Latin countries, with very few exceptions, pushed through unprecedented cuts in their real minimum wages during the 1980s. Almost all of them had real devaluations as well. Table 1-3 displays the underlying data for each of the fifteen countries: all but four countries (Colombia, Costa Rica, Panama, and Paraguay) cut their real minimum wage, five of them cut it by more than a third. All but two had a real devaluation. If one then asks, Is there any apparent relation between movements in the real minimum wage and the real exchange rate? the answer is no. The typical combination, a rise in the real exchange rate and a fall in the real minimum wage, happened in twelve of the fifteen countries.[2] But it was not universal. All four of the countries with a rising real minimum wage also had a real devaluation.

To see whether using the entire decade might have skewed the interaction between real wages and exchange rates, movements in these two variables were examined for only the period when the country was in its adjustment recession (defined as years when real output was falling). Altogether, there were twenty-one observations because of multiple periods of recession in several countries (see list above); the two-way breakdown is shown in table 1-4.

As before, the typical pattern was falling real wages and rising real exchange rates. There were, however, more cases of real appreciation

Table 1-3. Real Minimum Wages and Real Effective Exchange Rates, Fifteen Latin American Countries, 1981–1989

Country	1981	1982	1983	1984	1985	1986	1987	1988	1989
Argentina									
Minimum wage	98	104	155	168	114	111	121	94	42
Real effective exchange rate	112	122	203	175	194	217	238	261	297
Bolivia									
Minimum wage	76	51	81	75	27	25	29	30	27
Real effective exchange rate	79	73	80	61	36	121	126	133	138
Brazil									
Minimum wage	99	99	88	81	84	82	65	63	69
Real effective exchange rate	115	109	130	135	139	148	148	137	110
Chile									
Minimum wage	99	97	78	67	64	61	58	59	64
Real effective exchange rate	85	94	115	117	145	172	185	198	194
Colombia									
Minimum wage	98	103	108	113	109	114	113	108	110
Real effective exchange rate	93	87	88	96	110	147	165	171	177
Costa Rica									
Minimum wage	90	86	99	104	112	119	118	115	119
Real effective exchange rate	158	138	120	122	124	138	152	166	160
Ecuador									
Minimum wage	86	76	64	63	61	65	62	53	44
Real effective exchange rate	89	91	96	116	112	139	181	241	208
Guatemala									
Minimum wage	121	120	115	111	94	69	61	76	68
Real effective exchange rate	91	88	84	84	115	118	121	131	135

Table 1-3—Continued

Country	1981	1982	1983	1984	1985	1986	1987	1988	1989
Honduras									
Minimum wage	106	106	98	94	91	87	85	81	74
Real effective exchange rate	94	89	86	84	80	84	88	87	81
Mexico									
Minimum wage	100	89	74	68	67	61	56	49	47
Real effective exchange rate	84	115	125	103	99	145	158	130	119
Panama									
Minimum wage	93	89	102	102	101	101	100	99	100
Real effective exchange rate	97	95	93	93	92	101	108	116	121
Paraguay									
Minimum wage	104	102	94	94	99	109	120	134	136
Real effective exchange rate	93	105	113	120	139	138	171	166	217
Peru									
Minimum wage	94	82	89	69	61	62	64	51	25
Real effective exchange rate	87	89	100	103	127	111	98	100	65
Uruguay									
Minimum wage	103	105	90	90	94	91	91	85	79
Real effective exchange rate	89	85	138	144	150	152	156	165	158
Venezuela									
Minimum wage	86	78	74	66	95	91	111	93	77
Real effective exchange rate	89	83	91	107	111	133	186	167	196

Source: Cox Edwards, 1991; IADB, Economic and Social Data Base.

Note: 1980 = 100.

Table 1-4.   Observations of Movements of Real Minimum
Wages and Real Effective Exchange Rates,
Fifteen Latin American Countries, 1980–1989

Real Minimum Wage	Real Effective Exchange Rate		Total
	Depreciates	Appreciates	
Rises	3	3	6
Falls	13	2	15
Total	16	5	21

Source: See table 1-3.

during recession and also more cases in which real wages rose at the same time.

The evidence in table 1-4 suggests that some countries tried to protect real wages during their adjustments, while others did not. But one cannot find much of a correlation between the real minimum wage and either relative growth performance or the real exchange rate. Argentina and Panama defended this wage through most of the period and had low rates of growth. Costa Rica, Colombia, Paraguay, and Brazil (prior to 1987) maintained their minimum real wage and had relatively high rates of growth. Conversely, Chile, Ecuador, and Mexico pushed down their minimum wage and yet grew quite well, the latter two despite a drastic decline in the price of oil. With regard to the real exchange rate, the five countries with the largest real devaluations included both Venezuela and Argentina, two of the slowest growing countries.

Thus from the point of view of economic growth, it is not clear what significance attaches to the trends in real wages or exchange rates. (We look further at the link with poverty in chapter 6.) One thing, however, is clear, and that is that minimum wage rigidity was no barrier against real devaluation. Almost every country had a real devaluation, whether the real minimum wage was rising or falling. Indeed, one could use the Latin experience as a demonstration that real devaluation need not necessarily be accompanied by a reduction in workers' real purchasing power.

As is clear from table 1-3, real wages and real exchange rates were anything but rigid in the 1980s. Thus, it could not be rigidities that made balance of payments adjustments so difficult. All but Peru and Honduras had substantial real devaluations, most by 100 percent or more relative to 1980. In most cases, governments also ignored political pressure and adjusted their minimum wage by far less than the rate of inflation. While

Table 1-5.   Export Growth and Real Exchange Rates, Fifteen
Latin American Countries, 1980–1989

| | Real Effective Exchange Rate | | |
Exports	Depreciates	Appreciates	Total
Rise	10	1	11
Fall	3	1	4
Total	13	2	15

Source: See tables 1-2 and 1-3.
Note: Calculations are point to point. Exports are in constant
dollars.

this may well have had a large impact on the distribution of income, it
does not appear to have had any relation to relative growth performance.

Given that there is not a close relation between economic growth and
the real exchange rate, we might ask about the link between the exchange
rate and exports. Did real devaluations help exports? The data from the
fifteen countries show that the typical pattern (in ten countries) was for
exports to grow and for there to be a real devaluation (see table 1-5).
However, there are exceptions, such as Honduras, where exports rose in
spite of a real appreciation. Also, in three countries in the southwest
quadrant of the table (Guatemala, Bolivia, and Panama), exports fell despite real devaluation.

FISCAL POLICY DURING THE ADJUSTMENT

In 1980, many Latin American countries were running substantial government deficits; in at least five of them, they were greater than 5 percent
of GDP. Much of this deficit spending was financed by foreign borrowing, the external counterpart to current account deficits. When the capital
inflows stopped, a major part of the adjustment problem had to be the
elimination of those deficits. This would serve at least two purposes
simultaneously. First, it would reduce aggregate demand, which, as we
have seen, is a necessary element in making nominal devaluations into
real devaluations. Second, without foreign financing of the government,
eliminating the deficit was the only way to avoid either an inflationary rise
in the money supply or a severe crowding out of private sector credit.[3]

A third, perhaps less obvious, goal served by the elimination of deficits was a reduction in the size and scope of the government itself. Over the decade, a consensus seemed to form in the international development agencies, particularly the World Bank and the International Monetary Fund (IMF) that less government was better government. Shrinking the government became one of the express aims of many structural adjustment programs, not only because the macroeconomic problems caused by deficits were bad but because the government itself came to be regarded as an obstacle to the efficient operation of markets and the economy. The need to reduce the deficit was a handy club with which to beat back the government sector.

Measuring the deficit of a complex government sector is difficult in both accounting and conceptual senses. First, the public sector in Latin America includes a large number of state enterprises, whose profits and losses should be counted. They often do not enter in the national accounts definitions of the government, but since they have to be financed just as any other component of the government, they should be counted. Losses in state enterprises were a major source of rising deficits in several countries. Second, government investment, like any other government expenditure, has to be financed, but it differs from current expenditures in leaving an asset behind. Government borrowing to finance capital formation should be treated—and thought of—differently from borrowing to finance consumption. By the same token, eliminating government deficits by reducing government capital formation is very different from eliminating them by raising taxes or lowering current expenditures.

Another serious question is how to count nominal interest payments in a time of rising inflation. If nominal interest rates move with inflation, and if the government has a large outstanding debt, rising inflation essentially forces it to pay back its loans faster than expected. If it raises taxes by enough to cover the entire nominal interest payment, the real value of its outstanding debt falls by the inflation rate. Effectively, that part of the interest rate corresponding to inflation is an amortization payment. This is not important when the inflation rate is low, but it is when inflation accelerates rapidly, as it did in many Latin American countries in the eighties. Ideally, the government should issue bonds sufficient to keep the real stock of bonds constant and count only its real interest expenditures as part of the government deficit. This rule essentially ties the inflation component of the interest rate to bond financing—based on the rationale that the proportions of the public portfolio will then be unaffected by changes in the inflation rate.

Table 1-6. Fiscal Indicators, Thirteen Latin American Countries, 1980 and 1980s (percent of GDP)

Country	Consumption		Investment		Net Tax Revenue		Primary Deficit		Interest	
	1980	Around 1989	1980	Around 1989	1980	Around 1989	1980	Around 1989	1980	Around 1989
Argentina[1]	13.3	12.8	9.5	6.5	18.7	15.8	-4.1	-3.5	3.4	5.3
Bolivia[2]	16.3	12.8	7.3	6.6	18.4	13.1	-5.2	-6.3	2.6	2.0
Brazil[3]	9.2	12.6	8.8	7.9	18.0	19.4	0.0	-1.1	2.0	6.3
Chile[2]	11.9	7.3	7.3	10.3	25.4	20.2	6.2	2.6	0.8	2.9
Colombia[1]	9.1	9.7	7.1	7.1	15.3	18.6	-0.9	1.8	1.7	3.7
Costa Rica[2]	18.5	14.1	13.0	10.6	28.4	34.3	-3.1	9.6	5.0	6.3
Ecuador[2]	14.0	11.9	15.1	10.5	24.8	21.9	-4.3	-0.5	3.1	3.9
Guatemala[2]	6.4	5.8	5.6	2.1	7.9	8.0	-4.1	0.1	0.6	1.4
Mexico[1]	10.0	8.7	7.9	3.3	14.9	19.6	-3.0	7.6	3.5	13.0
Paraguay[3]	6.3	4.6	5.1	6.7	13.2	11.8	1.8	0.5	-0.5	1.4
Peru[1]	11.7	5.3	7.0	2.7	19.5	4.2	0.8	-3.8	4.7	1.7
Uruguay[2]	12.0	10.2	3.7	3.3	17.5	16.7	1.8	3.2	0.5	2.5
Venezuela[3]	16.2	10.9	16.4	12.1	43.4	21.3	10.8	-1.7	3.5	3.8

Source: Guillermo Perry, unpublished worksheets.

Note: Consumption and investment are from Perry. Net tax revenue is a residual, defined as the primary surplus tax plus the two expenditure items. It therefore includes all tax revenues and profits of state enterprises less all transfers other than interest payments. "Net" means taxes net of the total transfers and profits of state enterprises.

[1] Latest date is 1989.
[2] Latest date is 1987.
[3] Latest date is 1988.

Unfortunately, this is not the way deficits are usually calculated. They typically include all interest payments rather than simply the real component, which biases the apparent deficit upward when inflation accelerates. In the empirical analysis that follows, interest payments are separated to better show what was going on in the rest of the government, undistorted by this particular effect of inflation.

Table 1-6 displays the accounts of the government sector of thirteen principal Latin countries. As is obvious, the 1980s was a period of profound adjustment for the public sector in most countries. The government had been a major benefactor of the borrowing spree of the 1970s; now it was forced to stop borrowing and cut back, partly to meet interest payments and partly because recessions reduced government revenues. The revenue shocks were substantial. In the oil economies, the collapse of oil prices after 1982 drastically affected government income (it was a major factor in the deterioration of Venezuela's fiscal balance). Rising inflation had a dramatic effect on tax revenues in countries such as Peru, where the tax system was not adequately indexed. On the opposite side, real devaluation increased revenue in countries where the government itself was in the export business or got dollar-denominated export taxes.

Later, in most countries, the government made a substantial effort to put its house in order in spite of recession, interest rate shocks, and falling oil prices. Seven of the thirteen countries in the table were running deficits in 1980. Of those seven, six reduced or eliminated their deficits later in the decade. Mexico, Costa Rica, Guatemala, and Ecuador made particularly noteworthy efforts in this regard. Although Venezuela, Argentina, Peru, and Bolivia, in contrast, were clearly unsuccessful, almost everywhere government current expenditures were reduced, sometimes by a very large amount, as in Chile, Costa Rica, Peru, and Venezuela. Another victim was government investment, which fell in every country but Paraguay and Chile.

There was a much wider variation in net tax performance. Six countries increased tax revenues, eight reduced them, four by more than 5 percent of GDP. The reasons for their falling differ widely. In Venezuela the culprit was falling oil tax revenues, which fell by more than 11 percent of GDP, swamping a rise in the revenues from taxes per se. In Peru the Tanzi-Oliveira effect was the main problem.[4] Rising inflation after 1985 drastically reduced real tax revenue in unindexed tax systems with large collection gaps and lags. In Chile the reduction was part of a government effort to shrink the size of the public sector, and it took place in the context of a public sector that was running a substantial primary surplus. In Bolivia the problem was not the tax effort—it increased. Rather, it was losses in public enterprises, which rose by 7 percent of GDP over the period.[5]

The interest component of government expenditure is not included in the primary deficit figures shown in table 1-6, but one can calculate the total deficit of the public sector by adding interest to the primary deficit. As one can see, even in 1980, interest costs already were a significant fraction of GDP in many countries. In six of the thirteen countries, more than 3 percent of GDP was being spent on this item. Over the decade, that fraction rose in most countries, particularly in Brazil and Mexico. The picture would have been even worse in several other countries, notably Argentina and Peru, if they had been fully servicing their foreign debt obligations.

As for downsizing the government, in only five countries (Chile, Costa Rica, Mexico, Honduras, and Bolivia) did the government shrink relative to GDP (see table 1-7). And even among these five, Mexico and Honduras appear on the list only because of a reversal of trends in 1990.[6] In all the rest, the government acted as a shock absorber, an employer of last resort, during a decade when the availability of good jobs in the private sector was shrinking rapidly.[7] Since there was substantial privatization during the second half of the decade, the measure understates the reduction in the size of government. Nonetheless, the Latin experience indicates just how difficult it is to reduce government employment, particularly when the economy is not generating jobs.

An alternative reaction to the fiscal crisis and the pressure to downsize was in many cases to shrink government salaries. An estimate of the real value of the average government wage is shown in table 1-7. It was derived by taking the ratio of the real and nominal value of government services and deflating by the consumer price index. In only five countries did the real government wage go up. Of course, in many countries wages were falling across the board. Thus if one asks the alternative question, Were government wages allowed to fall faster than the minimum wage? one finds that did happen in five countries. In the other nine, government workers received a certain measure of protection from what was happening to unskilled labor in the private market.[8] In several cases, there was a sharp conflict between the table 1-7 source and other sources as to the real government wage indexes. In one publication, the average government salary for five countries (Colombia, Costa Rica, Panama, Uruguay, and

Table 1-7. Growth in Government Services, Wages, and
Gross Domestic Product, Fourteen Latin
American Countries, 1980s (percent)

Country	Real Government Services	Real GDP	Real Government Wage
Bolivia[1]	81.6	108.5	138.8
Brazil[2]	123.6	116.5	247.8
Chile[3]	95.9	115.4	61.4
Colombia[2]	163.3	143.3	102.8
Costa Rica[2]	109.6	125.2	116.0
Ecuador[2]	121.7	116.6	54.0
Guatemala[4]	118.3	98.1	69.5
Honduras[2]	111.1	125.5	100.1
Mexico[2]	116.4	117.6	63.3
Panama[2]	121.5	105.8	114.6
Paraguay[2]	162.4	136.6	96.5
Peru[2]	97.2	89.1	51.5
Uruguay[2]	129.7	101.4	71.6
Venezuela[2]	122.8	103.2	47.7

Source: ECLAC, various years, Statistical Yearbook.
[1] 1983–90.
[2] 1980–90.
[3] 1980–88.
[4] 1980–89.

Venezuela) was shown as a multiple of the poverty line over the decade (ECLAC 1993c, table 5). In all but Colombia, the average wage fell relative to the poverty line and in two cases (Venezuela and Costa Rica), quite drastically. Thus the two sources disagree about what happened to government wages for Costa Rica and Panama, leaving us with three of the fourteen observations in which government wages unambiguously increased and seven in which that wage rose relative to the minimum wage in the private sector.[9]

RISING INFLATION DURING THE EIGHTIES

The 1980s were a period of rising inflation in most of Latin America. Table 1-8 displays the annual change in the consumer price index for each of the fifteen countries over the decade: inflation rose in nine countries, rose

Table 1-8. Annual Inflation Rates (Consumer Price Index), Fifteen Latin American Countries, 1980–1992 (percent)

Country	1980	1981	1982	1983	1984	1985	1986	1987	1988	1989	1990	1991	1992
Argentina	101	105	165	344	627	672	90	131	343	3,079	2,314	173	23
Bolivia	47	29	133	269	1,282	11,748	276	15	16	15	17	21	12
Brazil	83	106	98	142	197	227	145	230	682	1,287	2,968	441	1,000
Chile	35	20	10	27	20	31	19	20	15	17	26	22	15
Colombia	27	27	25	20	16	24	19	23	28	26	29	30	27
Costa Rica	18	37	90	33	12	15	12	17	21	17	19	29	22
Ecuador	13	17	16	48	31	28	23	29	58	76	49	49	55
Guatemala	11	11	0	5	3	19	37	12	11	11	41	33	10
Honduras	18	9	9	8	5	3	4	2	5	10	23	34	9
Mexico	26	28	59	102	65	58	86	132	114	20	27	23	15
Panama	14	7	4	2	2	1	0	1	0	0	1	1	2
Paraguay	22	14	7	13	20	25	32	22	23	26	38	24	15
Peru	59	75	64	111	110	163	78	86	666	3,399	7,482	409	74
Uruguay	63	34	19	49	55	72	76	64	62	81	113	102	69
Venezuela	21	16	10	6	12	11	11	28	29	84	41	34	31

Source: IADB, various years, Economic and Social Progress Report.

and then subsided in three, was essentially constant in two, and fell in just one. The virulence of the inflation in several cases was like nothing previously experienced. The worst cases were Bolivia and Peru. Prices doubled every two months in Bolivia in 1985 and forced the government to undertake monetary reform. In Peru, populist policies and the collapse of the tax system fueled rapid monetary expansion and an inflation that reached 43 percent per month in 1989. Brazil and Argentina also experienced big increases in the inflation rate. Like Peru, in both cases the acceleration of inflation came in the latter part of the decade, when the electorate, released from military rule for the first time in many years, expressed its demands for more government services and higher employment and income levels after years of adjustment and recession. The new democratically elected governments were unable to resist this pressure, and the predictable result was a shift toward more populist policies and rising government deficits.

Despite the experience of Peru, Argentina, and Brazil, democracies were not generally more inflation prone than military governments. Consider Costa Rica, Colombia, Mexico, and post-Pinochet Chile. Colombia's inflation was constant over the decade. Mexico and Costa Rica both suffered a sharp rise in inflation during the period when they were adjusting to a severe balance of payments shock, but in both cases government efforts to control inflation through monetary discipline paid off. Costa Rica was back to its normal inflation rate by 1984. In Mexico the struggle took longer, and it took a change in government in 1988 to finally get the inflation rate below 30 percent for the first time since 1981. Chile gives the lie to the notion that replacing a tough military regime is always inflationary: Pinochet left office in March 1990, and as of this writing there has been no outbreak of inflation. Nor was there an outbreak of inflation in Ecuador in the early 1980s, after a democratically elected government replaced the military regime.

Balance of payments adjustments of the sort seen in Latin America generally lead to inflation. Remember that one essential characteristic of such an adjustment is shrinking aggregate demand relative to production so that the country generates a trade surplus. This is usually inflationary, and it usually leads to a recession, as well. Many of the policy measures required during such an adjustment are negative supply shocks, which shift the aggregate supply curve up and to the left. Real devaluation is the most obvious example; it directly raises the cost of imported inputs for all domestic producers. And because a devaluation raises the prices of all traded goods, it indirectly almost certainly raises wage demands, which drive up costs and shift the supply curve.

These unfavorable shifts in supply leave the monetary authorities with an unpleasant choice. They can either validate the cost increases or they can hold firm. If they do the former, there will be a rise in the inflation rate. If they do the latter, there will be a recession, until real wage and profit demands have been driven down to the point where they are compatible with the new level of costs. The more rigid the wage and profit demands are, the more likely adjustment will both raise the inflation rate and cause a recession. But it is important to emphasize that such supply shocks are not necessarily inflationary; inflation occurs after a devaluation or a hike in the real interest rate only when the supply shocks are validated by permissive monetary or fiscal policy.

The main distinguishing characteristic of inflations caused by supply-side and demand-side influences is what happens to output. In supply-side inflations, the leftward shift in supply dominates any upward shift in demand, so that the rise in inflation is accompanied by recession. In contrast, demand-side inflations are those in which the rightward shift in demand dominates, so that output and inflation are both increasing. With those patterns in mind, we can see that most changes in inflation in Latin America during the eighties were the result of supply-side shocks, as one would expect during periods of adjustment induced by shifts in the balance of payments.

This relation becomes clear when the inflation patterns in table 1-8 are combined with the cycle patterns in table 1-4. Altogether, there were twenty-four periods of falling per capita income during the 1980s in the fifteen economies. In eighteen of those twenty-four periods, there was rising inflation, in three there was essentially no change in inflation, and in three there was a decline in inflation. Only the latter three cases are inconsistent with supply-induced inflation, and they are fairly easy to explain. These three cases were Chile in 1981–84, Honduras in 1980–86, and Venezuela in 1981–83. Neither Honduras nor Venezuela had a real devaluation during these recession years. Chile did have one in 1983–84, when its fixed exchange rate regime collapsed, but inflation also doubled during those two years after having fallen earlier. Thus none of these three cases is a counterexample to the general pattern of supply-side, adjustment-induced inflation.

The recovery periods are a bit less clear. Where recovery is the result of relaxing monetary discipline, one would expect it to be associated with rising inflation. That was the case in six of the fourteen recovery observations in the sample. But in another six inflation fell during recovery, the pattern expected when favorable shifts in the supply curve of the economy dominate changes on the demand side. The six were Argentina in 1985–87; Chile, Costa Rica, and Mexico after their adjustments; Peru in 1984–87; and Venezuela after 1990. Presumably, in every case but Argentina and Peru, adjustment had a favorable effect on inflation and wage demands.

Chapter Two

Changes in Income Distribution and Poverty

Latin America has always had a very unequal distribution of income and a high level of poverty relative to its income. For most countries, adjustment during the 1980s made the situation worse on both counts. In most countries, the recessions that accompanied the adjustment process increased both earnings inequality and poverty.

Table 2-1 displays data on the distribution of income, as measured by the Gini coefficient.[1] Each row in the table represents an internally consistent time series of distribution statistics. In those countries for which there are Gini estimates for the beginning and end of the decade, there was in most cases a substantial rise in inequality. That means that the 1980s' recessions hit the poor harder than the rich.[2] But rising inequality was not universal; in four countries (Colombia, Costa Rica, Uruguay, and Paraguay) inequality went down.

That in itself is a significant finding, but it should not obscure the equally important fact that trends in inequality appear to have been significantly influenced by trends in per capita income. Countries in recession or with sharply declining per capita income generally had rising inequality, whereas countries in a recovery phase in 1989 enjoyed rising equality as well. Thus the four countries with rising equality had an average per capita income growth of 0.4 percent over the period of observation, whereas the five with rising inequality had an average 11 percent decline in per capita income.

One can say more than this. In Costa Rica and Uruguay, inequality fell despite falling per capital income, while in Brazil inequality increased despite a rise in per capita income (between 1981 and 1989). The difference between these cases is that in 1989 Costa Rica and Uruguay were both in strong and extended recovery phases after severe recessions earlier in the decade. They were beginning to enjoy the benefits of the painful adjustments they had both made between 1980 and 1985. Brazil, in contrast, was struggling to control its inflation and had had essentially no per capita income growth since 1986. The link between recession and inequality is borne out in three other cases: Colombia, Argentina, and Panama. Colombia did not have a severe recession during the 1980s and was growing, albeit slowly, in 1989. Argentina and Panama were both in severe recession.

Thus it would appear that not only the level, but also the rate of change, of per capita income during the period that a survey is taken has an effect on level of inequality. Recessions under Latin American conditions were inequitable in that the burden of falling incomes had an especially heavy impact on those at the bottom. Recoveries had the opposite effect. Not only did those at the bottom gain more than the better-off, in many cases they even improved their position relative to where they were at the start of the decade.

The advantage of the data in table 2-1 is that they permit one to understand the link between distribution and the economic cycle of recession and recovery; the data strongly confirm the relation between inequality and the economic cycle. In the vast majority of the cases for which there are comparable observations, recessions were accompanied by rising inequality, while inequality fell during recovery. A two-way table (table 2-2) categorizes the subperiods according to whether the real minimum wage fell and whether inequality rose or fell. For simplicity, a period of falling wages is labeled recession.

Inequality in almost every case was strongly countercyclical, rising in recession and falling in recovery. In twenty-one of the twenty-seven cases the wage fell in either the northeast or the southwest corners of the table, while only two fell in either of the opposite corners. Why do we find this strong relation? The hypothesis is that recession under conditions common in Latin America during the 1980s created severe downward pressure on wages and employment for those at the bottom of the income pyramid. With insignificant levels of unemployment insurance, workers were forced either to accept large real wage reductions, to be unem-

Table 2-1. Gini Coefficients for Thirteen Countries, 1979–1992

Country and Source	1979	1980	1981	1982	1983	1984	1985	1986	1987	1988	1989	1990	1991	1992
Argentina (Buenos Aires)														
Psacharopoulos et al. (1993)		0.41									0.48			
Fiszbein (1989)		0.40	0.43	0.40	0.40		0.40		0.43	0.45				
Bolivia (urban)														
Psacharopoulos et al. (1993)							0.52			0.52				
Brazil (total)														
Barros et al. (1993)	0.59				0.59	0.59	0.59	0.59	0.60	0.61	0.63	0.61		
Psacharopoulos et al. (1993)	0.59		0.58								0.63			
Chile														
Mujica and Larranaga (1993)	0.52	0.53	0.52	0.54	0.54	0.55	0.53	0.54	0.53					
Pardo et al. (1993)									0.53			0.54		0.47[1]
Colombia (urban)														
Psacharopoulos et al. (1993)		0.58									0.53			
Costa Rica (total)														
Gindling and Berry (1992)		0.40	0.40	0.42	0.38	0.38	0.37	0.36	0.42	0.42				
Psacharopoulos et al. (1993)			0.48								0.46			
Guatemala (total)														
Psacharopoulos et al. (1993)								0.58			0.59			
World Bank (1991)			0.48					0.53			0.57[2]			

Country / Source						
Mexico (total)						
Psacharopoulos et al. (1993)				0.51	0.52	
McKinley and Alarcon (1994)				0.43	0.47	0.47
Panama (total)						
Psacharopoulos et al. (1993)	0.49				0.56	
Paraguay (Asuncion)						
Psacharopoulos et al. (1993)		0.45			0.40	
Peru[3]						
Psacharopoulos et al. (1993)		0.34	0.39	0.43	0.44	
Escobal et al. (1992)	0.44	0.4	0.39	0.41	0.44	
Uruguay (urban)						
Psacharopoulos et al. (1993)		0.44	0.42		0.42	
Venezuela (total)						
Marquez et al. (1993)		0.40	0.44	0.46	0.44	
Altimir (1992a)[4]		0.39				
Psacharopoulos et al. (1993)			0.43	0.42	0.44	

Note: All Ginis from Psacharopoulos et al., 1993, are based on household income per capita, except for Peru, which is based on expenditure.

[1] Based on distribution of wage income only.

[2] Taken from IADB data worksheets.

[3] The 1985 observation is national, whereas all remaining observations are Lima only.

[4] Distribution of household income.

Table 2-2.   Distribution of Income and the Real Wage during Recession and Recovery

Distribution	Recession	Recovery
More equal		Chile 1983–87, real wage fell
		Chile 1990–92, real wage rose
		Colombia 1980–89, real wage rose
		Costa Rica 1983–86, real wage rose
		Costa Rica 1981–89, real wage rose
		Venezuela 1989–91, real wage fell
		Uruguay 1981–89, real wage fell
No change	Argentina 1980–82, real wage rose	Brazil 1983–86, real wage fell
	Argentina 1982–85, real wage rose	
	Brazil 1979–83, real wage constant	
Less equal	Argentina 1985–88, real wage fell	Guatemala 1986–89, real wage fell
	Argentina 1980–89, real wage fell	Chile 1987–90, real wage rose
	Bolivia 1986–89, real wage constant	
	Brazil 1986–89, real wage fell	
	Brazil 1979–89, real wage fell	
	Chile 1980–83, real wage fell	
	Costa Rica 1980–82, real wage fell	
	Guatemala 1981–86, real wage fell	
	Mexico 1977–84, real wage fell	
	Mexico 1984–89, real wage fell	
	Peru 1981–84, real wage fell	
	Peru 1984–89, real wage fell	
	Panama 1979–89, real wage constant	
	Venezuela 1981–89, real wage fell	

Source: Table 2-1.

ployed, or to work in the informal sector. For new entrants, the choices were equally stark. This group composed the bulk of rising unemployment, and for those who did find work, the evidence suggests a rise in the age-wage differential.[3]

Many of those interested in equity argue that maintaining or raising the minimum wage improves the distribution of income and alleviates poverty. To accept that argument requires two key assumptions: the poor must be working in minimum wage jobs, and the number of those jobs must be insensitive to the level of the minimum wage in real terms. Neither of these conditions holds in Latin America, where many people work in either the urban informal sector or agriculture, at wages well below the minimum. Such people would be helped, not hurt, if a decline in the minimum wage expanded job opportunities in the formal sector. However, if a decline in the minimum wage took place during a recession, in which the number of jobs in the formal sector declined, then the cost of the policy to workers in the formal sector would not be offset by gains to the newly employed. Furthermore, by affecting the distribution of income, the minimum wage might also affect the demand for formal sector output. Lowering the real wage might shrink the market for goods intended for the mass market, thus amplifying the reduction in labor income and worsening the adjustment recession. But these theories cannot be resolved theoretically. Rather, they require an appeal to experience, and in this regard Latin America offers a variety of patterns of real wages, adjustment, and poverty.

The data in table 2-2 show the direction of change in the real minimum wage during seventeen recessions and ten recoveries. In the southwest quadrant of the table (the combination of recession and rising inequality), real wages fell in fourteen cases and were essentially constant in two.[4] In all but one case (both in recession and recovery) where the real wage increased, the distribution also improved or stayed the same.[5] The bulk of those cases, not surprisingly, were also recoveries. The three cases that reverse this pattern (i.e., falling wages in recovery) were Venezuela, Uruguay, and Chile, where distribution improved during recovery despite a decline in the real minimum wage. In all three cases, the recovery was accompanied by an increase in employment and a rise in the average wage relative to the minimum.[6]

What all of this suggests is that there is a clear link between macroeconomic conditions and inequality. Inequality is countercyclical, and real minimum wages appear to have an equalizing effect on distribution. It is probably true that, in most cases, the real wage is also related to the economic cycle, falling during recession and rising in recovery. Thus, in most cases it is not an additional variable but is itself driven by economic conditions. But there are cases where the two do not move together (Argentina in 1982–85, Brazil in 1979–83, and Chile in 1983–87). In the first two, the improvement in the real wage may help explain why the distribution improved despite the severe recession both countries suffered in those years. Brazil's experience between 1979 and 1983, when per capita income fell 12.3 percent, is particularly instructive in this regard. Yet by policy design the real minimum wage was held virtually constant. This may have tempered the rise in inequality, which was relatively moderate compared to the experience of other countries suffering recessions of equal severity.

While changes in distribution tend to be dominated by what happens to wage distribution, changes in the factor shares of labor and capital must also have played a part in rising inequality in Latin America during the 1980s. Recessions in industrial countries have a large impact on profits because of the stickiness of wages and the tendency to stockpile labor when reductions in aggregate demand are expected to be temporary. No such safeguards to labor income seem to have been present in Latin America. There may have been some stockpiling of labor, but the reduction in real wages in most countries was so large that it swamped any reduction in profits. As a result, for almost every one of the countries for which there are data, the share of wages in GDP fell during the 1980s.[7]

In addition to wage repression, another factor raising the share of capital was a dramatic rise in real interest rates over the decade in some countries, particularly in Brazil. Many countries had established internal bond markets during the 1970s. As the financial picture of their governments worsened, they were forced to borrow to cover their deficits. Prior to 1982 some of that borrowing was external. Afterward governments were forced to borrow from their own citizens, and that forced up the real interest rate. While the higher rates reflected the understandable fear of lenders that they would not be fully repaid, the effect was to raise the return to capital. But the rise in real rates had another perverse effect—it pushed several unfortunate governments into a fiscal vicious circle, in which the rise in interest costs exacerbated deficits that required increased borrowing that further increased the real interest rate. Effectively, when a country gets into such a vicious circle, it is forced to raise taxes, most of which are levied on salaries and paid by the middle and working classes, to compensate bondholders, who are at the top of the distribution.

In countries where there was no internal bond market or where government deficits were not sizable, real interest rates rose to attract foreign capital to finance current account deficits or to slow capital outflow. In effect, the integration of Latin America into world capital markets meant that these economies had to pay owners of capital a rate reflecting what they could earn elsewhere, including a rate to compensate for the perceived risk of investing in Latin America.[8]

The point is that Latin America's increasing integration into a world capital market—where domestic returns adjusted for perceived risk competed with relatively safe rates on foreign assets, where governments were being pushed to transfer ownership of public sector companies to the private sector, and where governments were running large deficits that could be financed only internally—must have had a regressive effect on distribution. I say "must have," because the effect has not been measured with any greater precision than that of the national accounts data. None of the countries studied reports real interest payments separately, and the implied share of capital in the national accounts includes both earnings of the self-employed and return on capital. In countries such as Peru and Paraguay, where the share of the informal sector and subsistence farmers in GDP is large, one cannot be sure what a rise in the nonsalary share means. It could mean a rise in profits or a rise in the informal sector, with opposite implications for income distribution.

CHANGES IN POVERTY DURING THE 1980S

For changes in poverty during the 1980s, I rely mainly on poverty estimates reported in a World Bank report (Psacharopoulos et al., 1993). In broad strokes, the picture is as follows: First, there was a substantial increase in poverty between 1980 and 1989, an increase that raised the proportion of poor from approximately 26.5 percent to approximately 31.0 percent. Second, the rise was not uniform, either across countries or across time; at least four countries—Costa Rica, Colombia, Paraguay, and Uruguay—reduced their levels of poverty over the decade. Poverty followed the economic cycle, rising sharply in recession and falling, although less sharply, in recovery. Costa Rica and Colombia reduced poverty in large part because they had short and relatively mild adjustments to the debt crisis and were well into recovery by 1989.

The reforms of the 1980s and renewed growth after 1989 are having a positive effect on poverty in the 1990s. The year 1989 was probably the low point of the adjustment cycle in many countries.[9] Therefore, the estimates of poverty derived from 1989 household surveys, while showing the high short-run cost of the adjustment process, do not tell the full story. More recent estimates for Chile, Venezuela, and Argentina show that economic growth drove down their poverty ratios; poverty measurements are not available for countries like Panama that are growing once again, but one can be fairly sure that poverty is falling in these countries as well.

Much less optimism is possible for the poor who live in countries where adjustment is incomplete or where recovery was weak or delayed—which unfortunately account for some 70 percent of the continent's poor. Only two countries, Brazil and Peru, account for approximately 55 percent of the poor. Both were growing again in 1994, but only after long and deep recessions, which must have added millions to the poverty population. Another 15 percent of the poor are in Guatemala, Honduras, Bolivia, and Haiti, none of which is growing very rapidly, either because of policy failures or external conditions. Until macroconditions change for this group, even the modest reductions in poverty occurring elsewhere on the continent are unlikely.

THE LEVEL AND DISTRIBUTION OF POVERTY IN 1989

The poverty estimates that follow are based on the World Bank's household surveys of sixteen countries in 1989; probably the most comprehensive data available on the income and labor market status of households.[10] Even so, estimating poverty is fraught with problems. First, there is wide variability in underreporting and in the kind of income reported. Some countries include only labor income; almost none count in-kind income or the value of free housing. Second is the problem of defining poverty. Ideally, it should be a multidimensional measure and include not only income but also attributes such as education, health, nutrition, and the ability to find employment, all of which are important contributors to welfare. Since most of these other indicators correlate strongly with income, I here follow convention and arbitrarily adopt income as a single-dimensioned indicator.

Having done that, the problem remains of describing the poverty line. In Latin America the typical procedure has been to calculate the cost of a minimum-calorie market basket of food and then to define the poverty line as some multiple of that basket, the multiple generally being 2 in the city and 1.75 in the countryside. There is no adjustment for family composition.[11] Given this definition, one might suppose that poverty lines would be similar across countries after adjustment for differences in the cost of food, but this is far from the case. In richer countries, the so-called minimum-calorie market basket contains relatively high-cost commodities, so there tends to be a positive relation between the poverty line and per capita income. Each of these issues creates problems of interpretation and comparability in the measurement of poverty.

The World Bank took a different approach to the question of the poverty line. Rather than using market baskets, it arbitrarily set $60 per person per month in 1985 U.S. dollars (or $75 in 1991 dollars) as the poverty line; this amount was converted into local currency using the Summers-Heston purchasing power parity (PPP) exchange rates. A local consumer price index was then used to derive the poverty line for years other than 1985. Assuming that the PPP exchange rates accurately reflect the differences in the cost of buying a basic market basket, this procedure gives the amount of money required in each country to buy the same commodities. That in turn makes the Bank's poverty estimates comparable across countries in a way that the estimates based on national poverty lines are not. Using the uniform line, if the incidence of poverty is higher in one country than another, this will not be simply due to differences in the composition of the basic market basket.

Those with incomes less than $60 a month are designated as poor, but this amount may be far less than what people in a particular country consider a basic minimum standard. As a result, these poor may be far fewer than locally designated poor. Thus any definition of poverty is, of necessity, subjective. The one used here, however, does permit aggregation and comparisons between countries. Simply put, it shows how many people have less than $60 per month at their disposal, where they live, and what fraction they are of the total populations of their countries. That sort of aggregation is not possible with poverty lines that differ across countries.

Table 2-3 presents estimates of the size and distribution of the poor—those with incomes less than $60 per month. Because the incidence of poverty is higher in rural than urban areas, where possible, separate estimates for each area in each country were made. Overall, 31.0 percent of the 420 million Latin Americans—or 131 million people—were living on less than two dollars a day in 1989. For those who lived in the countryside, the probability of being poor was far higher than it was in the cities (53.4%, compared to 22.0%). However, because of the continued growth of the urban population during the 1980s, by 1989 more than half of the poor lived in the cities.

Because of the significance of the poverty profile in table 2-3, it is important that the reader understand how the estimates were obtained and how robust they are. Household surveys covered sixteen countries, ten of them covering both rural and urban areas. These sixteen country

Table 2-3.   Poverty in Twenty-five Latin American Countries, 1989

Country	Poverty Incidence (%)	Total Population (millions)	Population in Poverty (millions)	Share of Poverty Population (%)	Population Share (%)
Argentina (urban)[1]	6.4	27.387	1.753	1.3	6.5
Argentina (rural)	23.4[2]	4.496	1.050	0.8	1.1
Bahamas (urban)	2.3[2]	0.146	0.003	0.0	0.0
Bahamas (rural)	21.1[2]	0.102	0.022	0.0	0.0
Barbados (urban)	2.3[2]	0.113	0.003	0.0	0.0
Barbados (rural)	21.1[2]	0.142	0.030	0.0	0.0
Bolivia (urban)	54.0	3.605	1.947	1.5	0.9
Bolivia (rural)	76.3[2]	3.505	2.673	2.0	0.8
Brazil (urban)	33.2	111.867	37.140	28.4	26.5
Brazil (rural)	63.1	35.133	22.169	16.9	8.3
Chile (urban)	9.9	11.059	1.095	0.8	2.6
Chile (rural)	10.4	1.921	0.200	0.2	0.5
Colombia (urban)	8.0	22.537	1.803	1.4	5.3
Colombia (rural)	40.6[2]	9.798	3.977	3.0	2.3
Costa Rica (urban)	3.5	1.217	0.042	0.0	0.3
Costa Rica (rural)	3.2	1.518	0.049	0.0	0.4
Dominican Republic	24.1	7.002	1.687	1.3	1.7
Ecuador (urban)	24.2	5.784	1.400	1.1	1.4
Ecuador (rural)	47.4[2]	4.545	2.153	1.6	1.1
El Salvador (urban)	41.5	2.263	0.939	0.7	0.5
El Salvador (rural)	51.5[2]	2.880	1.482	1.1	0.7
Guatemala (urban)	54.8	2.925	1.603	1.2	0.7
Guatemala (rural)	79.4	6.021	4.780	3.7	1.4
Guyana (urban)	74.8[2]	0.273	0.204	0.1	0.1
Guyana (rural)	93.6[2]	0.527	0.494	0.4	0.1
Haiti (urban)	79.7[2]	1.891	1.507	1.2	0.4
Haiti (rural)	98.5[2]	4.477	4.408	3.4	1.1

Table 2-3—*Continued*

Country	Poverty Incidence (%)	Total Population (millions)	Population in Poverty (millions)	Share of Poverty Population (%)	Population Share (%)
Honduras (urban)	54.4	2.132	1.160	0.9	0.5
Honduras (rural)	82.6	2.849	2.353	1.8	0.7
Jamaica (urban)	4.4^2	1.239	0.055	0.0	0.3
Jamaica (rural)	18.3^2	1.157	0.212	0.2	0.3
Mexico (urban)	9.1	61.517	5.598	4.3	14.6
Mexico (rural)	31.6	23.923	7.560	5.8	5.7
Nicaragua (urban)	57.5^2	2.214	1.272	1.0	0.5
Nicaragua (rural)	76.3^2	1.526	1.164	0.9	0.4
Panama (urban)	26.9	1.287	0.333	0.3	0.3
Panama (rural)	36.8	1.083	0.399	0.3	0.3
Paraguay (urban)[3]	7.6	1.952	0.148	0.1	0.5
Paraguay (rural)	47.9^2	2.209	1.059	0.8	0.5
Peru (urban)	49.5	14.715	7.269	5.6	3.5
Peru (rural)	73.4	6.427	4.718	3.6	1.5
Suriname (urban)	2.3^2	0.205	0.005	0.0	0.0
Suriname (rural)	21.1^2	0.231	0.049	0.0	0.1
Trin. & Tobago (urban)	2.3^2	0.859	0.020	0.0	0.2
Trin. & Tobago (rural)	21.1^2	0.402	0.085	0.1	0.1
Uruguay (urban)	5.3	2.625	0.139	0.1	0.6
Uruguay (rural)	31.3^2	0.452	0.142	0.1	0.1
Venezuela (urban)	10.8	16.107	1.740	1.3	3.8
Venezuela (rural)	23.5	3.137	0.737	0.6	0.7
Total	31.0	421.382	130.827		
Urban	22.0	300.084	66.029		
Rural	53.4	121.297	64.798		

Source: Psacharopoulos et al., 1993.

Note: Poverty is defined as income of less than $60 a month.

[1] Gran Buenos Aires.

[2] Estimated from the poverty regression displayed in note 12.

[3] Asunción.

surveys covered 86 percent of the total population of Latin America, the biggest gap being Peru.[12] For the remaining countries without household survey data, the ratios of poor in rural and urban areas were estimated separately. The poverty ratio for the countries and regions for which observations were available was the dependent variable; per capita income and an urban dummy for these countries were the independent variables. This regression fit the data quite well, so it was used to obtain predicted poverty ratios for those countries and areas without observations. (In evaluating the data and patterns presented in table 2-3, one should keep in mind the macroeconomic circumstances in many of these countries in 1989, probably the nadir of the decade in terms of poverty. Argentina, Peru, Panama, and Venezuela experienced sharp declines in per capita income. In Mexico and Brazil, per capita incomes were stagnant, and there was an unacceptably high rate of inflation. Subsequently, Argentina, Venezuela, and Panama recovered, with beneficial effects on the levels of poverty.)

What, then, does table 2-3 tell us? First, more than half of Latin America's poverty was urban in 1989. Even though poverty was still far more prevalent in the countryside than in the cities, 50.5 percent of the poor were in the cities.[13] Any successful antipoverty program in Latin America will therefore have to have a significant urban component. Second, poverty was not homogeneous across either regions or countries. More than 45 percent of the poor were in Brazil, even though it had only approximately one-third of the continent's population. Brazil's 1989 situation was affected by recession, but that does not obscure the fact that Brazil has always had a relatively inequitable style of development, which means that it has a high level of poverty relative to its level of income.[14] Both its rural and urban poverty ratios were more than double those of Mexico, even though its per capita income was higher. It had an urban poverty index 50 percent higher than Ecuador's, even though Ecuador had only half of Brazil's per capita income. These deviations are significant. For example, if Brazil were to reach Mexico's poverty ratio, that alone would cut overall poverty by one-fourth and reduce the poverty population by 38 million people.

Another 9 percent of the poor were in Peru, and an additional 19 percent were in a group of small, relatively impoverished countries that, while not a part of the debt crisis per se, had falling or stagnant per capita income over the decade.[15] This group accounted for 74 percent of total poverty in Latin America, even though it had only 48 percent of the population. What is more serious from a policy point of view is that, as of 1992, these countries had not resumed a stable growth trajectory, so their situation is probably worse today than it was then.

That the incidence of poverty differed widely across countries reflects large differences in per capita income between countries. Most of the smaller and less industrialized economies had lower than average income levels and higher than average poverty levels. The household surveys of Bolivia, Guatemala, Honduras, and El Salvador back up that statement. Costa Rica, the Dominican Republic, and Jamaica appear to be exceptions to this general pattern; none had a particularly high per capital income level, but all had quite low levels of poverty.

WHAT HAPPENED OVER THE 1980S?

For most of the 1980s, Latin America struggled with the aftermath of the debt crisis: per capital income fell by 11 percent, real wages declined, and unemployment and underemployment sharply increased. In such an environment, it is to be expected that poverty would increase—and the country evidence suggests that this is exactly what happened. But other than national studies, each based on different poverty lines and methodologies, there are no estimates of what happened over the decade for the continent as a whole.[16] This study attempts to fill this gap. To accomplish this, the same methodology was used to determine the 1980 level of poverty as was used for the 1989 estimates. That is, the poverty ratios for 1980 were determined in the cases for which household surveys were available, and a regression was run to get estimates for those countries without household survey data.[17] The data for 1980 are a good deal less complete than those for 1989, so the estimates are somewhat more tentative; furthermore, several observations are for 1985 or 1986. Even so, these estimates, covering twelve countries and representing 81 percent of the Latin American population around 1980, are useful.

Table 2-4 presents these estimates. In all cases where a later observation was available, the regression coefficients and the observed change in income were used to estimate the 1980 poverty level.[18]

In 1980, before the debt crisis exploded, about 91.4 million people, or 26.5 percent of the population were below the poverty line. As in 1989, the incidence of poverty was far higher in the countryside than in the city, but unlike 1989, more than one-half of the poor were still rural. Table 2-5

Table 2-4.   Poverty in Twenty-five Latin American Countries, 1980

Country	Poverty Incidence (%)	Total Population (millions)	Population in Poverty (millions)	Share of Poverty Population (%)
Argentina (urban)	3.0	23.352	0.701	0.8
Argentina (rural)	11.5[1]	4.885	0.563	0.6
Bahamas (urban)	1.0[1]	0.113	0.001	0.0
Bahamas (rural)	2.1[1]	0.087	0.002	0.0
Barbados (urban)	4.9[1]	0.100	0.005	0.0
Barbados (rural)	10.5[1]	0.149	0.016	0.0
Bolivia (urban)	34.1	2.468	0.841	0.9
Bolivia (rural)	81.3[1]	3.102	2.521	2.8
Brazil (urban)	23.9	79.016	18.885	20.7
Brazil (rural)	55.0	39.984	21.991	24.1
Chile (urban)	15.9[1]	9.050	1.436	1.6
Chile (rural)	34.0[1]	2.095	0.712	0.8
Colombia (urban)	13.0	16.885	2.195	2.4
Colombia (rural)	58.4[1]	9.415	5.495	6.0
Costa Rica (urban)	9.9	1.037	0.103	0.1
Costa Rica (rural)	16.7	1.233	0.206	0.2
Dominican Republic	19.7[1]	5.697	1.124	1.2
Ecuador (urban)	19.2[1]	3.842	0.739	0.8
Ecuador (rural)	41.2[1]	4.281	1.764	1.9
El Salvador (urban)	23.6[1]	1.868	0.441	0.5
El Salvador (rural)	50.6[1]	2.633	1.332	1.4
Guatemala (urban)	35.7	2.256	0.805	0.9
Guatemala (rural)	52.7	4.644	2.447	2.7
Guyana (urban)	51.9[1]	0.228	0.118	0.1
Guyana (rural)	70.7[1]	0.532	0.376	0.4
Haiti (urban)	72.2[1]	1.328	0.959	1.0
Haiti (rural)	91.0[1]	4.072	3.703	4.1

Table 2-4—*Continued*

Country	Poverty Incidence (%)	Total Population (millions)	Population in Poverty (millions)	Share of Poverty Population (%)
Honduras (urban)	38.8	1.315	0.510	0.6
Honduras (rural)	70.6[1]	2.347	1.657	1.8
Jamaica (urban)	25.0[1]	0.983	0.245	0.3
Jamaica (rural)	53.5[1]	1.117	0.597	0.6
Mexico (urban)	9.4	46.746	4.394	4.8
Mexico (rural)	19.7	23.654	4.660	5.1
Nicaragua (urban)	24.3[1]	1.480	0.359	0.4
Nicaragua (rural)	52.0[1]	1.291	0.671	0.7
Panama (urban)	26.0	0.954	0.248	0.3
Panama (rural)	33.0	0.946	0.312	0.3
Paraguay (urban)	9.0	1.312	0.118	0.1
Paraguay (rural)	58.4[1]	1.835	1.071	1.2
Peru (urban)	30.9	11.159	3.448	3.8
Peru (rural)	46.0	6.142	2.825	3.1
Suriname (urban)	3.4[1]	0.159	0.005	0.0
Suriname (rural)	7.4[1]	0.197	0.014	0.0
Trinidad & Tobago (urban)	1.6[1]	0.555	0.009	0.0
Trinidad & Tobago (rural)	3.4[1]	0.513	0.018	0.0
Uruguay (urban)	6.2	2.436	0.151	0.2
Uruguay (rural)	13.5[1]	0.464	0.063	0.1
Venezuela (urban)	2.5	13.023	0.326	0.4
Venezuela (rural)	9.0	2.462	0.222	0.2
Total	26.5	345.440	91.404	
Urban	16.8	227.360	38.167	
Rural	45.1	118.080	53.238	

Source: Psacharopoulos et al., 1993.
Note: Poverty is defined as income of less than $60 a month.
[1] Estimated from the poverty regression displayed in note 17.

Table 2-5.   Rural and Urban Poverty in Latin America, 1980
            and 1989

Year	Total Population (millions)	Population in Poverty (millions)	Poverty Incidence (%)
1980			
Total	345.5	91.4	26.5
Urban	227.4	38.2	16.8
Rural	118.1	53.2	45.1
1989			
Total	421.4	130.8	31.0
Urban	300.1	66.0	22.0
Rural	121.3	64.8	53.4
Change, 1980–89			
Total	76.0	39.4	
Urban	72.7	27.8	
Rural	3.3	11.6	

Source: See tables 2-3 and 2-4.

helps the reader to evaluate the changes in poverty over the decade. Overall, the ratio between the population in poverty and total population rose by around 17 percent over the decade. While poverty rose almost everywhere, it rose much faster in the cities than in the countryside: urban poverty rose by almost a third, whereas rural poverty rose by only 18 percent. For the region as a whole, poverty increased by just under 40 million people; of that increase, 28 million were urban and nearly 12 million were rural.

The fact that poverty in the rural sector rose more slowly than in the cities does not necessarily mean that the rural poor received more income. Rather, it may have resulted from the continued migration from the countryside to the cities; virtually the entire increase in population between 1980 and 1989 was urban. In almost every country, rural poverty rose less than urban poverty (see table 2-6), but this may simply reflect the transfer of the poverty problem from the countryside to the city rather than any real improvement in the rural sector. One would need more information on income differentials and movements in relative wages to decide which of these two possibilities reflects conditions in the rural sector during the 1980s.

To help focus on the large changes in poverty, let us decompose the

Table 2-6.   Changes in Rural and Urban Poverty, by Country, 1980–1989

Country	Change in Poverty Population, 1980–1989 (millions)	Percentage Change in Total Poverty	Country	Change in Poverty Population, 1980–1989 (millions)	Percentage Change in Total Poverty
Argentina (urban)	1.052	2.7	Haiti (urban)	0.548	1.4
Argentina (rural)	0.487	1.2	Haiti (rural)	0.705	1.8
Bahamas (urban)	0.002	0.0	Honduras (urban)	0.650	1.6
Bahamas (rural)	0.020	0.1	Honduras (rural)	0.696	1.8
Barbados (urban)	−0.002	0.0	Jamaica (urban)	−0.191	−0.5
Barbados (rural)	0.014	0.0	Jamaica (rural)	−0.386	−1.0
Bolivia (urban)	1.105	2.8	Mexico (urban)	1.204	3.1
Bolivia (rural)	0.152	0.4	Mexico (rural)	2.900	7.4
Brazil (urban)	18.255	46.3	Nicaragua (urban)	0.913	2.3
Brazil (rural)	0.178	0.5	Nicaragua (rural)	0.492	1.2
Chile (urban)	−0.341	−0.9	Panama (urban)	0.085	0.2
Chile (rural)	−0.512	−1.3	Panama (rural)	0.086	0.2
Colombia (urban)	−0.392	−1.0	Paraguay (urban)	0.030	0.1
Colombia (rural)	−1.518	−3.9	Paraguay (rural)	−0.011	0.0
Costa Rica (urban)	−0.060	−0.2	Peru (urban)	3.281	9.7
Costa Rica (rural)	−0.157	−0.4	Peru (rural)	1.892	4.8
Dominican Rep.	0.564	1.4	Suriname (urban)	−0.001	0.0
			Suriname (rural)	0.034	0.1
Ecuador (urban)	0.661	1.7	Trin.&Tob. (urban)	−0.011	0.0
Ecuador (rural)	0.389	1.0	Trin.&Tob. (rural)	0.034	0.2
El Salvador (urban)	0.498	1.3	Uruguay (urban)	−0.012	0.0
El Salvador (rural)	0.150	0.4	Uruguay (rural)	0.079	0.2
Guatemala (urban)	0.798	2.0	Venezuela (urban)	1.414	3.6
Guatemala (rural)	2.333	5.9	Venezuela (rural)	0.516	1.3
Guyana (urban)	0.086	0.2			
Guyana (rural)	0.117	0.3	Total	39.422	

Source: Psacharopoulos et al., 1993.

changes in poverty by country and region. For the region as a whole, the poverty population rose by 39.5 million, 46 percent in the cities of Brazil, another 14.5 percent in Peru. These countries plus the group of small, stagnant, and poor economies identified in note 15 account for 85 percent of the change in poverty over the decade.[19] This from a group of countries with only 48 percent of the total population in 1980. Mexico, which accounted for another 11 percent of the poverty increase, had a relatively low incidence of poverty in 1989, thanks to its urban sector. But it had very slow growth during the entire Salinas administration, so its poverty problem worsened both relative to the more rapidly growing countries and, perhaps, absolutely as well.

Were the large increases in poverty during the 1980s due to a decline in income or to increases in inequality? That is, were there more poor in 1989 than in 1980 because income was lower or because income was transferred from the poor to the rich? The World Bank household surveys can help answer this question by permitting calculations of what the poverty index would have been in 1989 with the observed growth in per capita income and the 1980 distribution. In this counterfactual exercise, each percentile of the 1980 population is allotted its percentage of the national average increase or reduction in income. The hypothetical number falling below the poverty line is then counted. Table 2-7 shows this calculation for all those countries for which there is a 1980 household survey. Columns 1 and 3 repeat the actual percentages from tables 2-3 and 2-4. Column 2 was derived by applying the observed growth rate in income to the 1980 population.

In the urban sector, six of the countries (those with minus signs in column 5) had a lower poverty level in 1989 than would be expected based on changes in their income. In the rural sector, the picture is less favorable. There are only six observations, and in only two, Panama and Costa Rica, did improvements in the distribution make the 1989 poverty level better than expected based on income growth.

The worse-than-expected countries are those with positive entries in column 5—Argentina, Bolivia, Brazil, Guatemala, Honduras, and Venezuela. The divergence due to rising inequality was largest in Brazil, no doubt due to a very sharp increase in income inequality after 1987. Prior to that, Brazil had a relatively good record on poverty and growth.

Table 2-7.   Predicted and Actual Poverty, Twelve Countries, 1989

Country	Actual Poverty Incidence, around 1980 (1)	Hypothetical Poverty Incidence, 1989 (2)	Actual Poverty Incidence, 1989 (3)	Change Due to Change in Income[1] (4)	Change Due to Change in Distribution[2] (5)
Argentina[3]	3.0	5.4	6.4	2.4	1.0
Bolivia (urban)	51.1[2]	53.7	54.0	2.7	0.3
Brazil (urban)	23.9	22.0	33.2	−1.9	11.2
Brazil (rural)	55.0	52.0	63.1	−3.0	11.1
Colombia (urban)	13.0	12.1	8.0	−0.9	−4.1
Costa Rica (urban)	9.9	9.1	3.5	−0.8	−5.6
Costa Rica (rural)	16.7	15.7	3.2	−1.0	−12.5
Guatemala (urban)[4]	48.7	48.3	54.8	−0.4	6.5
Guatemala (rural)	71.8	71.4	79.4	−0.4	8.0
Honduras (urban)[4]	48.7	47.5	54.4	−1.2	6.9
Mexico (urban)[5]	12.9	15.8	9.1	2.9	−6.7
Mexico (rural)	27.0	30.1	31.6	3.1	1.5
Panama (urban)	26.0	31.7	26.9	5.7	−4.8
Panama (rural)	33.0	39.5	36.8	6.5	−2.7
Paraguay (Asunción)[6]	13.1	14.6	7.6	1.5	−7.0
Uruguay (urban)	6.2	6.9	5.3	0.7	−1.6
Venezuela (urban)	2.5	5.9	10.8	3.4	4.9
Venezuela (rural)	9.0	19.5	23.5	10.5	4.0

[1] Figure in column 2 minus figure in column 1.
[2] Figure in column 3 minus figure in column 2.
[3] Gran Buenos Aires.
[4] Figure is poverty in year of earliest survey, 1986.
[5] Figure is poverty in year of earliest survey, 1984.
[6] Figure is poverty in year of earliest survey, 1983.

CHARACTERISTICS OF POOR FAMILIES

There are many reasons why people are poor. Some are demographic and personal, others are economic. First and foremost, the labor market penalizes workers with a low level of education, so that members of families whose workers are poorly educated are likely to be poor. Second, many family heads are not in the labor force either because they are retired or because they are women with many dependent children. Finally, even if adult family members are in the labor force, wages never fully reflect demographic factors. Thus if one happens to be born into a large family or one with few working adults one is also likely to be poor.

The difference between economic and demographic factors is important. Investment in education can alleviate differences in educational attainment across the labor force and perhaps even narrow the educational wage differential. This is a source of income inequality that the market economy can do something about. But the market cannot solve income inequalities stemming from differences in the dependency ratio as long as workers are paid according to the work they do rather than the income they need to support their families. Nor will it eliminate inequalities that result from families headed by retired people or nonworking women. These sources of poverty and inequality can be solved only by direct government subsidy, a solution that most governments in Latin America can afford.

The relation of demographic and economic factors can be seen in the World Bank household surveys (Psacharopoulos et al., 1993), in which the education and gender of family heads were ranked by quintile of family income per capita. Some of the key differences between those in the bottom quintile and the rest of the population are examined below.

Education

Differences in education are an important determinant of a worker's earnings. Wage differentials across education classes are large, and therefore education plays a key role in where workers are placed in the earnings pyramid.[20] Table 2-8 displays the percentages of workers in the bottom income quintile by their levels of education. Overall, 56 percent of those with no education were in the bottom quintile, while 9 percent of those with a secondary school education were in that income bracket. If one has a low level of education, one is more likely to be in the bottom quintile in Argentina and Panama, where the average educational level is high, than in Honduras and Bolivia, where it is low.

The data in table 2-8 quite convincingly show the impact of education on workers' earnings, but that is not the same thing as its effect on family income per capita, which is a better measure than earnings per worker, because the family is the social unit that distributes income for final use by

Table 2-8.   Percentages of Household Heads in Each Educational Level and in Both
Gender Categories in the Bottom 20 Percent of Income Distribution, Ten
Countries, 1989

Country	None	Primary School	Secondary School	University	Male	Female
Argentina	69	36	13	6	13	37
Bolivia	42	27	14	9	13	33
Brazil	54	19	5	2	14	37
Colombia	67	32	9	4	16	27
Costa Rica	55	25	8	4	16	34
Guatemala	36	14	5	2	16	35
Honduras	43	15	4	1	16	34
Panama	83	45	12	4	13	34
Uruguay	65	31	10	4	13	34
Venezuela	50	25	10	5	15	38
Regional average	56	27	9	4	15	34

Columns grouped under *Educational Level* (None, Primary School, Secondary School, University) and *Sex* (Male, Female).

Source: Psacharopoulos et al., 1993.

individuals. One can think of several reasons why the effect of education on relative family income might be different from its effect on workers' earnings. Poorly educated workers could earn less but have smaller families; or they could be in families in which several people work. In either case, the effect of education on relative family income would be diluted.

We look now at how years of schooling is related to income, defined as family income per person. Table 2-9 shows three measures: years of schooling of all adult family members, the percentage of those over fifteen years of age who are either illiterate or have no schooling, and an education deficit index for children (explained below). On average, adults in the bottom income quintile have between one-half and one-third the education as those in the top quintile, underscoring the risk one has of being poor if one is in a family whose adults have low levels of education. Illiteracy rates exhibit an even wider variation between the top and bottom quintiles. These two indexes together leave no doubt that differences in education play a big role in determining family income inequality as well as which families will be poor.

Comparisons between countries are for the most part not possible with these data, because some of the samples are urban while others are national. However, the differences in education across income classes seem

Table 2-9.   Education Statistics, by Income Quintile, Thirteen Countries, 1989

Country	Income Quintile			
	1	3	5	All
Argentina (Buenos Aires)				
Years of schooling (adults)	6.6	7.9	11.0	8.5
Illiteracy (%)	4.4	2.5	0.6	2.3
Education deficit index (children)	0.2	0.2	0.1	0.2
Bolivia (17 urban centers)				
No schooling (%)	10.5	6.4	3.2	6.6
Brazil (national)				
Years of schooling (adults)	2.1	4.3	8.7	5.2
Illiteracy (%)	43.0	18.0	3.5	18.8
Education deficit index (children)	0.6	0.4	0.2	0.4
Chile (national)				
Years of schooling (adults)	6.1	7.7	10.9	8.3
No schooling (%)	11.5	7.2	3.2	6.8
Education deficit index (children)	0.2	0.1	0.1	0.1
Colombia (urban)				
Years of schooling (adults)	5.8	7.2	11.0	8.0
No schooling (%)	6.2	3.4	0.9	3.2
Education deficit index (children)	0.4	0.3	0.2	0.3
Costa Rica (national)				
Years of schooling (adults)	4.8	6.2	9.4	6.8
No schooling (%)	13.6	7.5	2.7	7.0
Education deficit index (children)	0.4	0.4	0.3	0.4
Guatemala (national)				
Years of schooling (adults)	1.0	2.3	7.0	3.2
Illiteracy (%)	64.0	42.7	13.2	39.7
Education deficit index (children)	0.8	0.6	0.4	0.6
Honduras (national)				
Years of schooling (adults)	2.1	3.1	7.5	4.2
Illiteracy (%)	40.6	30.7	8.1	25.4
Education deficit index (children)	0.7	0.6	0.3	0.6
Panama (national)				
Years of schooling (adults)	5.1	8.0	11.7	8.5
No schooling (%)	13.2	5.3	1.4	5.6
Education deficit index (children)	0.3	0.2	0.1	0.2
Paraguay (Asuncion)[1]				
Years of schooling (adults)	6.3	8.0	11.2	8.7
No schooling (%)	3.6	3.6	0.5	2.2
Education deficit index (children)	0.6	0.6	0.6	0.6

Table 2-9—*Continued*

Country	Income Quintile			
	1	*3*	*5*	*All*
Peru (Lima)[1]				
Years of schooling (adults)	7.1	9.3	11.1	9.4
No schooling (%)	20.3	7.8	0.5	9.1
Education deficit index (children)	0.3	0.2	0.2	0.2
Uruguay (urban)				
Years of schooling (adults)	6.1	7.2	10.4	7.9
No schooling (%)	5.0	4.1	1.0	3.5
Education deficit index (children)	0.3	0.2	0.1	0.2
Venezuela (national)				
Years of schooling (adults)	6.3	7.4	9.9	8.0
No schooling (%)	18.3	8.8	2.9 *	8.9
Education deficit index (children)	0.3	0.2	0.1	0.2

Source: Psacharopoulos et al., 1993.

Note: The education deficit index is (the age of the child minus six minus years of schooling) divided by (age minus six).

[1] 1990.

far greater in countries like Brazil and Guatemala, where the overall average educational level is low, than they are in countries with a higher overall average. What that says is that, if a country raises the minimum education level of adults—thereby reducing the variance of educational attainment—the influence of this variable on relative income will be reduced. Noneducational factors, both demographic and personal, will then play a bigger role in determining which families end up at the bottom.

Another important question is how much education poor families give their children. If the children of the poor are taken out of school and pushed into the job market by either economic pressure or the low expectations of poorly educated parents, they too run a high risk of being poor when they become adults. A society's best chance of breaking the intergenerational inheritance of poverty is to make sure that the children of the poor have the same chance to attend school as everyone else and that the schools they attend meet at least a minimum quality standard.

To measure the educational attainment of children, the World Bank devised the education deficit index, defined as (age minus six minus years of schooling)/(age minus 6). The denominator is the maximum years of school a child can have; the numerator is the difference between the child's maximum possible schooling and his or her actual schooling, or the education deficit. The index (dividing the deficit by maximum schooling) puts the measure into relative terms. The index was calculated and averaged for all children between the ages of seven and seventeen in each household survey. In Brazil, for example the deficit index for poor families is 0.61, which tells us that children of poor families are getting only 39 percent of their potential schooling. In every country, there is a difference between the deficit in poor and rich families, confirming the expectation that, through high school, one has a much lower probability of attending school if one comes from a poor, rather than a rich, family.

The differences in the education deficit index between income classes vary inversely with the average educational level of the labor force. Compare Brazil, Honduras, and Guatemala, three low-education countries, with Chile and Panama, two high-education countries. The samples for all five of these countries is national, so the comparison is not biased by rural-urban differences. In the three low-education countries, the deficit indexes are 0.61, 0.67, and 0.75, for poor families, more than twice the deficit indexes in Chile (0.16) and Panama (0.31). Thus, poor families are turning out poorly educated children, children who then are highly likely to be the poor of the next generation.

A comparison of the education deficit indexes across countries and income classes shows the seeds for a continuation of extreme inequality in the low-education countries. For example, in Brazil the deficit in the top quintile is only one-third that of the bottom quintile, while in Chile, not only are both deficits much smaller in absolute value, the difference between the top and the bottom quintiles are also smaller. Whatever the sources of inequality and poverty are in Chile, they are far less likely to be passed along from generation to generation. In Brazil, a good deal of poverty is likely to be intergenerational, passed along from poorly educated parents to poorly educated children.

A determined government can do something about this source of poverty and inequality. Equalizing the educational level of the labor force by guaranteeing a minimum level of education to everyone is a powerful income equalizing force. Indeed, for the purpose of reducing income inequality, distribution of education matters as much as level of education. Neither Paraguay and Costa Rica, two countries with relatively low Gini coefficients, has a particularly well-educated labor force—but neither are their education deficits very different across income classes. It probably also matters that in both countries the industrial sector, generator of high-skill, high-wage jobs, is small relative to agriculture.

Demographic Factors

One of the reasons people are poor is that they are members of families headed by poorly educated workers. But often they are poor because their families are large or because their families have relatively few workers (when working-age family members are either not in the labor force or cannot find work). A summary statistic that combines both of these factors is the dependency ratio, defined here as the number of family members per working adult. Families with high dependency ratios will have lower income per capita unless there is a very high positive correlation between the ratio and the education of workers.

Table 2-10 shows how the components of the dependency ratio vary across both income class and country. In every country the pattern is the same: the dependency ratio is generally two to three times higher in the bottom quintile than in the top quintile, which means that, even if workers in the two groups were educationally indistinguishable—which they are not—per capital income in the lowest quintile would be only one-half to one-third that of the highest quintile simply because it has to be divided among more family members. Three factors contribute to this finding: poor families are larger, poor families have fewer members in the labor force, and poor families have higher unemployment rates. Of the three factors, unemployment appears to be the least important, because unemployment rates in general are not very high in Latin America. To determine how important these differences in dependency ratios are as a source of inequality, the question was asked, What would the earnings differential per family member have been between the top and bottom income classes if each had the national average dependency ratio? This calculation eliminates variations in the dependency ratio as a source of inequality across families. Actual and hypothetical earnings differentials per family member are shown in table 2-11.

Differences in the dependency ratio have a very large effect on inequality; in almost every country, equalizing the dependency ratio cuts earnings inequality by at least 50 percent, which implies that variations in family size and participation rates in the labor market are responsible for a large part of income inequality. The data support this, but one should keep in mind that the calculation is only for labor earnings, not total

Table 2-10. Dependency Ratios and Workforce Participation, by Income Quintile, Eleven
Countries, 1989

| Country | Income Quintile | | | |
	1	3	5	All
Argentina				
Dependency ratio	7.4	3.7	2.7	3.8
Participation (%)	44.3	48.8	63.4	51.6
Unemployment (%)	13.2	7.1	3.1	6.7
Bolivia				
Dependency ratio	12.1	6.1	4.1	6.0
Participation (%)	37.4	51.1	59.6	51.0
Unemployment (%)	20.7	8.3	3.1	8.4
Brazil				
Dependency ratio	6.9	3.2	2.5	3.4
Participation (%)	50.5	56.9	62.8	56.8
Unemployment (%)	4.5	3.2	1.3	2.8
Chile				
Dependency ratio	9.6	4.2	3.7	4.6
Participation (%)	42.4	52.4	61.3	53.3
Unemployment (%)	11.9	5.5	1.9	5.3
Colombia				
Dependency ratio	5.9	3.8	3.0	4.0
Participation (%)	50.3	55.9	64.9	56.9
Unemployment (%)	16.9	9.3	3.1	9.1
Costa Rica				
Dependency ratio	5.5	3.5	2.3	3.3
Participation (%)	45.6	53.6	64.0	54.4
Unemployment (%)	7.2	3.8	1.2	3.3
Panama				
Dependency ratio	14.9	4.8	2.6	4.7
Participation (%)	54.5	56.6	64.8	58.0
Unemployment (%)	20.4	21.1	7.3	17.2
Paraguay				
Dependency ratio	7.3	3.7	3.7	4.2
Participation (%)	61.6	69.1	75.5	68.9
Unemployment (%)	17.5	4.8	1.9	6.3
Peru				
Dependency ratio	15.8	6.0	3.8	6.0
Participation (%)	65.7	59.7	66.7	62.7
Unemployment (%)	2.6	5.2	3.1	4.2

Table 2-10—*Continued*

Country	Income Quintile			
	1	*3*	*5*	*All*
Uruguay				
Dependency ratio	5.7	3.3	2.6	3.4
Participation (%)	52.5	54.7	66.4	57.4
Unemployment (%)	16.7	8.4	2.8	8.0
Venezuela				
Dependency ratio	9.7	4.7	2.7	4.5
Participation (%)	39.7	48.1	66.0	51.4
Unemployment (%)	6.9	5.3	1.9	4.7

Source: Psacharopoulos et al., 1993.

Table 2-11. Earnings Differential per Family Member between the Top and Bottom Income Quintiles, Eleven Countries, 1989

Country	*Actual Differential*	*Hypothetical Differential*	*Ratio of Family Income per Capita, Top Quintile / Bottom Quintile*
Argentina	9.3	4.1	12.6
Bolivia	16.1	6.3	16.4
Brazil	90.6	40.1	32.6
Chile	12.3	5.4	17.0
Colombia	10.4	6.0	16.9
Costa Rica	11.2	5.7	12.7
Panama	39.0	8.8	29.7
Paraguay	4.6	2.6	7.8
Peru	17.4	5.0	8.9
Uruguay	6.2	3.3	8.9
Venezuela	8.3	2.9	10.2

Source: Psacharopoulos et al., 1993.

Note: Hypothetical is defined as $[E^1 / (1 + d^a)] / [E^0/(1 + d^a)] = E^1 / E^0$, where E^1 and E^0 are the labor earnings per worker in the top and bottom classes, and d^a is the average dependency ratio. *Actual* is $[(E^1 / E^0) (1 + d^0)] / (1 + d^1)$, where d^1 and d^0 are the dependency ratios in the two classes.

income (for which an equivalent estimate was not possible). Nonetheless, since labor earnings compose the bulk of household income, the same significant influence of demographic factors should be observable on total income as well as on earnings.

Dependency is a source of inequality that the government and the market can do little about. The government can equalize educational opportunities, and the market can reward productive workers, but compensation for dependents is not available. If a government wished to reduce this source of inequality and subsidize education at the same time, it could pay children to stay in school. Even if such a subsidy were not means-tested, more of it would go to poor families than to rich ones, because poor families are larger and have more school-age children. At the same time, it would help poor parents avoid sending their children to work to supplement family incomes. Such a policy would reduce both intergenerational inheritance of poverty and current income inequality.

Other Factors

One of the reasons families are poor is because their adults have lower workforce participation rates. A natural further question is whether this is because such families are headed by retirees. An answer to that can be found in table 2-12, which gives the fraction of households headed by those over sixty-five years of age. As is clear from the numbers, poverty is not concentrated among older families—it is not a result of inadequate retirement income. Because of the relative youthfulness of Latin American populations, the absolute number of older households is small. More to the point here, the fraction of older households is smaller in the bottom quintile than the top in eight of the eleven cases. Whatever the causes of poverty are, they mainly affect families with working-age heads.

The evidence is slightly more mixed with respect to female-headed households. Given that women earn a good deal less than men, even after correcting for differences in education, one would expect there to be an inverse relation between the proportion of female-headed households and income level. But the data do not support this expectation very strongly in most cases; in ten cases the proportion of female-headed households is higher in the bottom quintile than for the country as a whole. But the difference is large in only four countries (Bolivia, Costa Rica, Peru and Venezuela). The conclusion is that gender is not a particularly significant separate source of poverty in most countries.

Table 2-12. Labor Force and Head of Household Characteristics, by Income Quintile,
Thirteen Countries, 1989 (percent)

| Country | Income Class Quintile | | | |
	1	3	5	All
Argentina				
Employees	58.0	73.6	69.7	68.8
Self-employed	26.5	21.1	21.1	22.5
Older head of household[1]	6.5	12.7	11.8	11.3
Female head of household	16.3	23.2	23.0	21.9
Bolivia				
Employees	43.5	48.2	47.2	47.7
Self-employed	43.1	39.0	35.4	38.5
Employed in informal sector	66.2	60.1	50.8	57.9
Older head of household[1]	4.4	2.3	2.9	4.0
Female head of household	22.3	16.3	12.2	16.1
Brazil				
Employees	46.5	70.6	68.9	66.0
Self-employed	30.0	21.8	17.4	21.9
Employed in informal sector	72.8	40.8	27.9	40.7
Older head of household[1]	6.9	3.2	2.5	3.4
Female head of household	20.8	21.3	17.4	20.1
Chile				
Employees	49.9	67.4	55.9	61.9
Self-employed	37.8	23.4	18.9	23.9
Older head of household[1]	4.1	7.1	9.0	6.7
Female head of household	22.2	20.3	21.4	20.9
Colombia				
Employees	64.8	67.7	58.4	64.0
Self-employed	27.0	23.3	20.1	23.5
Female head of household	23.1	23.2	25.3	23.6
Costa Rica				
Employees	48.2	68.9	75.3	67.3
Self-employed	28.9	19.5	16.0	19.9
Employed in informal sector	73.0	46.3	30.7	46.8
Older head of household[1]	6.8	4.5	5.0	4.9
Female head of household	23.1	14.2	19.1	17.8
Guatemala				
Employees	8.4	56.2	69.1	49.0
Self-employed	54.6	29.8	21.9	33.2
Employed in informal sector	96.3	62.7	43.6	65.3
Female head of household	11.1	15.3	20.0	15.7

Continued next page

Table 2-12—*Continued*

Country	Income Class Quintile			
	1	3	5	All
Honduras				
Employees	16.9	42.7	59.0	42.9
Self-employed	56.2	40.3	23.3	38.3
Employed in informal sector	92.0	70.8	37.3	64.4
Older head of household[1]	2.6	3.3	2.9	2.9
Female head of household	19.2	19.1	17.1	17.9
Panama				
Employees	20.3	69.0	86.8	67.2
Self-employed	56.8	27.2	8.6	25.8
Employed in informal sector	92.5	46.5	22.7	45.6
Older head of household[1]	5.9	5.4	8.6	6.2
Female head of household	25.2	25.4	21.2	24.6
Paraguay				
Employees	55.7	64.5	51.0	58.9
Self-employed	30.2	21.0	19.6	22.2
Employed in informal sector	67.1	52.4	49.7	54.2
Older head of household[1]	5.0	6.1	6.5	5.5
Female head of household	21.3	21.4	18.1	19.5
Peru				
Employees	19.0	46.3	56.0	44.3
Self-employed	21.1	44.1	40.2	38.1
Older head of household[1]	4.4	3.8	4.0	4.1
Female head of household	15.8	6.0	3.8	6.0
Uruguay				
Employees	67.2	76.4	69.3	73.1
Self-employed	26.5	17.6	16.2	18.4
Employed in informal sector	18.5	14.9	15.5	15.6
Older head of household[1]	6.9	16.6	13.5	13.6
Female head of household	25.0	24.0	22.6	24.2
Venezuela				
Employees	53.3	69.8	70.7	67.1
Self-employed	34.7	22.5	16.1	22.4
Employed in informal sector	62.5	40.0	29.8	40.0
Older head of household[1]	2.9	2.9	3.4	3.1
Female head of household	24.0	18.7	15.3	18.7

Source: Psacharopoulos et al., 1993.

[1] Sixty-five years of age or older.

It is also interesting to examine labor force characteristics of workers— the proportion who are employees, who are self-employed, and who work in the informal sector.[21] In table 2-12, the proportion of self-employed is generally higher and the proportion of employees lower in the bottom quintile than in the top quintile. But it is also true that the absolute proportion of employees is higher than 40 percent in nine of the countries, which indicates that inadequate wages in the formal sector must be a significant source of poverty for many households.

Also, the self-employed have a better than average chance to be poor. The figures on the informal sector make it clear why: the informal sector includes all the self-employed except for professionals. In every country, a higher-than-expected number of labor force members of poor households worked in the informal sector. Only Uruguay had less than 60 percent of its bottom quintile in the informal sector. The proportion is over 90 percent in three cases. The informal sector is therefore an important source of supplementary income and employment of last resort for the poor in most countries.

Chapter Three

Social Indicators and Social Expenditures

The development crisis that engulfed Latin America in the 1980s reduced per capita income and increased poverty levels in almost every country. Government budgets were under severe pressure as a result of the debt crisis and falling tax receipts. What happened to important nonincome measures of welfare, such as education, health, and nutrition? How did societies cope with economic turbulence in areas important for welfare, and what role did the government play? This chapter examines three areas: education, health, and emergency social programs.

EDUCATION

Despite the broad recession of the 1980s, Latin America continued to make significant progress in upgrading the educational level of its population and labor force. What is slightly puzzling is that it apparently did this while actually reducing public education expenditure, both per capita and as a fraction of GDP. That is, those education expenditures that can be measured fell in real terms, while at the same time the output of the educational system seems to have increased.

Let us look first at the evidence on the output, or results, side. Table 3-1 shows the gross and net enrollment rate for children of primary school age and the gross enrollment rate for children of secondary school age.

Because of the presence of repeaters, it is difficult to interpret changes in the gross enrollment rate, particularly at the primary level. A fall in the ratio could mean that a smaller fraction of the age group was attending school or it could mean that the school system was becoming more efficient in educating students, that is, that it had fewer repeaters. The net enrollment rate is a better measure, at least for primary school, because it measures the proportion of children of primary school age in primary school, thus excluding older students doing remedial work or repeating grades. This measure is unavailable for children of secondary school age. But even the net enrollment rate fails to show an important measure of performance, namely, the ability of the school system to graduate its students. A poor school could have a high net enrollment rate, but many of its students might be stuck in lower grades and fail to graduate. Thus a better measure is school completion rate, defined as the ratio of students completing primary school to students starting at entry level t years earlier.

The data in table 3-1 show that most countries were well on their way to realizing the goal of universal primary schooling by the beginning of the 1980s and that they continued to make progress over the decade. The average net participation rate of the twelve countries with observations spanning the decade was 85 percent in 1980, and only two of these twelve, Chile and Costa Rica, had a decline in that rate between 1980 and 1989. Of perhaps greater significance, only one country (Guatemala) had a decline in its primary completion rate. Many other countries had very significant gains in the efficiency of their primary school systems, notably Chile, Colombia, Peru, and Bolivia. The data on completion rates also illustrate the tragic waste of human resources in many countries. Brazil failed to graduate four-fifths of those who entered primary school! The situation was not too much better in Guatemala, Honduras, and Bolivia.

Secondary school enrollment ratios show a similar picture of continued improvement over the 1980s. A great deal of progress was made during the 1970s in offering more children a secondary school education. All fifteen countries save Venezuela had an increase in enrollment ratios during that decade, and this trend continued during the 1980s, although at a slower rate. Only Bolivia, Costa Rica, and Panama had a decline in enrollment. Some of the gains elsewhere are impressive, in particular those in Chile, Uruguay, and Argentina. In only one country, Costa Rica, did the adjustment of the 1980s seem to lead to an absolute deterioration in the educational system. Uruguay and Chile had slight reductions at the

Table 3-1. Measures of Educational Attainment (percent)

Country	Primary School Gross Enrollment Rate				Primary School Net Enrollment Rate				Secondary School Gross Enrollment Rate				Primary School Completion Rate		
	1970	1980	1985	1989	1970	1980	1985	1989	1970	1980	1985	1989	1975–1982	1980–1986	1986–1989
Argentina	105	106	107	112	95	94	99	99	44	56	71	74	70	66	66
Bolivia	76	84	87	82	68[1]	77	79	79	24	36	37	34	30	32	50
Brazil	83	99	101	108	62	81	82	88	26	34	36	38	30	20	22
Chile	107	109	106	98	93	98	92	86	39	53	67	74	59	58	77
Colombia	108	118	107	107	64[1]		69	73	25	41	46	52	37	37	56
Costa Rica	110	105	97	102	89	89	84	87	28	48	40	41		75	77
Ecuador	97	113	116	113	79		93	94	22	51	55	56	59	50	63
Guatemala	57	71	76	78	48	58	62	64	8	18	19	21	37	38	36
Honduras	87	93	102	107	68[1]	74	85	88	14	30	35	32	27	27	43
Mexico	104	115		112	81	95	100	98	22	46	53	53	83	66	70
Panama	99	106	105	107	74	89	89	92	38	61	59	59	89	73	79
Paraguay	109	104	103	107	88	87	87	95	17	26	30	29	48	48	57
Peru	107	114	122	126	78	86	97	87	31	59	63	66	51	51	70
Uruguay	112	107	107	106	80[1]		88	86	59	62	72	77	87	88	93
Venezuela	94	93	95	92	77	86	86	89	33	22	24	35	68	68	70

Source: UNESCO, various years, Statistical Yearbook; UNICEF, 1985.
[1] Data for 1975.

Table 3-2.   Labor Force Education, Seven Countries

Country	Percentage of Labor Force with Fewer Than Eight Years of Schooling		Average Years of Schooling	
	ca. 1980	*1989*	*ca. 1980*	*1989*
Argentina[1]	72.1	64.9	8.7	9.6
Brazil	83.2	73.5	4.4	5.8
Colombia[1]	63.4	51.8	7.3	8.5
Costa Rica	70.9	66.7	6.9	7.3
Panama	51.4	39.1	8.7	10.0
Uruguay[1]	59.9	52.2	7.8	8.5
Venezuela	73.4	61.3	6.3	7.6

Source: Psacharopoulos et al., 1993.
[1] Urban only.

primary school level but had significant improvement at the secondary school level. Colombia, Bolivia, and Panama, which had reductions in enrollment rate, made up for that with improvement in primary completion rates. All the rest of the countries had growing enrollment ratios at both levels, in some cases at rates faster than in the 1970s.

Changes in the educational level of the workforce over the eighties is displayed in table 3-2. Note that there was both a substantial increase in the average years of schooling of the labor force and a reduction in the percentage of the labor force with fewer than eight years of education. Some of these gains were very large, particularly in Panama, Colombia, and Venezuela.

What happened to school participation rates during the crisis? Were children pushed into the labor force to supplement falling family incomes, or did they continue to go to school? We cannot answer these questions with complete precision, since surveys do not distinguish between students who work part time and full-time workers. Nonetheless, the evidence is suggestive, and the answer appears to be no, children were not pushed into the labor force (ECLAC, *Statistical Yearbook 1992*, tables 15 and 16). Between 1980 and 1985, the last year for which data are available, the school participation rates of ten-to-fourteen-year-old males fell in every Latin American country. For fifteen-to-nineteen-year-olds, it fell in all but Uruguay and Venezuela. These participation rates are consistent with the patterns found earlier. Despite the crisis, in most countries a larger fraction of the children went to school, and they stayed in school longer rather than entering the labor market. As a result, there were substantial improvements in the educational level of the labor force. Thus, far from suffering a decline in educational level due to the adjustment crisis, most if not all Latin American countries continued to make improvements, albeit at a slower rate than in the 1970s. In fact, progress in education, as measured by net enrollment and completion rates, appears to have been made despite a general cutback in real per capita government expenditure on education. The data are displayed in table 3-3.

When trends in expenditure as a fraction of GNP are combined with what is known about trends in income, it becomes clear that educational spending per capita fell over the 1980s in all but four countries. This finding is consistent with the estimate that, for Latin America as a whole, per capita public expenditures on education fell by around 12.5 percent in real terms between 1980 and 1988, the latest year for which data are available (Hicks, 1992, table A-5). In eight countries, expenditures on education rose as a fraction of GDP and total government spending; however, the overall shrinkage in GDP and in government spending was so great that in only four countries (Brazil, Colombia, Honduras, and Uruguay) did educational spending per capita go up in real terms. Spending reductions in Bolivia, Costa Rica, and Ecuador were particularly severe (more than 40 percent in real terms per capita), paralleling the relatively poor performance of their primary and secondary educational systems (see table 3-1). Two reasons underlie this trend: GDP declined and the share of GDP devoted to education was reduced.

How was it possible to increase primary and secondary education while reducing public expenditure per capita on education? There could have been an increase in the student-teacher ratio, a shift from public to private schools, a reduction in teachers' pay, or a shift in the public education budget from universities to lower levels of education. One can rule out the first possibility; data show that if anything, the student-teacher ratio declined during the 1980s (ECLAC, *Statistical Yearbook 1992*, table 32).[1] This pattern is corroborated by data on the absolute number of teachers which show a faster rate of growth than either the number of students or the GDP in most countries (ibid., tables 363 and 365).[2]

One way there could have been a rise in the number of teachers and a fall in public expenditure is a shift from public to private schools, but there are no data to confirm or deny this possibility. That leaves the possibility that teachers' pay declined relative to the average wage, and this trend can be confirmed. In a recent study (made available to author) of teachers'

Table 3-3.   Public Expenditures on Education, Fifteen Countries, 1980 and 1989

| | Expenditure as Percent of GNP | | Expenditure as Percent of Total Public Spending | | Expenditure per Student, 1989 (dollars) | |
| | | | | | Primary Schools | Secondary Schools |
Country	1980	1989	1980	1989		
Argentina	3.6	3.4	15.1		207	304
Bolivia	4.4	3.0	25.3	20.1	51	57
Brazil	3.6	3.9		17.7	209	261
Chile	4.6	3.7	11.9	12.0	163	155
Colombia	1.9	2.9	14.3	21.4	79	142
Costa Rica	7.8	4.4	22.2	20.8	158	342
Ecuador	5.6	3.0	33.3	21.3	71	130
Guatemala	1.9	2.3	16.6	19.3	47	98
Honduras	3.2	4.6	14.2	15.9	110	202
Mexico	4.7	3.3		7.4	88	216
Panama	5.2	6.0	19.0	15.6	246	316
Paraguay	1.5	1.0	16.4	12.1	22	45
Peru	3.1	3.5	15.2	22.8	77	145
Uruguay	2.3	3.3	10.0	15.1	196	268
Venezuela	4.4	4.8	14.7	21.1	218	1,095

Source: UNESCO, various years, Statistical Yearbook; and author calculations.

pay in eight Latin American countries, the World Bank finds that it fell in five (Brazil, Argentina, Bolivia, Uruguay, and Venezuela), was constant in one (Panama), and improved in two (Colombia and Honduras). Grosh (1990, box 3-2) finds the same relative deterioration for teachers in Costa Rica.

There was also some shifting in public budgets between university education and the lower levels, but that does not explain how countries were able to educate more students with less money. The share going to universities rose in Argentina, Mexico, Bolivia, and Costa Rica, and that is one of the reasons the latter two countries provided so poorly for their primary and secondary schoolchildren.[3] Brazil and Chile were the only two countries that redirected a significant fraction of public spending away from higher education, which is one way these countries, particularly Chile, was able to dramatically increase enrollment ratios in secondary school without a large increase in per capita expenditure.

For most countries, the continued improvements in education despite reduced expenditures were made possible by cutting investment, teaching materials, and teachers' salaries at the same time that both private and public schools expanded, a fact not covered by expenditure surveys. In Brazil and Chile there was also a shift of expenditure away from the universities to primary and secondary schools.

HEALTH

The pattern of health and nutrition indicators during the 1980s is the same pattern as for education. Table 3-4 shows mortality rates for infants and for children under five years of age, measured as deaths per 1,000 live births—a particularly good health indicator, because it reflects nutrition, immunization, and maternal care. The trend in both infant and child mortality was downward; Chile and Costa Rica, in particular, made large gains after 1960.

Other health indicators show similar improvements in the 1980s. Grosh (1990, p. 61) collected information on the percentage of under-weight children for many countries in Latin America; all had a reduction in malnutrition save Chile, which started out with the lowest index but had a slight increase. Similarly, there was an increase in life expectancy (ECLAC, *Statistical Yearbook 1992*, table 10).

How were countries able to continue making progress in the health area despite the recession? Available data suggest that, while expenditures by the public sector in health were held about constant in real terms, there was a rise in the availability of health services as measured by a decline in the number of inhabitants per physician and per hospital bed (see table 3-5). Despite some questions regarding comparability of data across time, the evidence is clear that Latin American societies continued to make basic investments in their health system despite the recession. These improvements in health and increases in inputs to the health system in most countries do not seem to have been made by the public health system. One estimate for fifteen Latin American countries is that health expenditures as a share of GDP rose slightly, from 1.7 percent to 1.85 percent (Hicks, 1992). But since GDP fell in real terms by just about the same percentage, those numbers imply that government spending per capita stayed about constant in real terms.

There appears to be great heterogeneity across countries. There was a sharp drop in per capita government expenditures in Argentina, Costa Rica, and Chile and an equally large increase in Venezuela and Brazil (Grosh, 1990, app. 3, 4). But there does not seem to be any relation be-

Table 3-4.   Mortality Rates, under Two Years of Age and under Five Years of Age,
Thirteen Countries (per 1,000 live births)

Country	Under Five Years of Age			Under Two Years of Age		
	1960	1980	1989	1970–75	1980–85	1985–90
Argentina	75	46	36	49	36	32
Bolivia	282	207	165	151	109	98
Brazil	160	103	85	90	71	63
Chile	142	43	27	70	24	18
Colombia			50	73	41	40
Costa Rica	121	31	22	53	19	16
Guatemala			97	95	70	59
Honduras			103	103	78	68
Mexico			51	68	49	41
Panama			33	43	26	23
Paraguay			61	55	53	49
Uruguay			27	46	33	24
Venezuela	114	50	44	49	39	36

Source: Grosh, 1990, p. 58; UNDP, 1993, table 11; ECLAC, *Statistical Yearbook 1991*, table 26.

Table 3-5.   Hospital Beds and Physicians, Fourteen Countries, 1980 and 1988

Country	Physicians (inhabitants per doctor)		Hospital Beds (beds per thousands of inhabitants)	
	1980	ca. 1990	1980	1990
Argentina	356	373	5.3	4.5
Bolivia	1,956	2,222	1.8	2.0
Brazil	830	735	4.2	3.6
Chile	1,143	909	3.4	4.5
Colombia	1,621	917	1.7	1.5
Costa Rica	1,473	793	3.0	2.5
Guatemala	1,773	1,282	1.8	1.1
Honduras	3,021	1,428	1.4	1.2
Mexico	1,192	588	0.8	0.7
Panama	1,074	610	3.8	2.5
Paraguay	1,283	1,538	1.0	1.7
Peru	1,391	943	1.7	1.7
Uruguay	328	274	6.0	4.8
Venezuela	924	617	2.8	2.3

Source: ECLAC, various years, *Statistical Yearbook*, and PAHO (1994) for 1990 observations.

tween these expenditure patterns and either of the indicators of health status: hospital beds and physicians per capita. Some countries made improvements in their health system using the public sector, others through the private sector. But whether public or private, all countries continued to make improvements even when their standards of living were falling. Health, even more than education, is of such value to societies that they find the resources to continue bringing their systems up to industrial world standards even when their incomes are declining. Given the abysmal state of public finances in most Latin American countries during the 1980s, a good part of those improvements must have come in the private health system.

EMERGENCY SOCIAL PROGRAMS

During the 1980s it did not take a social scientist armed with household surveys to realize that recession and adjustment were driving a significant fraction of the population into poverty. Unemployment and underemployment soared, and cases of malnutrition became common as family incomes deteriorated, particularly at the bottom of the income pyramid. Particularly worrisome from a political perspective was the fact that many of the families so affected were new to the experience of poverty. A substantial fraction of the rural population had always been poor; now for the first time in decades this same sort of poverty reached well into the urban population as well. These "new poor" were thought to be a potent source of political instability and unrest.

No doubt because of this threat and also because this sort of poverty was new and expected to be temporary, governments all over the region created or expanded emergency employment and income transfer programs in an attempt to shield the most vulnerable from the full impact of adjustment. The biggest and best known of these programs are the emergency employment programs in Chile, Bolivia, and Peru, but these were not the only programs established in the region; almost every country set up some sort of emergency program. Many were simply food transfer schemes, such as the Beca Alimentaria in Venezuela; others were emergency social funds, modeled after the highly regarded Bolivian Emergency Social Fund (Fondo de Emergencia Social, or FES). But none of them, with the possible exception of the Chilean program, was big enough to reverse the regressive impact of recession and adjustment on the income of the poor; they helped dull the pain, but they were no substitute for a resumption of growth. One can distinguish three sorts of programs: some offered emergency employment; some offered transfers of various sorts, generally food; and some, more recent and generally of a less temporary and emergency nature, supported social investment projects.

The first and most successful of the special employment programs was Chile's PEM (Programa de Empleo Mínimo). Created in 1975 in response to rising unemployment during Pinochet's first adjustment program, the PEM had three defining characteristics.[4] First, it was a targeted program, achieved by paying a very low wage (one-quarter of the minimum wage), reflecting the government's determination to target social expenditure to the most needy. Second, the work was low skilled and temporary, reflecting the government's view that the unemployment problem was a result of economic adjustment rather than a structural problem, which would have required a retraining component. Finally, the program was top-down and authoritarian. That is, the government chose the communities to which it transferred funds, and projects often benefited the rich rather than the poor or served political purposes more than poverty alleviation. The program was also large. In 1982, at the height of the recession, with open unemployment running at 19.6 percent, the PEM employed over 336,000 workers, or 9.6 percent of the labor force (Graham, 1991a, p. 13).

In 1982–83, in response to the severe recession, the government created several additional employment programs, the most important being the POJH (Programa Ocupacional para Jefes de Hogares, or Employment Program for Heads of Households). As its name implies, this program was designed to complement the PEM program, which provided jobs mainly for secondary family members because of its low wage rates. POJH workers had to be heads of household, and they had to have had some stable job before the crisis. Wages were somewhat higher than in the PEM. By 1984 this program was employing over 200,000 people, three-fourths of whom were men. At their maximum in 1983 these two programs plus several additional smaller ones were creating 500,000 jobs, or 11 percent of the Chilean labor force (ibid., p. 13). All of these emergency employment programs were eliminated in 1989 following Chile's rapid recovery from the deep adjustment recession of the mid-1980s.

The Chilean emergency programs were controversial. The work was often unskilled and menial, and some workers felt they were treated in an authoritarian and demeaning manner. There was little or no attempt to build human capital through training, and jobs in these programs did not often lead to other employment. Nonetheless, the programs did have two extremely positive benefits: they were cheap and they were effective. Thanks to the low level of wages paid, in 1983 the government had to spend only 1.5 percent of GDP to employ 11 percent of the labor force (World Bank, 1990b, p. 119). That is a far lower price per job created than any other programs examined here achieved.

As to effectiveness, the low wages meant that the programs were also quite effectively targeted to the poor. The World Bank estimates that 71 percent of the jobs in the PEM and the POJH went to those in the bottom 40 percent of income distribution (Grosh, 1994, p. 120). These programs must also be a primary cause of Chile's reduction in poverty during the most contractionary phase of the recession of the early 1980s. A measure of poverty in Greater Santiago with observations during the years when the PEM and the POJH were active (see table 6-1, the PREALC measure) shows that poverty declined between 1980 and 1982, despite a 12 percent reduction in per capita income. Poverty increased again between 1982 and 1985, when per capita income was constant but when the employment programs were cut in half. No other country in Latin America was able to reduce poverty during a recession as severe as that in Chile, and at least part of the explanation has to be its massive and well-targeted emergency employment programs.

Peru was the second country in the region to experiment with a national emergency public works program. Peru's program, the PAIT (Programas de Apoyo de Ingreso Temporal), was started by Alan Garcia in 1985 and lasted for three years.[5] It was never as big as the Chilean programs, employing at its maximum in 1986 only 3.5 percent of the Peruvian labor force, at a cost of 0.2 percent of GDP (World Bank, 1990b, p. 119). The program provided three-month-long jobs at the minimum wage in such activities as reforestation, rehabilitation of educational centers, park beautification, and water and sewer construction. Given the relatively high wages, there was an excess demand for PAIT jobs, which were allocated by lottery. The bulk of PAIT workers (75%) were female; only one-third were household heads.

Although the PAIT did provide needed income support and some socially useful infrastructure, it was forced to close in 1988, due partly to the general fiscal crisis that overwhelmed the Garcia government and partly to failures in its own organization and implementation.[6] Like the Chilean program, the choice of projects came from the central government rather than the communities themselves; that is, the implementation was top-down and authoritarian. Furthermore, the program was discredited by allegations that it was being used for blatantly political purposes: its budget was increased just prior to elections and allowed to wither thereafter, projects were directed to politically supportive mayors and towns, and in several cases PAIT workers were used to break strikes (Graham, 1994, pp. 153–55). Perhaps even more serious, the program was never allowed to have its own separate budget but rather was financed out of general government funds (Graham, 1991b, p. 100), which made it difficult to develop a coherent, long-run strategy and made funding a function more of the political needs of the government than of the level of poverty in the population. Also, the program cost too much for the number of jobs it created; in 1986 the cost per job was 4,153 intis.[7] If each job lasted the entire quarter and paid the minimum wage of 737 intis per month, the cost per job was almost double the minimum wage. If one is trying to create a large number of jobs in a short period of time, that is too high a price for a financially constrained government to pay.

Bolivia's emergency social fund, the FES, represented a different, innovative approach to the alleviation of poverty during the adjustment process. It was established by the newly elected Paz Estenssoro government in late 1985 as a part of a tough stabilization plan designed to end Bolivia's hyperinflation. It lasted for four years and has generally received high marks for its efficiency and transparency. It differed from the Peruvian and Chilean programs in several key respects.

Most important, it was a demand-driven rather than a top-down program, a feature that has been widely copied in social funds in other countries. Communities could take project proposals to the FES which operated as a coordinator or a financial intermediary and did not directly participate in the implementation of projects. While the choice of which communities should receive grants was left to FES officials, the choice of what to do with FES funds as well as project implementation was left to the communities themselves. Thus the FES relied on projects conceived by local governments and nongovernmental organizations.[8] This characteristic of the program ensured that projects were likely to be useful to communities and to be successfully completed, but it was also criticized by some because there was no guarantee that the poorest communities would make successful proposals, thus compromising the program's aim of poverty alleviation.[9] Nor would the program necessarily reach the tin miners, who were the most adversely affected by the adjustment program.

A second distinguishing feature of the FES was that it financed mainly social investment projects rather than make-work. Clearly, the FES had two complementary goals—creating employment and building social infrastructure—but it put a higher priority on the second than the Peruvian and Chilean programs did. Finally, unlike either of the other programs, it relied heavily on foreign financing.[10]

The FES program has been widely praised for its efficiency, relative lack of corruption, and separation from politics. At its peak in 1990 it generated 20,000 man-months of employment and contributed a bit over 1 percent to the overall growth of GDP, a sizable impact for a small program (Jorgensen et al., 1992, p. 47). It was directed by a small, able, and well-paid staff, and its administrative costs amounted to only 3.5 percent of total costs. Project approval was rapid, and benefit-cost ratios for projects were generally well above 1 (ibid., p. 45).

As for targeting, one can calculate either the benefits of the jobs to the workers in the program or the benefits of the projects built by the program to those who use them. At the outset, a decision was made that the ESF would not pay a below-market wage, as the Chilean program had. Instead, it paid the minimum wage for heavy construction labor, hoping by that means to ensure a supply of workers skilled enough to build FES projects. While that decision meant less self-targeting, the general economic conditions in Bolivia were such that three-fourths of the workers in the program could have been expected to be in the poorest 40 percent had it not been for the program (ibid., p. 40).[11] On the benefits side, far more projects were approved in the richest than in the poorest areas.[12] Even so, Graham (1994, p. 392) estimates that over its four-year lifetime the FES built projects that benefited over 1 million poor, a substantial amount in a population of only 7 million.

IN-KIND TRANSFER PROGRAMS

Many governments established or expanded programs other than emergency employment schemes to transfer resources to the poor. Most of these programs were in the form of in-kind transfers of food, health, and day care. Typically, they were directed at either children or families with pregnant women or nursing mothers. There also was a concerted effort in many countries to shift from general subsidies to transfers targeting the poor.

Chile, Mexico, and Venezuela are good examples of what happened. Chile had always had a relatively well-developed social welfare system until 1973, when the Pinochet government cut social spending. But because of the tough approach to targeting in its public employment programs, it actually managed to increase social spending per capita in the bottom two income deciles of the population.

Chile had a complementary feeding program, the PNAC, which had been started in 1954. The Pinochet government cut back the coverage of this program to only the poorest families; eligibility was determined by a person's position on a poverty index based on a number of personal characteristics other than income.[13] Chile also had a school lunch program, which had been started in 1964 and which had covered all school-children. That program was cut back to children under six years old and to pregnant women and nursing mothers (Graham, 1991a, p. 10). The government also created a new program (JUNJI) to provide food, day care, and a subsidy of 4,000 pesos per month per child for children in families in the bottom poverty class. That subsidy was a relatively large one, amounting to 60 percent of the minimum wage of the period (ibid).

In Venezuela in 1989, the newly elected government of Carlos Andres Pérez was faced with large government deficits and rising inflation. Like other Latin countries, Venezuela had a widespread system of general price subsidies on imported food and on many other commodities, such as electricity and oil, sold by government enterprises. In 1987 these subsidies were estimated by the World Bank (1990a, p. 70) to be costing the government $1 billion per year. The Pérez government, as a part of its general reform program, took the politically difficult step of eliminating most of these subsidies and replacing them with subsidies targeted to the poor.[14] The key element in its targeted subsidy strategy was the PEP (Plano de Enfrentamiento a la Pobreza). As originally planned, the program had four components: nutrition and medical care (for mothers and their infants, preschool and primary education, employment support and infrastructure, and urban development.

The employment component of the PEP never developed satisfactorily, and thus the main element of the program became its nutrition, health, and school programs.[15] Of these, the largest by far were the Beca Alimentaria (food vouchers) and the PAMI (a nutrition program for nursing and pregnant women administered through local health posts). The food voucher program distributed food vouchers to all primary school students in school districts designated as poor on a 1981 poverty map.

Attendance in school had to be certified by the local school administration, vouchers were limited to three per family, and they were redeemable at local banks. The vouchers must have had a substantial impact on the budgets of poor families: in 1989 each voucher was worth 500 bolivares, so for a family of three, this subsidy amounted to about 25 percent of the minimum wage.[16] Aside from its effect on the income level of poor families, this subsidy must also have had a positive effect on primary school dropout rates, which are large in Venezuela. Given the contribution to the income of a poor family that these vouchers made, they must have been a powerful inducement for students to stay in school.

Overall, the PEP nutrition programs were large and efficient. The food voucher program alone cost the government about $400 million per year by 1991, and when one adds in the other food and maternal health programs, Venezuela was spending almost $1 billion, or 1.8 percent of GDP, on these targeted programs (IADB, 1993b, p. 22).[17]

The PEP programs also appear to have been quite well targeted, reaching 2.5 million children in primary school. Estimating that more than 80 percent of the benefits went to the poor, most poor children in the country must have been reached by the program (ibid., p. 24). While the various PEP programs may not have completely offset the harmful effects of the elimination of food price subsidies, they must have had a substantial positive impact particularly for large poor families.

Like Venezuela, Mexico prior to the debt crisis relied on general food and agriculture subsidies to help the poor. Before 1982 these subsidies had amounted to 1.4 percent of GDP, or almost $3 billion. In the general austerity of the mid-1980s these subsidies were cut to under $500 million, while several targeted programs were expanded under the de la Madrid food program PRONAL (Programa Nacional de Alimentación). However, general subsidies were permitted to grow again to almost $1 billion in 1989, as the government struggled to control rising inflation (Friedman et al., 1992, p. 13). Not surprisingly, these general subsidies were poorly targeted. The World Bank estimates that 80 percent went to families earning more than 1.5 times the minimum wage (Levy, 1991, p. 78). The main components of the targeted program were the sale of fixed amounts of milk and tortillas to families earning less than two minimum wages at subsidized prices.[18] In the rural sector, distribution was achieved through a system of stores operated by the government's food marketing and distribution agency, CONASUPO. It sold basic staples at a significant price discount. In addition, a number of other nutrition and health programs provided free food and basic health coverage to families in areas of extreme poverty and to families with pregnant and nursing women. Altogether, these targeted programs in Mexico in 1989 (the last year for which there are data) were much smaller in both absolute and relative terms than those in Venezuela. The two largest, the *tortibonos* and *liconsa* programs, in 1988 together cost $195 million, and all the targeted programs together cost no more than $500 million in 1989, or a bit less than 0.3 percent of GNP (ibid., pp. 72–73). If all of the targeted urban subsidies reached the poor (using the estimate of the 1989 urban poverty population in table 2-3, which shows 5.5 million below the $60-a-month poverty level), these subsidies amounted to only $35 per year, or around 5 percent of the poverty level of income, far less than the subsidies of the PEP programs in Venezuela.[19] And this was only for the urban sector; the rural programs were far less generous than those in the cities (Friedman et al., 1992, p. 27).

The Salinas government, as part of its general program of government reform, combined all of the targeted subsidy programs under a program called PRONASOL (Solidarity) and shifted resources from general subsidies to programs targeted to the poor.[20] Most other countries in the region also established or expanded targeted food or health programs in response to the economic crisis, but given the fiscal constraints facing all governments during the 1980s, these transfer programs tended to be small, much smaller than in Chile, Venezuela, and Mexico.

In 1982, in the midst of its worst downturn of the twentieth century, Costa Rica established a social emergency plan (Programa Nacional de Compensación Social, or PNCS). This was a temporary or emergency program, with three main components: housing, employment, and nutrition. It was a small program, spending altogether only $24 million, most of which went for temporary employment projects, with about $3.2 million going to nutrition (PAHO, 1992, p. 77).

Prior to the debt crisis, Argentina had a social nutritional program (PPSN), which distributed food through the schools. It provided funds for school lunches everywhere but the capital and reached about 15 percent of the nation's students (Queisser et al., 1993, p. 50). In 1984 an additional food program (PAN) was established by the Alfonsín government; it distributed food packages and subsidized milk in rural and low-income areas. Nutrition supplement programs also distributed food to pregnant and nursing mothers through health clinics (ibid., pp. 50–51). In real terms, these transfer programs multiplied almost ten times between

1982 and 1989, in the latter year reaching 1.2 million families, probably the majority of those with unmet basic needs.[21] Even so, the amount of assistance provided by the PAN must have been small; at its peak in 1989 it spent only $150 million, which is about 0.1 percent of GDP or about $10 per family per month (FIEL, 1994, p. 15).

Brazil presents roughly the same picture as Argentina. A large school food program (PNAE) had been in existence since 1954; it reached about 15 million children in 1980, before the debt crisis began.[22] The 1980s crisis forced a substantial expansion of this and other food programs; Coverage doubled even before the military regime left office in 1985 and then rose an additional 68 percent under the Sarney government. At the same time, the Sarney government increased the amount spent per recipient from $14 to $21 (per year!) and the share of GDP devoted to these programs from 0.1 percent to 0.25 percent. While this increase was admirable and worthwhile, it should be clear from the size of the transfer that these programs did not provide much of an income supplement to families living below the poverty line. Recall that even the World Bank poverty line, which was lower than those used in the region itself, was $60 per month, or $720 per year (in 1985 dollars).[23] After 1990 the Collor government made an effort to reduce the size of these various nutrition programs and to target them better.[24] In late 1993 all such programs were combined under a new program, the PCFM (Plano de Combate a Fome e a Miseria, or plan to combat misery and hunger). Its eventual goal is to reach 32 million indigent people, or almost one-fifth of the Brazilian population. It is too early to judge whether it will be able to reach this goal.

SOCIAL INVESTMENT FUNDS

Another outgrowth of the crisis of the 1980s was the establishment of social investment funds in a large number of countries. Most were modeled after the ESF program in Bolivia, with the difference that they are smaller in relative size and are planned to be permanent. They are all demand-driven, like the Bolivian fund, and they aim at poverty elimination through the creation of capital or social infrastructure rather than poverty alleviation through emergency make-work projects.

All of these programs, with the exception of FINSOCIAL in Brazil are recent developments, begun at the end of the 1980s or later. The best known and the largest of these social funds is Mexico's PRONASOL, or

Solidarity, begun at the end of 1988 by the newly elected Salinas govern-ment.[25] The goal of Solidarity was to promote social mobilization by eliciting the organized participation of individuals and local communities through small Comités de Solidaridad. The hope was to reduce the socio-logical aspect of poverty by giving people a sense that they could help to choose and oversee projects in their own communities. Solidarity was staffed by special appointees outside the civil service and had directorates in all regions of the country.

In addition to the transfer programs described above, Solidarity set up investment funds in three areas: production, social well-being, and re-gional development. The program is demand-driven; local communities develop and write up project applications. If the project is approved, Solidarity gives a grant of about one-fifth of the cost of the project, the community puts up a substantial contribution, and then Solidarity helps the community arrange commercial bank financing for the balance of the cost of the project (Sahota, 1991, p. 38). In that way, Solidarity's own funds go further, and both the community and local banks have a stake in the success of the project. As of 1990, most of Solidarity's projects were what could be called social infrastructure—health clinics, schools, water and sewer systems, roads, and rural electrification (Lustig, 1992, p. 6). It spent about $850 million in 1989 and $2.2 billion in 1990, which was about 0.5 percent of GDP in 1989 and 0.9 percent in 1990 (ibid., table 3 and p. 7).

It appears that most Mexicans are happy with the Solidarity program.[26] Nonetheless, two criticisms have been made of the program, and they undoubtedly apply with equal force to other social investment funds. First, the funds may not reach the poorest communities, which may be unable to develop a successful project application or may be too alienated or too uneducated to try. Second, there is a high risk of political manipula-tion and corruption. Governments have an understandable tendency to reward their own supporters, and Solidarity has been criticized for hav-ing been used to buy political support. Furthermore, if projects are under local control, there is a danger that funds may be used to solidify the position and reward the supporters of local party officials rather than to help the most needy people in the community.

Many other countries have social investment funds that follow the general example of the ESF in Bolivia. All are smaller than that fund and than Solidarity. Chile's fund is FOSIS, set up by the Allwyn government in 1989. It had a budget of only $20 million in 1991.[27] Venezuela set up FONVIS (Fondo de Inversión Social) in 1990. Despite its optimistic plan to spend $400 million (mostly externally provided) over the four years 1990–94, it has been criticized as being a low-visibility, low-profile program with a weak staff that failed to mobilize much local interest or support (IADB, 1993c, p. 25).

In Peru in 1991 the Fujimori government established a national fund for development and social compensation (Fondo Nacional de Compensación y Desarrollo Social, or FONCODES). However a manager was not appointed until mid-1992. FONCODES did fund slightly more than 3,000 projects at a cost of $75 million in that year, but all its expected external funding was withheld until a less political management structure was set up in 1993 (Graham, 1994, p. 160). In addition, there are social funds in Nicaragua, Honduras, Uruguay, El Salvador and Brazil, and small funds are pending in Guatemala and Panama.

Chapter Four

Case Studies: Poverty and Adjustment in Argentina and Venezuela

Argentina and Venezuela were severely impacted by contraction in the 1980s. They started the decade with levels of per capita income among the highest and levels of poverty among the lowest in all of Latin America, but severe and extended adjustment changed all that—few Latin countries suffered so large a decline in per capita income or so sharp a rise in inequality and poverty. We now look more carefully at this human tragedy, using both macroeconomic data and household surveys from the beginning and the end of the decade.

ARGENTINA

The 1980s were a disastrous decade for Argentina.[1] Per capita income fell by 26 percent, there were two periods of severe inflation, and foreign debt grew from less than 20 percent to 100 percent of GDP. This section examines how this ruinous decade affected the Argentine poor, using the same household surveys used in constructing the poverty indexes for Latin America as a whole. Here however, the ECLAC country-specific poverty lines are used rather than the $60 poverty line used in chapter 3. This procedure permits the use of ECLAC's careful corrections for under-reporting and of a poverty line based on the cost of a minimum market basket of commodities chosen by those in the region. My measures of poverty for 1980 and 1986 will coincide with those reported by ECLAC in its study of poverty (ECLAC, 1990a).

Household survey tapes are available for the city of Buenos Aires for three years: 1980, a relatively good year; 1986, a year of partial recovery after three years of recession; and 1989, one of the worst years of the twentieth century. The percentage of people in poverty in Buenos Aires increased from 6 percent in 1980 to 11 percent in 1986 to 22 percent in 1989. While one can quibble with these estimates of poverty growth, there is no doubt that the poor have been very severely affected by Argentina's dismal economic performance in the 1980s.

Some of the key patterns of Argentina's macroeconomic performance and labor market are displayed in table 4-1 and the tables in chapter 2. The central fact is the steady decline in per capita income that took place over the decade, relieved only by a weak recovery in the years 1985–87. Overall, the decline was so severe that only countries in the midst of revolution or civil war—such as El Salvador, Nicaragua and Peru—did as badly.

Like the rest of Latin America, Argentina was forced to shift from financing a substantial part of its investment with foreign saving to financing a large trade surplus from domestic sources. As table 4-1 makes clear, this was done primarily by sharply reducing capital formation rather than consumption. Given that exports did not increase much, the rise in foreign savings must have been the result of a significant contraction in imports. The only way that Argentina was able to generate the foreign savings necessary to pay the interest on its foreign debt was by a contraction in domestic demand and a recession severe enough to produce the necessary trade surplus. One can see the clear connection between the trade surplus and domestic activity in table 4-1: from 1980 to 1985, as per capita income declined, the trade surplus steadily expanded, reaching 3.8 percent of GNP in 1985; then, as the economy recovered during the subsequent three years, the surplus evaporated, increasing again only when the economy fell back into recession in 1988 and 1989.

Through 1987, workers in the formal sector appear to have been protected from the full impact of the downturn. Despite a fall in per capita income, both the real minimum wage and the wage in manufacturing actually increased.[2] There was also evidence of substantial labor stockpiling; in 1985, for example, manufacturing output was 20 percent below its 1980 level, yet salaried employment fell by only 1 percent.

The recession of 1988–89 was far more regressive. Real wages in the manufacturing sector were cut in half, and the minimum wage fell by one-

Table 4-1.   Indicators of Economic Performance, Argentina, 1980–1989

Year	GDP per Capita (1980 = 100)	Investment (% of GDP)	Foreign Savings (% of GDP)	Terms of Trade (1980 = 100)
1980	100	25.4	4.2	100
1981	93	22.6	3.2	97
1982	89	19.5	−1.6	85
1983	91	18.6	−2.2	82
1984	91	17.6	−1.7	99
1985	84	15.5	−3.8	81
1986	89	16.7	−1.9	73
1987	90	18.7	−0.9	64
1988	87	18.6	−3.0	67
1989	81	15.0	−4.8	68

Source: IADB, Economic and Social Data Base.

third, thanks in part to efforts to control hyperinflation by lagging wage adjustments. At the same time, there were concerted efforts to shrink employment in the public sector. Both open unemployment and under-employment rose sharply as the economy suffered through the century's worst combination of declining output and hyperinflation.

Another feature of the period was the informalization of the labor force. As one can see from table 4-2, there was virtually no job growth in the salaried (or formal) sector through 1987: 82 percent of the increase in employment came in the self-employed (or informal) sector.

Despite the difficulties most countries have in changing the real ex-change rate, Argentina had a substantial real devaluation (see table 1-3). In contrast to the real wage, the biggest part of this depreciation of the real exchange rate happened prior to 1985, during the decade's first recession. Unfortunately, this did not seem to affect exports, which rose only 5 percent between 1980 and 1985 despite a doubling of the real exchange rate. The responsiveness of exports to relative prices appears to have increased after 1985, but almost all the improvement in the trade balance was due to falling imports, primarily because of declines in income and investment.

To summarize: during the 1980s Argentina suffered through two seri-ous recessions, punctuated by a short and shallow recovery. These reces-sions were part of a macroeconomic adjustment to a very unfavorable shift in external conditions caused by rising interest rates, falling terms of

Table 4-2.   Macroeconomic Data on Employment and Wages, Argentina, 1980–1989

Year	Employment (thousands)		Unemployment Rate (%)	Real Wage Indexes	
	Self-Employed	Salaried		Minimum	Average
1980	2,276	6,325	26	100	100
1981	2,433	6,192	47	98	89
1982	2,601	6,182	53	104	80
1983	2,781	6,312	47	155	101
1984	2,973	6,349	46	168	127
1985	3,120	6,270	61	114	108
1986	3,245	6,442	56	111	110
1987	3,407	6,571	59	121	103
1988			63	94	92
1989			78	42	83

Source: ECLAC, Economic Survey 1994.

trade, and a collapse of external financing. While the country managed to produce a significant depreciation of the real exchange rate depreciation and a reduction in the real wage (two central policy prescriptions in most adjustment programs), through 1989 the results of adjustment were disappointing. The country had hyperinflation despite nine years of virtually no growth in formal sector employment, a 25 percent fall in per capita income, and a 50 percent reduction in the real wage. These were not auspicious conditions for the poor.

The reader should keep in mind that the year 1989 was the low point of the adjustment process. Scattered evidence indicates that the recovery under Menem, which started in 1990, at least partially reversed the unfavorable trends in wages and distribution of income. Not only did real income per capita rise by 20 percent between 1989 and 1993, but there was also a rise in the real wage and a reduction in poverty.[3] Thus, when changes in poverty between 1980 and 1989 are measured, a somewhat misleading picture of the adjustment process may emerge, for all short-run costs of the adjustment on the poor are shown while subsequent improvements are left out.

There were two primary studies of Argentine poverty in the 1980s, one by ECLAC (1990a), the other by the Argentine census bureau (INDEC, 1990). The ECLAC study defines the poverty line as twice the amount required to purchase a minimum basket of food. Its estimates of income were based on household income surveys, which were corrected for un-

Table 4-3.   Poverty Population, Argentina, 1980–1988, Various Years

| | Percentage of Population below Poverty Line | | | Percentage of Population below Indigence Line | |
| | Greater Buenos Aires | | All | Greater | All |
Year	INDEC, 1990	ECLAC, 1990a	Argentina (ECLAC, 1990a)	Buenos Aires (ECLAC, 1990a)	Argentina (ECLAC, 1990a)
1980	10.1	6	10	2	3
1982	28.0				
1985	20.6				
1986		11	16	3	5
1987	25.2				
1988	27.9				

derreporting by comparing their totals with those from the national accounts. The census bureau study was done early in 1988 and used a poverty line comparable to that of ECLAC when adjusted for inflation; its figures, however, were not adjusted for underreporting, which is the apparent reason that its estimates of poverty are so much higher than those of ECLAC. Table 4-3 gives poverty estimates from the two studies for Greater Buenos Aires, the only area of the country for which household surveys were available. The indigence line in the ECLAC study is one-half the poverty line, or in other words an income just sufficient to purchase the basic food basket. ECLAC's poverty estimates for the rest of Argentina are based on national surveys for 1970 and "educated guesses about what happened in the rural sector during the 1980s" (Feres and Leon, 1990, p. 141).

There is an inescapable degree of arbitrariness in the establishment of poverty lines and the treatment of underreporting. Unfortunately, poverty measures in most cases are highly sensitive to a researcher's choices in regard to these two factors. Thus one should not be particularly concerned by the large differences between studies at any point in time but instead should use a series to suggest trends in poverty over time.

Several things are clear from table 4-3. First, there was a big increase in poverty during the 1980s, starting well before 1989. This trend confirms the patterns reported in this chapter. Second, poverty was higher outside of Buenos Aires than in the capital. Third, poverty was sensitive to level of economic activity, but there appear to have been other important determining factors at work as well: poverty increased dramatically in the initial recession between 1980 and 1982, as one would expect, but thereafter poverty and the economy unexpectedly appear to have moved in the same direction. Poverty fell along with the economy between 1982 and 1985 and then rose along with the economy up until 1987. Why that occurred and whether it was due to measurement or to a mix of real wage movements and unemployment is impossible to say. Finally, Altimir's estimates of rural poverty suggest that rising poverty was primarily urban, confirming the pattern noted for other countries in chapter 3 (Altimir, n.d.)

Measurements of Poverty

The data upon which this case study is based are tapes taken from household surveys of metropolitan Buenos Aires. The dates of the surveys were October 1980, October 1986, and May 1989. When using these same surveys for its study, ECLAC (1990a) compared the total amount of income, by type, from the surveys with the equivalent measure from the national accounts and found a serious problem of underreporting. ECLAC adjusted the survey by expanding each income source by the degree of underreporting. We (Morley and Alvarez, 1992c) did not have access to these estimates. To make our estimates comparable to ECLAC's, we used a single underreporting factor for all income, which would make our poverty estimate equal to ECLAC's. For 1980, that required an expansion in reported income of 75 percent and, for 1986, of 47 percent.

The year 1989 poses particularly difficult problems, because there is no ECLAC poverty estimate and, therefore, no independent method of verifying the accuracy of the expansion factor. Nor can one compare total labor income from the national accounts to that from the surveys because of the severe inflation in Argentina during the year. The survey was taken in May, but with inflation running at practically 50 percent per month, nominal income expanded very rapidly over the balance of the year, leaving no way to distinguish between the effect of inflation and underreporting. The 1989 estimate is therefore just that, a number comparable to the expected level of poverty, given the level of per capita income. Note that for 1989, if a degree of underreporting similar to 1980 or 1986 was assumed, the estimate of poverty would have been much larger.[4]

The other problem with the data was accelerating inflation over the decade. Monthly inflation was so high in 1989 that one can get a very large difference in estimated poverty by using a price index off by one month from the time when income was reported. Thus it mattered whether people, responding to the survey, reported their current or their last month's income. In this volume, the latter was used, since it implies the use of price indexes for September 1980, September 1986, and April 1989. Had the concurrent month's income been used, the poverty indexes for 1989 would have been far greater than those reported, simply because the poverty line would have been much higher in nominal terms.

Chapter 3 uses the simplest possible poverty measurement: the fraction of individuals with less than a poverty level of income. But this index both is insensitive to transfers of income within the poverty population and shows a drop in poverty when transfers from the poor to those just at the line move a little over the line. Clearly, an index sensitive to the intensity of poverty and that registers an increase whenever there is a transfer from someone who is poor to someone who is less poor is preferred.[5] An index satisfying this requirement has been developed by Foster, Greer, and Thorbecke (1984). This so-called FGT index is defined as

$$P\alpha = \frac{1}{n} \sum_{i=1}^{q} \left(\frac{Z - Y_i}{Z} \right) \alpha, \tag{1}$$

where

n = number of individuals in the population,
q = number of individuals below the poverty line,
Z = the poverty line,
Y_i = income of individual i, and
α = degree of poverty aversion.

The FGT index is the summation of the percentage gap between the income of each member of the poverty population and the poverty line, raised to a power that depends on the degree of poverty aversion. Note that if we set α equal to zero, implying that we have no interest in the intensity of poverty, the index becomes the poverty ratio. That is

$$P0 = \frac{q}{n}. \tag{2}$$

Similarly, if we set α equal to 1, the index is the poverty gap:

$$P^1 = \frac{1}{n} \sum_{i=1}^{q} \left(\frac{Z - Y_i}{Z} \right). \qquad \text{Or}$$

$$P^1 = \frac{q}{n} \frac{(Z - \tilde{Y}_p)}{Z}. \tag{3}$$

P^1 is the percentage by which the average income of the poor falls short of the poverty line multiplied by the percentage of the population in poverty. P^1 is an improvement on P^0, since it is sensitive to changes in distribution, which increase the poverty gap even if they reduce the poverty ratio. But P^1 is still insensitive to transfers within the poverty population as long as they leave the average income of the poor unchanged. To incorporate a concern for the intensity of poverty, one can calculate the FGT index for α equal to 0, 1, and 2. A comparison of the FGT index with these three exponents will indicate those sectors with high proportions of the very poor.

Another advantage of the FGT indexes is that they are decomposable, which makes them a good tool for determining sources of poverty and changes in poverty over time.[6] One can divide up the poor into k mutually exclusive groups and construct the index for each such group. Call that index P_k^α. Suppose further that m_j is the size of the jth subgroup. Then it is easy to show that the national index is a weighted sum of the individual sectoral indexes, where the weights are the fraction of the overall population in each sector. That is

$$P^\alpha = \sum_{j=1}^{k} m_j P_j^\alpha. \tag{4}$$

Since equation 4 is an exact decomposition, the contribution of the kth group to the national index is $m_k P_k^\alpha / P^\alpha$. This decomposability property of the FGT indexes allows an understanding of the sources of the big rise in poverty in Argentina during the 1980s.

Estimates of Poverty

Tables 4-4, 4-5, and 4-6 present poverty measures and decompositions across a number of household-head categories for 1980, 1986, and 1989.

Table 4-4.   Decomposition of the P^α Class of Poverty Measures, by Head of Household
Characteristics, Greater Buenos Aires, 1980

Characteristic	P^0	P^1	P^2	Share of Population	Contribution to National Poverty P^0	P^1	P^2
Educational level							
Illiterate	.336	.116	.054	.068	.365	.447	.513
Grade school	.053	.013	.005	.598	.508	.456	.409
High school	.030	.007	.002	.231	.109	.089	.076
University	.012	.001	.000	.094	.018	.007	.002
Total	.063	.018	.007				
Age in years							
Less than 15	.276	.055	.011	.006	.007	.005	.002
16–20	.000	.000	.000	.002	.000	.000	.000
21–25	.027	.011	.006	.030	.013	.018	.026
26–30	.081	.023	.008	.075	.097	.096	.088
31–35	.088	.024	.010	.117	.164	.159	.154
36–40	.068	.022	.010	.112	.122	.141	.152
41–45	.058	.017	.008	.136	.125	.135	.151
46–50	.089	.026	.011	.127	.181	.188	.198
51–55	.048	.011	.004	.111	.085	.071	.060
56–60	.072	.018	.007	.099	.113	.100	.098
61–65	.022	.007	.002	.062	.022	.024	.021
66 and older	.035	.009	.003	.127	.072	.062	.050
Total	.063	.018	.007				
Gender							
Women	.040	.008	.002	.125	.081	.054	.035
Men	.066	.019	.008	.874	.919	.945	.965
Total	.063	.018	.007				
Employment							
Formal labor market	.083	.026	.011	.506	.666	.742	.803
Informal labor market	.043	.008	.002	.267	.181	.125	.088
Unemployed	.068	.005	.000	.006	.007	.002	.000
Inactive	.041	.010	.004	.221	.145	.131	.109
Total	.063	.018	.007				

Source: Author calculations from government household survey data tapes.
Note: Last three columns may not sum to 1.00 due to rounding.

Table 4-5. Decomposition of the P^α Class of Poverty Measures, by Head of Household Characteristics, Greater Buenos Aires, 1986

Characteristic	P^0	P^1	P^2	Share of Population	Contribution to National Poverty		
					P^0	P^1	P^2
Educational level							
Illiterate	.346	.115	.057	.072	.231	.077	.038
Grade school	.121	.035	.015	.528	.589	.171	.075
High school	.063	.020	.010	.279	.161	.051	.025
Technical school	.048	.035	.026	.015	.006	.005	.003
University	.013	.004	.003	.101	.012	.004	.003
Total	.109	.033	.016				
Age in years							
16–20	.306	.080	.026	.003	.009	.008	.005
21–25	.130	.036	.016	.027	.032	.029	.027
26–30	.103	.037	.019	.073	.070	.080	.087
31–35	.159	.052	.025	.105	.153	.163	.169
36–40	.124	.038	.018	.137	.157	.158	.156
41–45	.103	.032	.017	.140	.133	.133	.150
46–50	.116	.036	.018	.113	.121	.122	.129
51–55	.108	.034	.015	.102	.101	.103	.094
56–60	.094	.027	.010	.087	.076	.069	.057
61–65	.090	.026	.011	.082	.068	.063	.060
66 and older	.066	.018	.008	.130	.079	.072	.064
Total	.109	.033	.016				
Gender							
Women	.110	.035	.016	.139	.141	.144	.143
Men	.108	.033	.016	.861	.859	.856	.857
Total	.109	.033	.016				
Employment							
Formal labor market	.102	.030	.013	.493	.463	.436	.412
Informal labor market	.097	.031	.015	.283	.252	.260	.279
Unemployed	.446	.159	.080	.019	.079	.091	.099
Inactive	.110	.035	.016	.205	.206	.213	.210
Total	.109	.033	.016				

Source: Author calculations from government household survey data tapes.
Note: Last three columns may not sum to 1.00 due to rounding.

Table 4-6.   Decomposition of the P^α Class of Poverty Measures, by Head of Household
Characteristics, Greater Buenos Aires, 1989

Characteristic	P^0	P^1	P^2	Share of Population	Contribution to National Poverty P^0	P^1	P^2
Educational level							
Illiterate	.514	.254	.161	.045	.108	.140	.169
Grade school	.270	.100	.051	.556	.697	.682	.664
High school	.133	.046	.023	.273	.169	.154	.146
Technical school	.052	.013	.005	.017	.004	.003	.002
University	.043	.015	.008	.109	.022	.020	.020
Total	.215	.081	.043				
Age in years							
16–20	.279	.117	.083	.004	.005	.006	.008
21–25	.120	.051	.030	.030	.017	.018	.021
26–30	.279	.096	.043	.069	.089	.082	.069
31–35	.308	.112	.057	.109	.156	.150	.145
36–40	.277	.110	.060	.134	.173	.182	.189
41–45	.253	.100	.056	.143	.168	.176	.187
46–50	.184	.076	.042	.112	.096	.104	.109
51–55	.184	.078	.042	.106	.091	.101	.104
56–60	.139	.042	.019	.087	.056	.045	.039
61–65	.163	.060	.033	.077	.058	.057	.060
66 and older	.151	.050	.023	.129	.091	.080	.069
Total	.215	.081	.043				
Gender							
Women	.194	.081	.044	.148	.134	.148	.153
Men	.219	.081	.043	.852	.866	.852	.847
Total	.215	.081	.043				
Employment							
Formal labor market	.201	.071	.035	.471	.439	.411	.383
Informal labor market	.235	.096	.054	.299	.327	.353	.375
Unemployed	.475	.222	.133	.025	.054	.067	.076
Inactive	.188	.067	.035	.205	.180	.169	.166
Total	.215	.081	.043				

Source: Author calculations from government household survey data tapes.
Note: Last three columns may not sum to 1.00 due to rounding.

Overall, the poverty ratio, or the fraction of the population of Buenos Aires below the poverty line, rose from 6 percent in 1980 to 21.5 percent in recession year 1989. The increase in poverty was more widespread and severe in the second half of the decade than in the first.[7] The percentage increase in P^1 and P^2 over the decade was even greater than that of P^0, implying that severe poverty rose even faster than the number in poverty. Clearly, by any measure, the 1980s, particularly the latter half, were a calamitous period for the poor of Buenos Aires.

One can ask how sensitive the indexes are to errors in measurement. Foster and Shorrocks (1988) show that, under conditions satisfied by the FGT index, when the cumulative percentage of the population below each value of income rose between two points in time (i.e., if the frequency distribution for the later year lay entirely above the initial year), then regardless of the poverty line or the degree of poverty aversion (choice of α), poverty rose between the two years. The initial year is said to "first-order dominate" the terminal year.

The frequency distributions for the sample for the each of the three years pass this test. The year 1989 lies entirely above 1986, which in turn lies entirely above 1980. This means that poverty unambiguously increased during the time periods, regardless of how different parts of the poverty population are weighted or where the poverty line is set. Errors in measurement, such as differences between the inflation rate for the poor and the nonpoor and degree of income underreporting by the poor, could affect this comparison. However, the horizontal distance between the frequency distributions at the poverty line tells us by how much reported income at that point would have to be adjusted for there to have been no change in the poverty ratio. For 1986 the correction would have to be 23 percent and for 1989 a whopping 54 percent. Measurement errors of this magnitude are unlikely.

Frequency distributions also permit one to see how sensitive the poverty indexes are to changes in the poverty line. The ratio is very sensitive to where the poverty line is placed because of the large numbers of people in that part of the income distribution. For example, if the poverty line is raised by 20 percent, the 1980 ratio would jump from 6.3 percent to 9.3 percent. By the same token, changes in the indexes are not very sensitive to the choice of a poverty line, and that is of more concern. Had both the 1980 and 1989 poverty lines been raised by 20 percent, poverty would have been shown to increase by 207 percent, which is not dramatically different than the 241 percent rise actually shown.

Tables 4-4, 4-5, and 4-6 indicate who the poor were and the incidence of poverty in various subgroups of the population. We concentrate here on the 1989 figures, reserving analysis of changes in poverty for the following section. The three columns on the left-hand side of each table show the incidence of poverty, and those on the right show the decomposition of each index. Thus for example table 4-6 tells us that in 1989, 27 percent of those in households whose head had only a grade school education were poor but that this group comprised 69.7 percent of all those below the poverty line.

Across age cohorts, one finds that the incidence of poverty was higher among young households but that most of the poor were not in such households, because young households made up a small proportion of the total population. When the sample is split by sex of the household head, we surprisingly find that the incidence of poverty was lower among households headed by females. However, looking at P^2 rather than P^0, we find that the incidence of severe poverty was slightly higher among females.

Look now at the poverty measures classified by the employment of the head of the household.[8] As is to be expected, the informal labor market had a higher incidence of poverty than the formal labor market, but the differences are surprisingly small. That pattern is repeated in the decomposition indexes, where in all three poverty measures the share of the formal sector is higher than that of the informal sector. This tells us that the poverty problem in Buenos Aires was not simply a matter of people being pushed into the informal sector, where they took low-paying jobs. Indeed, the share of the labor force in the informal sector rose by only 3 percent between 1980 and 1989. Rather, productivity and the real wage in the formal sector fell so far that almost half of these workers were unable to earn even a poverty-level income in 1989. At the same time, poverty incidence grew more rapidly in the informal sector than in the formal sector, as one would expect.

The indexes for unemployed and inactive household heads (not in the labor force) tell us, first, that while the incidence of poverty and of extreme poverty was very high for the unemployed, poverty was not primarily a problem of lack of jobs; only 5.4 percent of poor heads of household were unemployed in 1989. Nor was poverty mainly confined to the retired or the elderly; even assuming that all of the inactive household heads were retired, only 18.8 percent of the poor were in this category, and only 15 percent were over sixty years old.

Decomposing the Changes in Poverty Between 1980 and 1989

The data showing that Argentina suffered a sharp increase in poverty over the 1980s, particularly during the recession at the end of the period, come only from Greater Buenos Aires, but there is no reason to believe that the picture would look much different were we able to look at the entire country. Indeed, reverse migration to the countryside may well bias downward the estimates of changes in urban poverty over the decade.

In this section, the question asked is, Where did this massive increase in poverty come from? In the following section, the question is, How much of it was caused by recession? In the previous section, the FGT poverty indexes were decomposed to show sectoral contributions to poverty. Here they are decomposed to show the source of changes in the overall poverty index. For convenience, the poverty aversion superscripts are not shown.

For any index P we can decompose changes between two points in time as follows:

$$P_t - P_o = \sum_{j=1}^{k} [m_{jo}(P_{jt} - P_{jo}) + P_{jo}(m_{jt} - m_{jo}) + (P_{jt} - P_{jo})(m_{jt} - m_{jo})]. \quad (5)$$

| within | between | cross-product |
| groups | groups | |

The first term on the right-hand side of the equation is the contribution of changes in the poverty indexes within each group j and the second represents changes due to movements of the population between groups. The third, or cross-product, term tells whether expanding groups have rising or falling poverty indexes. If the cross-product is positive, it means that expanding (contracting) sectors have rising (falling) poverty.

Table 4-7 displays the decomposition of changes in P^0, P^1, and P^2 between 1980 and 1989 for various characteristics of household heads. Of the total increase of 15.2 percent in the poverty ratio between 1980 and 1989, 12.9 percent (or 85% of the total increase) came from increases in poverty in households headed by those with no more than a primary school education. This fraction is far greater than the share of the group in the poverty population of 1980 (51%), which means that the unfavorable trends over the decade had a concentrated and particularly negative effect

Table 4-7. Changes in Poverty Level, by Head of Household Characteristics, Greater Buenos Aires, 1980–1989

| | P^0 | | | P^1 | | | P^2 | | |
Characteristic	Between Groups	Within Groups	Cross-Product	Between Groups	Within Groups	Cross-Product	Between Groups	Within Groups	Cross-Product
Educational level									
Illiterate	-.0078	.0121	-.0041	-.0027	.0094	-.0032	-.0013	.0073	-.0025
Grade school	-.0023	.1295	-.0091	-.0006	.0517	-.0037	-.0002	.0277	-.0020
High school	.0013	.0239	.0044	.0003	.0090	.0017	.0001	.0047	.0009
Technical school	.0000	.0000	.0009	.0000	.0000	.0002	.0000	.0000	.0001
University	.0002	.0029	.0005	.0000	.0013	.0002	.0000	.0007	.0001
Total	-.0086	.1685	-.0075	-.0029	.0714	-.0047	-.0014	.0404	-.0033
Change		.1523			.0637			.0357	
Age in years									
Less than 15	-.0004	-.0004	.0004	-.0001	-.0001	.0001	.0000	.0000	.0000
16–20	.0000	.0007	.0005	.0000	.0003	.0002	.0000	.0002	.0001
21–25	.0000	.0028	.0000	.0000	.0012	.0000	.0000	.0007	.0000
26–30	-.0005	.0148	-.0012	-.0001	.0055	-.0004	-.0001	.0026	-.0002
31–35	-.0007	.0256	-.0017	-.0002	.0102	-.0007	-.0001	.0055	-.0004
36–40	.0015	.0235	.0046	.0005	.0099	.0019	.0002	.0057	.0011
41–45	.0004	.0266	.0014	.0001	.0112	.0006	.0001	.0065	.0003
46–50	-.0013	.0120	-.0014	-.0004	.0063	-.0007	-.0002	.0039	-.0005
51–55	-.0002	.0150	-.0006	-.0001	.0073	-.0003	.0000	.0042	-.0002
56–60	-.0009	.0066	-.0008	-.0002	.0024	-.0003	-.0001	.0012	-.0001
61–65	.0003	.0088	.0021	.0001	.0033	.0008	.0000	.0019	.0005
66 and older	.0001	.0148	.0002	.0000	.0053	.0001	.0000	.0026	.0000
Total	-.0017	.1507	.0034	-.0003	.0629	.0012	-.0001	.0351	.0007
Change		.1523			.0637			.0357	

Continued next page

Table 4-7—Continued

Characteristic	P^0			P^1			P^2		
	Between Groups	Within Groups	Cross-Product	Between Groups	Within Groups	Cross-Product	Between Groups	Within Groups	Cross-Product
Gender									
Women	.0009	.0193	.0035	.0002	.0092	.0017	.0000	.0053	.0010
Men	.0015	.1336	-.0035	-.0004	.0545	-.0014	-.0002	.0303	-.0008
Total	-.0006	.1529	.0000	-.0003	.0637	.0003	-.0001	.0356	.0002
Change			.1523			.0637			.0357
Employment (urban)									
Formal labor market	-.0029	.0596	-.0041	-.0009	.0228	-.0016	-.0004	.0118	-.0008
Informal labor market	.0013	.0515	.0061	.0003	.0235	.0028	.0001	.0138	.0016
Unemployed	.0013	.0026	.0075	.0001	.0014	.0040	.0000	.0008	.0024
Inactive	-.0006	.0324	-.0023	-.0002	.0125	-.0009	-.0001	.0069	-.0005
Total	-.0009	.1461	.0072	-.0007	.0600	.0043	-.0004	.0333	.0028
Change			.1523			.0637			.0357

Source: Author calculations from government household survey data tapes.

on those with the least education. We will get a better idea of why and how this happened when we look at changes in wage differentials in the next section.

When poverty indexes are decomposed by employment, another dimension of the rise in poverty over the decade becomes clear. In 1980, the informal sector had a lower incidence of poverty than the formal sector. This dramatically changed during the recession, as the ratio in the informal sector rose from 4.3 percent to 23.5 percent. In 1980 only 18 percent of the poor came from the informal sector; yet the informal sector contributed over one-third of the rise in P^0 over the decade. When the index is adjusted by the poverty aversion factor α, the impact of the recession on the informal sector is even more marked. In 1980, the informal sector had a share of extreme poverty far lower than its share of the population (8.8%, compared to 26.7%). Yet between 1980 and 1989, 38.5 percent (0.0118/0.0357) of the increase in P^2 came from the informal sector. Recession pushed people into the informal sector and drove down disproportionately the incomes of those who worked there.

In 1980, unemployment among household heads was not a big cause of poverty: only 7 percent of the unemployed heads of households were poor, and less than 1 percent of poverty, using any of the three poverty indexes, came from this source. In 1989, this group had a far higher likelihood of being in poverty, but still very few household heads in the labor force were unemployed. Thus, despite the rise in the incidence of poverty among this group, only 6.5 percent of the overall rise in the ratio came from the unemployed (counting both within-product and cross-product terms).

A slightly different picture emerges for the inactive class. In 1980, 22 percent of the population and 14.5 percent of the poor were in this group. Over the decade, the incidence of poverty in the group rose from 4.5 percent to 18.8 percent, implying that 21.3 percent of the increase in the ratio was caused by rising poverty among heads of household not in the workforce. Thus poverty rose during the 1989 recession partly because wages went down for working people in both the formal and informal sectors and partly because retirement incomes and transfers were inadequately indexed for inflation. Unemployment per se was not a particularly significant additional source of poverty.

Finally, consider the patterns of poverty across age and sex. Not surprisingly, since most households are headed by males, most poverty and changes in poverty came from these households as well. But there was an important change over the decade. In 1980, the incidence of poverty was lower in households headed by females than in those headed by males. That pattern partially reversed over the decade. The ratio was still higher for men than for women in 1989, but that was not true for either P^1 or P^2. This implies that a disproportionate number of female-headed households were pushed into extreme poverty over the decade. In 1980, only 3.5 percent of the extreme poverty (P^2) came from female-headed households, but 15 percent of the rise in this index came from that source. Clearly, the recession had a severe impact on households headed by women.

Recession was particularly hard on younger households. Both in 1980 and 1989, these household had a higher than average incidence of poverty, not a surprising pattern considering the age-earnings profile and the high dependency ratio of younger households. Still, the extent to which the increase in poverty was concentrated in this group is surprising. For example, 62 percent of the rise in poverty came from households whose head was less than 46 years old, even though this group contained only 47 percent of the 1980 population. This decomposition implies that not only was there a substantial age-wage differential but also that those with more experience were better positioned than younger workers to defend their incomes against recession. More evidence for this implication in the age-wage differential is shown in the next section.

Earnings Differentials

To go beyond simple decomposition in order to understand better the link between the adjustment, the labor market, and poverty, one can measure the wage differentials during the adjustment. To do this, reported nominal earnings for 1986 and 1989 were deflated by a common cost-of-living index and expressed relative to their 1980 level (which equals 1; see tables 4-8 and 4-9).[9]

The patterns are the same for all characteristics: real wages fell for everyone. Wage differentials first narrowed between 1980 and 1986 and then widened quite sharply over the next three years. Either the recovery in 1986 permitted a recovery of wages at the bottom, or there was a significant difference in the adjustment process between the early and the late 1980s. In the early years, the adjustment was progressive, whereas in the downturn of 1988–89, the real wage deterioration was heavily concentrated among those with the least education and in the least skilled jobs.

Table 4-8.   Indexes of Real Household Income, by Decile,
Greater Buenos Aires, 1986 and 1989 (1980 = 1)

Income Decile	1986	1989
1	0.93	0.28
2	0.97	0.35
3	0.96	0.35
4	0.97	0.33
5	0.94	0.32
6	0.91	0.31
7	0.92	0.31
8	0.93	0.33
9	0.85	0.33
10	0.88	0.41

Source: Author calculations from government household survey data tapes.

In looking for explanations for the shift from progressive to regressive adjustment over the decade, one cannot help but be struck by the similarity between what happened to real wages and what happened to wage differentials. Recall that the minimum and the average real wage rose between 1980 and 1986 and then fell sharply to 1989 (see table 4-2). Wage differentials moved in the opposite direction. While this historic co-movement is far from a proof of causation, it does suggest that maintaining a real wage floor tends to buffer the impact of adjustment on those at the bottom. In contrast, an adjustment like that of 1988–89, which produces a significant reduction in real and minimum wages, seems likely to lead to a regressive widening of wage differentials.

The Effect of Recession and Adjustment

The 1980s were not one homogeneous adjustment period. Rather, there were two periods of stabilization separated by a short and partial recovery in 1986–87, after the Austral Plan. The first attempt at stabilization came after the collapse of the Tablita experiment and the onset of the debt crisis in 1982. This stabilization lasted until 1985 and was strongly progressive. Wages and output had fallen sharply between 1980 and 1982, when what might be termed the period of populist adjustment began. From that point until 1986, both the minimum wage and the average wage

Table 4-9.   Index of Real Wages by Worker Characteristics,
Greater Buenos Aires, 1986 and 1989 (1980 = 1)

Characteristic	1986	1989
Age in years		
Less than 15	0.89	0.33
16–20	0.87	0.44
21–25	0.92	0.46
26–30	0.91	0.51
31–35	0.95	0.51
36–40	1.09	0.54
41–45	0.92	0.51
46–50	0.86	0.55
51–55	0.77	0.45
56–60	0.83	0.48
61–65	0.73	0.52
66 and older	0.78	0.46
Economic sector		
Agriculture	1.04	0.28
Industry	0.95	0.49
Utilities	0.93	0.65
Construction	0.84	0.44
Commerce	1.03	0.53
Transportation	0.99	0.56
Finance	0.87	0.55
Services	0.92	0.51
Educational level		
Illiterate	1.01	0.49
Grade school	0.93	0.47
High school	0.89	0.48
Technical school	0.89	0.48
University	0.83	0.51

Source: Author calculations from government household
survey data tapes.

sharply increased, the former by 13 percent and the latter by 28 percent.[10]
Since this increase took place in the context of an economy where per
capita income was still shrinking, it caused a significant reduction in
inequality.

There is a good deal of evidence to back this statement. Beccaria (1991)
shows that the income share of the bottom 30 percent of households rose
from 10.1 percent to 10.4 percent between 1981 and 1985. During the same
period, the share of the top income group fell from 33.5 percent to 31.3

percent (ibid., p. 333).[11] One can see the same progressivity in the share of labor in national income. It fell from 35 percent in 1980 to 22 percent in 1982 and then rose back to 35 percent in 1986 (ibid., p. 323). Income and wage trends show the same progressive pattern. Real wage differentials were calculated by age, education, and income class, and all told the same story—a significant shrinking of wage differentials between 1980 and 1986 (Morley and Alvarez, 1992c, table 7).

More relevant is the question of what happened to poverty—and here is one of the rare cases where poverty and income both fell at the same time. According to census bureau surveys for Buenos Aires, the ratio fell from 0.28 to 0.206 between 1982 and 1985 (see table 4-3). Since there had been a sharp rise in poverty between 1980 and 1982, this reversal was not enough to make up that early loss, which is why, over the entire period 1980–86, poverty rose.

The second stabilization, during 1987–90, was completely different from the first. Where the latter had been progressive, the new stabilization was regressive. Earlier, real wages had risen; now they fell precipitously, especially in the inflation-racked year of 1989 (see table 4-2). Where the wage differential narrowed between 1980 and 1986, now it widened (ibid.). Where the distribution had become more equal, now it became sharply less equal.[12] Since all of this took place at a time when per capita income was suffering declines relative even to the 1985 trough, it was to be expected that poverty would increase. And increase it did (see table 4-3).

When one compares these two stabilization phases, it is tempting to conclude that maintaining the real wage during a period when income is shrinking is a good way of deflecting the cost of adjustment from the poor. The evidence is certainly consistent with this conclusion. But the issue is more complex than that, because inflation is left out of the picture. In Argentina the populist stabilization of 1982–85 unleashed a virulent inflation. It rose from 165 percent in 1982 to 672 percent in 1985 before the Austral Plan of that year put an artificial and temporary damper on price increases.

The subsequent stabilization of 1987–90 was primarily directed at the inflation problem rather than the balance of payments. Such stabilizations are always regressive. Wages were de-indexed and held down to reduce cost pressures on prices, with disastrous effects on both poverty and the distribution of income. The question we cannot answer is the extent to which the outburst of inflation in 1982–85, which made the subsequent stabilization necessary, was due to the previous rise in real wages. If it was, it would be incorrect to conclude that raising the real wage in an adjustment program would help the poor. That may be true in the short run but not in the long run, if raising the wage leads to the sort of inflation that Argentina had after 1986. Such an inflation requires a wage-reducing stabilization, which inevitably hurts the poor by offsetting any short-run gains they may have enjoyed during a previous populist stabilization.

VENEZUELA

We turn next to the story of adjustment in Venezuela, the quintessential mineral economy.[13] For decades, Venezuela was carried along by rising oil prices and one of world's largest oil deposits. It prospered, but it never developed alternative economic activities that could sustain it when the oil bonanza collapsed. Throughout the sixties and seventies, the country grew and borrowed, running enormous current account deficits to fund ambitious and often wasteful investment projects. By 1980 it was the most highly urbanized, the richest, and the second-most-indebted country in Latin America.

In 1983 this pleasant process abruptly stopped. Oil prices fell by 12 percent and new loans dried up; Venezuela was forced to start a painful process of adjustment. The succeeding decade was the most painful in the country's history. Per capital income and real wages fell by one-fourth, inflation rose from 10–15 percent in the 1970s to a peak of 84 percent in 1989, and interest payments on the debt rose to almost 70 percent of exports by mid-decade. Heavily dependent on oil revenue, the government was forced to drastically curtail expenditures on investment projects, social programs, and subsidies.

The process of adjustment began in earnest in 1983. The first phase (1983–86) brought a real devaluation, the first in twenty years, and a sharp drop in the government budget deficit and in both public and private investment (see table 4-10). The resulting contraction in aggregate demand caused a recession, which pushed down real wages and incomes and raised the unemployment rate to over 14 percent (table 4-11). This first phase of the adjustment process has been called "adjustment without structural change," meaning that the contraction was not accompanied by

Table 4-10. Indicators of Economic Performance, Venezuela, 1980–1989

Year	GDP per Capita (1980 = 100)	Investment (% of GDP)	Current Account Deficit (% of GDP)	Terms of Trade (1980 = 100)
1980	100	28.0	12.8	100
1981	97	28.1	16.0	103
1982	95	31.4	19.3	95
1983	88	16.2	1.9	104
1984	83	23.3	6.2	116
1985	83	23.8	5.1	111
1986	86	23.5	3.1	54
1987	87	25.7	3.6	66
1988	91	27.9	5.7	54
1989	81	14.5	–2.5	64

Source: IADB, Economic and Social Data Base.

either an opening up of the economy or a reduction in government intervention (Cline, 1991).

In the period 1986–88, the new Social Democratic government reversed the contractionary policy of its predecessor, attempting to emerge from recession by a policy of debt-financed growth. Despite a continued reduction in oil revenues, the government increased its spending, which grew from 21 percent to 26.5 percent of GDP. It also raised the minimum wage, which had been frozen from 1980 to 1984 and which had fallen by 33 percent in real terms. The new government raised the nominal wage by enough to offset all of its loss in real purchasing power since 1980. All of these expansionary measures revived the economy (GDP grew by 16.7% in the years 1986–88); but they also led to an ominous rise in the inflation rate, the current account, and the government deficit.

In 1989 the new government of Carlos Andres Pérez reversed policy again, putting in place a new policy of adjustment, this time based on a reduction in aggregate demand coupled with structural changes. One of the main components of the new program was a sharp fiscal contraction. The government deficit was cut from 7.4 percent to 1 percent of GDP, due mainly to a large cut in expenditures, which fell by 5 percent of GDP. But the policy changes were not limited to the traditional areas of monetary and fiscal policy. There was also a concerted effort to reduce the role of government in the economy. Price controls were abolished, as were many

Table 4-11. Macroeconomic Data on Urban Employment,
Venezuela, 1980–1990

Year	Employment (thousands)	Unemployment Rate (%)
1980	4,646	6.0
1981	4,803	6.2
1982	4,928	7.1
1983	4,934	10.0
1984	4,938	13.0
1985	5,106	14.1
1986	5,396	11.0
1987	5,694	9.0
1988	6,033	7.3
1989	6,154	9.2
1990	6,233	

Source: ECLAC, various years, Economic Survey.

restrictions on imports and the system of multiple exchange rates. Tariffs were lowered, and a far-reaching process of privatization was initiated.

The first results of the new program could not have been very comforting for the new government. Thanks partly to the elimination of price controls, the 1989 inflation rate rose to 84 percent, and GDP fell by almost 9 percent. Investment shrank to its lowest level in twenty years. Labor was particularly hard-hit: real wages fell by around 20 percent, and the unemployment rate rose by 2 percent. According to official sources, real income per urban worker fell to less than half its 1980 level, this in a country where at least 90 percent of the labor force is urban (ECLAC, Economic Survey 1985, 1989). If these statistics are accurate, no other country in Latin America has had so severe an adjustment in labor incomes.

These difficult conditions form the background against which the 1989 observations of poverty were taken. Family incomes were recorded during the first year of what must have been a wrenching structural adjustment. The fact that this came at the end of almost ten years of stagnation only made the situation more difficult, for the buildup of unemployment and poverty in the first half of the decade could hardly have been dissipated by the short recovery of 1986–88. The 1989 recession was followed by a fairly vigorous recovery, in which per capita income grew by over 17 percent between 1989 and 1992, inflation dropped to around 30 percent, and there was a significant reduction in poverty (see table 4-12).

Table 4-12. Population in Poverty, Three Estimates, Venezuela, 1981–1991, Various Years
(percent)

Year	World Bank (1990a)[1]			ECLAC (1990a)[1]			Marquez (1992)[2]		
	Urban	Rural	Total	Urban	Rural	Total	Urban	Rural	Total
1981				20	43	25	15	26	18
1982	25	58	33						
1985							23	47	25
1986				30	42	32			
1987	38	71	44				28	49	32
1989	49	74	53				38	60	41
1991							31	53	35

[1] Households.
[2] Individuals.

Estimates of Poverty

Table 4-11 displays estimates of the percentage of the population receiving less than a poverty level of income. All of the sources on which the table is based used the same basic methodology to measure poverty; first a poverty line was defined as twice the cost of a basket of food meeting basic calories and protein requirements; then a household survey was taken to determine per capita income. The estimates differ because of the treatment of underreporting of income, the composition of the basic food basket, and the price deflator.[14] Because the estimates are sensitive to these definitions, the figures should not be compared; rather they suggest trends in poverty, for changes in the percentages over time are much less sensitive to bias in measurement than level of poverty at any point in time.

The figures suggest the same broad picture: poverty declined during the long oil boom between 1970 and 1982, then rose rapidly, the deterioration being relatively worse in urban areas than in rural areas.[15] Possibly by 1986 and certainly by 1989, the absolute level of poverty had risen to a point higher than at any time since 1970. As we have seen, between 1980 and 1989, per capita income and real wages both fell by more than 20 percent. The table data show the severe impact of those changes on the poor.

Decomposing the Changes in Poverty

Tapes of household surveys were available for 1981, 1986, and 1989. The year 1981 is a good proxy for the situation prior to the adjustment because, while there was a slight reduction in GDP/per capita in that year, the really severe adjustment started in 1983. The year 1986 was a year of partial recovery from the trough in economic activity in 1985; and, as in Argentina, the year 1989 coincides exactly with the second trough of the decade. Thus a comparison of the years 1981 and 1989 should show quite clearly the effect of the contraction phase of the adjustment process. Unlike Argentina, the Venezuelan surveys covered the whole nation, allowing direct observation of trends in both rural and urban poverty.

Tables 4-13, 4-14, and 4-15 present poverty estimates across a number of household categories of 1981, 1986, and 1989.[16] Data in the tables confirm the dramatic increase in poverty in all categories shown by the other studies. Both these results and those of Marquez indicate that, while poverty increased rapidly in both periods, the biggest increase was in the second period, 1986–89. Much of that increase must have occurred in 1989, when a renewal of adjustment led to large reductions in government spending, big declines in per capita income and real wages, and big increases in unemployment and the inflation rate. The impact of adjustment was especially pronounced on the very poor. The P^0 measure doubled between 1981 and 1989, but P^2 almost tripled. For both measures, the rate of increase in poverty was particularly rapid after 1986. By any standard, the 1980s was a terrible decade for those at the bottom of the income pyramid in Venezuela.

Comparisons over time are always fraught with uncertainty because of changes in sampling, measurement error, and so on. Thus it is natural to wonder how firm these conclusions about poverty increases are. This question is addressed in two ways: Foster and Shorrocks (1988) show that, under conditions satisfied by the FGT index, when the frequency distribution for the later year lies entirely above the initial year, then regardless of the poverty line or the degree of poverty aversion (choice of α), poverty rose between the two years.

The frequency distributions constructed for the sample for each of the three years pass this test. The year 1989 lies entirely above 1981, which means that poverty unambiguously increased, regardless of how different parts of the poverty population are weighted or where the poverty line is set. That fact does not tell about errors in measurement, such as

Table 4-13. Decomposition of the P^i Class of Poverty Measures, by Head of Household Characteristics, Venezuela, 1981

Characteristic	P^0	P^1	P^2	Share of Population	Contribution to National Poverty P^0	P^1	P^2
Educational level							
Illiterate	.436	.163	.083	.171	.311	.348	.372
Grade school	.243	.078	.036	.530	.538	.516	.499
High school	.096	.024	.009	.194	.077	.058	.048
University	.021	.005	.002	.055	.055	.003	.002
Not specified	.333	.119	.061	.049	.068	.073	.079
Ignored	.271	.114	.050	.001	.001	.001	.001
Total	.240	.080	.038				
Age in years							
16–20	.231	.081	.040	.004	.004	.004	.004
21–25	.204	.061	.027	.037	.031	.028	.026
26–30	.213	.065	.028	.096	.085	.078	.071
31–35	.256	.080	.037	.122	.130	.122	.119
36–40	.277	.097	.047	.148	.171	.179	.182
41–45	.259	.092	.045	.148	.159	.169	.176
46–50	.236	.078	.037	.125	.123	.122	.121
51–55	.219	.071	.033	.113	.103	.101	.098
56–60	.213	.069	.034	.088	.079	.076	.079
61–65	.224	.076	.038	.054	.050	.051	.053
66 and older	.238	.083	.042	.066	.065	.068	.072
Total	.240	.080	.038				
Gender							
Women	.303	.110	.056	.165	.208	.227	.244
Men	.227	.074	.034	.835	.792	.773	.756
Total	.240	.080	.038				
Employment (urban)							
Formal labor market (public)	.163	.041	.015	.207	.177	.149	.123
Formal labor market (private)	.144	.038	.015	.261	.197	.173	.153
Informal labor market	.184	.057	.026	.376	.365	.372	.381
Unemployed	.567	.225	.120	.016	.048	.063	.075
Inactive	.286	.100	.049	.141	.212	.244	.269
Total	.189	.057	.026				
Geographical area							
Metropolitan	.132	.037	.015	.271	.149	.124	.106
Urban	.220	.068	.032	.517	.473	.441	.429
Rural	.427	.164	.083	.212	.378	.435	.465
Total	.240	.080	.038				

Source: Author calculations from government household survey data tapes.

Table 4-14. Decomposition of the P^i Class of Poverty Measures, by Head of Household
Characteristics, Venezuela, 1986

				Share of	Contribution to National Poverty		
Characteristic	P^0	P^1	P^2	Population	P^0	P^1	P^2
Educational level							
Illiterate	.479	.182	.095	.120	.197	.215	.229
Grade school	.334	.116	.056	.493	.566	.565	.561
High school	.188	.057	.026	.260	.168	.146	.135
University	.031	.010	.005	.089	.010	.009	.008
Ignored	.441	.170	.087	.038	.058	.065	.067
Total	.290	.101	.049				
Age in years							
16–20	.287	.101	.045	.003	.003	.003	.003
21–25	.305	.089	.036	.035	.037	.031	.026
26–30	.273	.085	.038	.097	.091	.082	.074
31–35	.282	.097	.047	.143	.139	.137	.137
36–40	.307	.106	.052	.164	.174	.173	.172
41–45	.323	.114	.057	.133	.147	.150	.152
46–50	.282	.097	.047	.106	.103	.101	.101
51–55	.260	.094	.048	.100	.089	.093	.097
56–60	.281	.102	.050	.090	.087	.091	.090
61–65	.264	.094	.046	.057	.052	.053	.053
66 and older	.313	.123	.066	.071	.076	.086	.095
Total	.290	.101	.040				
Gender							
Women	.371	.145	.044	.825	.224	.251	.273
Men	.273	.092	.077	.175	.775	.748	.727
Total	.290	.101	.049				
Employment (urban)							
Formal labor market (public)	.236	.074	.032	.193	.167	.154	.136
Formal labor market (private)	.242	.075	.033	.406	.362	.326	.304
Informal labor market	.314	.120	.062	.340	.393	.436	.471
Unemployed	1.000	.066	.004	.000	.001	.000	.000
Inactive	.343	.129	.065	.061	.077	.085	.089
Total	.272	.093	.045				
Geographical area							
Metropolitan	.189	.053	.022	.341	.221	.180	.154
Urban	.325	.119	.059	.529	.592	.621	.635
Rural	.416	.154	.080	.130	.186	.198	.211
Total	.290	.101	.049				

Source: Author calculations from government household survey data tapes.

Table 4-15. Decomposition of the P^i Class of Poverty Measures, by Head of Household Characteristics, Venezuela, 1989

Characteristic	P^0	P^1	P^2	Share of Population	Contribution to National Poverty P^0	P^1	P^2
Educational level							
Illiterate	.703	.329	.194	.128	.186	.217	.236
Grade school	.551	.224	.121	.481	.550	.555	.554
High school	.355	.118	.056	.269	.198	.163	.143
University	.117	.038	.018	.086	.021	.017	.015
Ignored	.605	.264	.152	.036	.045	.049	.052
Total	.482	.194	.105				
Age in years							
Less than 15	.678	.211	.112	.000	.000	.000	.000
16–20	.464	.165	.082	.004	.004	.003	.003
21–25	.469	.167	.082	.035	.034	.030	.027
26–30	.472	.183	.094	.087	.086	.082	.078
31–35	.522	.206	.111	.125	.135	.133	.132
36–40	.505	.202	.108	.163	.171	.169	.168
41–45	.489	.196	.106	.143	.146	.145	.145
46–50	.466	.193	.107	.115	.112	.115	.117
51–55	.437	.179	.100	.097	.088	.089	.091
56–60	.444	.192	.108	.084	.077	.083	.086
61–65	.458	.183	.098	.064	.061	.060	.059
66 and older	.514	.215	.120	.082	.088	.091	.094
Total	.482	.194	.105				
Gender							
Women	.530	.232	.135	.180	.198	.215	.230
Men	.471	.186	.099	.802	.802	.758	.770
Total	.482	.194	.105				
Employment (urban)							
Formal labor market (public)	.344	.113	.052	.166	.128	.108	.093
Formal labor market (private)	.385	.132	.063	.347	.299	.265	.238
Informal labor market	.485	.201	.111	.310	.337	.359	.375
Unemployed	.766	.386	.244	.033	.056	.073	.086
Inactive	.560	.236	.134	.144	.180	.195	.208
Total	.447	.174	.092				
Geographical area							
Metropolitan	.316	.113	.057	.210	.138	.123	.114
Urban	.491	.194	.104	.627	.638	.625	.619
Rural	.664	.303	.174	.162	.223	.252	.267
Total	.482	.194	.105				

Source: Author calculations from government household survey data tapes.

differences between the inflation rate for the poor and the nonpoor and changes in the degree of relative underreporting of income by the poor. However, in 1989 the correction would have to be about 40 percent to reverse the finding that poverty increased. Measurement errors of this magnitude are unlikely.

Tables 4-12, 4-13, and 4-14 give us some idea of who the poor are and the incidence of poverty in various subgroups of the population. The first three columns show the incidence of poverty or the probability of being poor for any member of a subgroup; the last three columns show who the poor were. For example, in 1989, 70 percent of illiterates were poor, and they composed 18.6 percent of the overall poverty population in 1989. The first pattern that strikes one, when looking at the tables, is that most of Venezuela's poverty was urban. Even though poverty incidence was higher in the countryside, the population living there was so small that 78 percent of the poor were urban.[17] This probably means that any targeted antipoverty programs will have to be predominantly urban and non-agricultural.

It is quite clear from these tables that the effect of structural adjustment reached well up into the labor pyramid. Its impact was not confined to the unemployed, even though they composed 21 percent of the poor. Nor is it limited to illiterates or workers in the informal sector. According to table 4-14, 43 percent of the poor were in households whose heads worked in the formal sector, compared to 33 percent in households whose heads worked in the informal sector. Fully 22 percent of the poor in 1989 had a high school or university education, not much fewer than their number in the population. This is quite a striking pattern and indicates the severity of conditions in 1989. It is likely that the high incidence of poverty among the well educated (those with at least a high school education) reflects the large increase in the supply of well-educated new entrants in the stagnant labor market of 1989.

The decomposition formula (eq. 5) can be used to address more systematically the question of which groups were most affected by the large increase in poverty between 1981 and 1989 in Venezuela. Table 4-16 displays the decompositions of changes in P^0, P^1, and P^2 between 1981 and 1989 for various groupings of households. Virtually the entire 24 percent increase in poverty between 1981 and 1989 in the geographical area grouping was due to rising poverty in the urban sector; 78 percent (19/24) of the increase was caused by rising poverty in the base period population, and another 15 percent came from a population expansion in the

Table 4-16. Changes in Poverty Level, by Head of Household Characteristics, Venezuela, 1981–1989

	P^0			P^1			P^2		
Characteristic	Between Groups	Within Groups	Cross-Product	Between Groups	Within Groups	Cross-Product	Between Groups	Within Groups	Cross-Product
Educational level									
Illiterate	−.0188	.0456	−.0115	−.0070	.0284	−.0072	−.0036	.0191	−.0048
Grade school	−.0119	.1628	−.0150	−.0038	.0777	−.0072	−.0018	.0454	−.0042
High school	.0072	.0502	.0196	.0018	.0182	.0071	.0007	.0090	.0035
University	.0007	.0053	.0029	.0002	.0018	.0010	.0000	.0009	.0005
Not specified	−.0047	.0137	−.0039	−.0017	.0072	−.0021	−.0009	.0046	−.0013
Total	−.0276	.2776	−.0079	−.0106	.1334	−.0083	−.0054	.0790	−.0063
Change			.2421			.1145			.0673
Age in years									
16–20	−.0001	−.0010	−.0001	.0000	.0004	−.0000	.0000	.0002	.0000
21–25	−.0004	.0098	−.0006	−.0001	.0039	−.0002	−.0001	.0020	−.0001
26–30	−.0018	.0249	−.0022	−.0006	.0112	−.0010	−.0002	.0063	−.0006
31–35	.0009	.0323	.0009	.0003	.0153	.0004	.0001	.0090	.0003
36–40	.0042	.0338	.0035	.0015	.0155	.0016	.0007	.0091	.0009
41–45	−.0011	.0339	−.0009	−.0004	.0154	−.0004	−.0002	.0090	−.0002
46–50	−.0023	.0287	−.0022	−.0008	.0145	−.0011	−.0004	.0088	−.0007
51–55	−.0035	.0245	−.0035	−.0011	.0121	−.0017	−.0005	.0075	−.0011
56–60	−.0009	.0204	−.0010	−.0003	.0109	−.0005	−.0002	.0066	−.0003
61–65	.0022	.0126	.0023	.0008	.0058	.0011	.0004	.0032	.0006
66 and older	.0039	.0181	.0046	.0014	.0086	.0022	.0007	.0052	.0013
Total	.0011	.2402	.0008	.0006	.1137	.0002	.0004	.0669	.0001
Change			.2421			.1145			.0673

Continued next page

Table 4-16—Continued

Characteristic	P^0 Between Groups	P^0 Within Groups	P^0 Cross-Product	P^1 Between Groups	P^1 Within Groups	P^1 Cross-Product	P^2 Between Groups	P^2 Within Groups	P^2 Cross-Product
Gender									
Women	.0046	.0373	.0035	.0017	.0201	.0019	.0009	.0129	.0012
Men	-.0035	.2039	-.0037	-.0011	.0937	-.0017	-.0005	.0539	-.0010
Total	.0012	.2412	-.0003	.0006	.1138	.0001	.0003	.0668	.0002
Change			.2421			.1145			.0673
Employment (urban)									
Formal labor market (public)	-.0065	.0375	-.0073	-.0017	.0148	-.0029	-.0006	.0075	-.0015
Formal labor market (private)	.0124	.0630	.0209	.0033	.0246	.0082	.0013	.0125	.0042
Informal labor market	-.0121	.1133	-.0198	-.0037	.0542	-.0095	-.0017	.0320	-.0056
Unemployed	.0094	.0032	.0033	.0037	.0026	.0027	.0020	.0020	.0020
Inactive	.0008	.0385	.0008	.0003	.0192	.0004	.0001	.0118	.0002
Total	.0040	.2554	-.0021	.0019	.1154	-.0012	.0011	.0658	-.0006
Change			.2573			.1161			.0663
Geographical area									
Metropolitan	-.0079	.0499	-.0111	-.0022	.0207	-.0046	-.0009	.0114	-.0025
Urban	.0242	.1401	.0299	.0075	.0649	.0138	.0035	.0374	.0080
Rural	-.0214	.0504	-.0119	-.0082	.0295	-.0070	-.0042	.0192	-.0045
Total	-.0051	.2404	.0069	-.0029	.1151	.0023	-.0016	.0680	.0009
Change			.2421			.1145			.0673

Source: Author calculations from government household survey data tapes.

urban sector. Thus 93 percent of the increase in poverty came from the urban sector, even though only 80 percent of the 1981 population was urban. The dominance of urban poverty is slightly less marked for the P^1 and P^2 indexes, suggesting a significant rise in severe poverty in the countryside.

There was an increase in poverty in households headed by both sexes, with females contributing only slightly more than their 1981 population share to the overall rise in poverty. Educationally, the surprising result is the extent of poverty in relatively well-educated households. Even though people with at least a high school education composed only one-fourth of all households in 1981, they contributed 35 percent of the rise in poverty over the decade.[18] Not surprisingly, the bulk of rising poverty came from those with the least education, but even education was not a guaranteed defense against the impact of structural adjustment in Venezuela.

Decomposing change in poverty in the urban labor market permits us to concentrate on the role of the informal sector during structural adjustment. According to the theory, the informal sector should offer emergency employment at low wages during hard times. That apparently did not happen, for if it had, both employment and the number of poor in the informal sector would have risen. Instead, the informal sector shrank from 42 percent to 35 percent of the labor force, and the proportion of the change in poverty (47%) coming from the formal sector was just about equal to its 1981 share of the urban households.[19] Ironically, the increase in emergency, low-wage employment seems to have been in the formal sector rather than the informal. There was a significant increase in employment and a reduction in the urban real average wage between 1981 and 1989 (table 4-10), and the share of the informal sector fell over the decade. Thus most of the expansion in employment must have been in the formal sector, and much of it at wages below the poverty line. Another conclusion is that rising urban unemployment was not a major cause of the increase in poverty. Despite a high incidence of poverty among the unemployed, overall they accounted for not more than 15.6 percent of the change in urban poverty between 1981 and 1989. For the economy as a whole, the picture is somewhat different. Morley and Alvarez (1992b) find that nationally, unemployment accounted for 23 percent of the change in poverty, implying that rural unemployment was a significant cause of poverty.

Finally, consider the age distribution of changes in poverty displayed in table 4-15. Both young and old households suffered a slight relative increase in poverty, but overall the differences across age cohorts were quite small. This tells us that rising poverty was not primarily a problem for either the retired or the young. About 18 percent of the rise in poverty was in households headed by those over sixty years, while 70 percent was in households headed by thirty-to-sixty-year-olds. The rest (12%) was in households headed by those younger than thirty, which is just about equal to their share in the 1981 labor force.

Earnings Differentials

Tables 4-17 and 4-18 display the deflated earned income of individuals by several characteristics (no correction was made for underreporting, since what we are interested in here is wage differentials rather than real wage movements, per se). Based on other indexes of real wages, there was an increase in underreporting in 1989 relative to the two earlier years, implying that table 4-16 overstates the drop in real wages in all labor categories.

Two striking and somewhat inconsistent patterns are displayed in the table. The first is a significant rise in earnings inequality and the second is a simultaneous reduction in the education or skill differential. Income inequality rose, with a sharp rise in earnings at the top of the pyramid

Table 4-17. Real Income, by Household Income Decile, Venezuela, 1986 and 1989 (1981 = 1)

Income Decile	Total		Urban		Rural	
	1986	1989	1986	1989	1986	1989
1	.76	.09	.71	.05	.66	.20
2	.74	.27	.70	.27	.84	.35
3	.77	.36	.71	.35	.77	.40
4	.73	.36	.72	.36	.74	.43
5	.75	.38	.71	.37	.72	.43
6	.74	.39	.72	.39	.74	.42
7	.75	.40	.74	.40	.71	.41
8	.77	.41	.75	.41	.71	.40
9	.77	.42	.76	.41	.68	.39
10	.89	.46	.89	.47	.76	.41

Source: Author calculations from government household survey data tapes.

Table 4-18. Real Wages, by Worker Characteristic, Venezuela, 1986 and 1989 (1981 = 1)

Characteristic	Total		Urban		Rural	
	1986	1989	1986	1989	1986	1989
Age in years						
Less than 15	.74	.45	.68	.44	.89	.52
16–20	.75	.50	.74	.51	.74	.47
21–25	.75	.46	.74	.46	.75	.46
26–30	.76	.45	.74	.44	.75	.45
31–35	.80	.43	.78	.42	.73	.43
36–40	.85	.45	.82	.44	.81	.47
41–45	.86	.47	.85	.46	.72	.45
46–50	.90	.48	.88	.48	.69	.41
51–55	.86	.50	.82	.50	.90	.45
56–60	.88	.48	.85	.47	.68	.47
61–65	.85	.50	.84	.49	.66	.51
66 and older	.92	.51	.88	.51	.76	.45
Economic sector						
Agriculture	.80	.46	.71	.41	.73	.45
Mining	.98	.47	.97	.47	1.06	.45
Industry	.87	.52	.85	.51	.94	.56
Basic services	.92	.48	.89	.47	1.26	.48
Construction	.78	.48	.76	.47	.76	.46
Commerce	.80	.48	.79	.48	.68	.44
Transportation	.81	.44	.80	.44	.79	.47
Finance	.97	.50	.96	.50	1.29	.45
Services	.83	.47	.82	.46	.83	.50
Educational level						
Illiterate	.74	.47	.73	.47	.71	.47
Grade school	.73	.44	.73	.44	.67	.42
High school	.77	.46	.77	.46	.75	.43
University	.88	.41	.88	.41	1.11	.35

Source: Author calculations from government household survey data tapes.

relative to the bottom. The same pattern can be seen for the urban and rural sectors. In addition, there was a widening of the urban-rural differential, caused entirely by the rise at the top of the urban sector: wages in the best paying jobs in the urban sector held their value in spite of the adjustment, while wages across the rest of the labor pyramid, both urban and rural, fell sharply.

The picture is in conflict with rising inequality, for there was a quite significant narrowing of the education differential, particularly at the university level. Illiterates did best of all, but this group made up only 17 percent of the 1981 labor force. High schoolers did slightly better than grade schoolers, but more important, both did better than university graduates. This result is very different from that found in Argentina. It implies that skill differentials are negatively related to the economy. The pattern was confirmed in a standard earnings regression reported in Morley and Alvarez (1992b).

There was a narrowing in age differentials both for men and for women. One might have expected the opposite pattern, given that so many of the young entered the labor force with high levels of education at a time when the education differential was narrowing. To look more carefully at all this, a cross-tab of real wages was run by age and educational level, which indicates that the increase in the average education level of younger households (twenty-one–thirty years of age) was so great that it more than offset the narrowing of education differentials. Fully 86 percent of the new entrants into this age group had either a high school or university education, compared to 55 percent of the 1981 group. This change in the composition raised the average wage, even though the return to education was falling.[20]

By any standard, the adjustments in Argentina and Venezuela have had a very severe impact on the poor. The poverty ratio tripled in Buenos Aires and doubled in Venezuela, and not only because per capita income fell in these two countries. Almost every country in Latin America endured extended periods of recession and adjustment, and many suffered equal or greater shocks than Argentina and Venezuela. Some had equivalent declines in per capita income. But none, with the possible exception of Chile in 1973–76 and 1982–84 and Peru after 1987, had greater percentage increases in poverty. This poor relative performance becomes clearer when put into a comparative perspective, as we shall now do by looking at examples of more successful adjustment in Costa Rica and Colombia.

Chapter Five

Case Studies:
Successful Adjustment in
Colombia and Costa Rica

Colombia and Costa Rica are two of the four countries that managed to both reduce poverty and improve the distribution of income during the 1980s.[1] We now take a closer look at these two cases, searching for clues about the differences in economic conditions or policies from those in countries like Argentina and Venezuela, which had so difficult a time during their adjustments.

COLOMBIA

Luckily for Colombia, it discovered debt-led growth later than the rest of Latin America. Because of its conservative policy in the 1970s, by 1980, when other countries were already reeling under excessive debt burdens, Colombia still had manageable ratios between its debt and interest and its exports. However, between 1980 and 1983 the country made up for lost time (see table 5-1 for key macroeconomic indicators for the period). Increasingly large government deficits and very high fixed investments were financed to a large extent by foreign borrowing.

The mechanism by which this was accomplished is by now familiar. Essentially, the government followed a policy that stimulated demand but not production. Government deficits financed mainly by capital inflows caused an appreciation of the real exchange rate, which depressed pro-

Table 5-1. Indicators of Economic Performance, Colombia, 1980–1989

Year	GDP per Capita (1980 = 100)	Investment (% of GDP)	Foreign Savings (% of GDP)	Terms of Trade (1980 = 100)
1980	100	23.8	2.2	100
1981	100	26.4	4.1	85
1982	99	27.5	5.5	87
1983	99	26.4	4.8	94
1984	100	24.0	3.0	101
1985	102	20.9	0.4	92
1986	106	20.5	−1.1	120
1987	110	21.2	−1.4	92
1988	113	22.0	−1.3	92
1989	114	19.7	−2.6	89

Source: IADB, Economic and Social Data Base.

duction of tradable goods, and output in general, and caused a significant rise in the current account deficit. Exports fell in absolute value, imports increased, and the growth rate of production in the economy fell to the lowest level in the entire postwar period. The net result was a big increase in absorption and foreign debt but not production. On the price side, limitations on an increase in the nominal exchange rate and a significant rise in imports caused a real appreciation and kept rising demand from driving up the inflation rate. Indeed, the drop in inflation has been credited by some for the rise in real wages during those years.[2]

By mid-1984, the deteriorating fiscal and balance of payments situation forced the government to stabilize. A new finance minister was named to design and implement a plan. By any measure, this new plan was a striking success, reinvigorating the economy and eliminating both the balance of payments and fiscal deficits, all without lowering the real wage or causing a burst of inflation. Although supported by the IMF and the World Bank, in some important respects the plan was heterodox. The key elements were (1) a real devaluation, which was carried out in three steps in order to avoid igniting a round of catch-up wage increases or inflation (6% in 1984, 28% in 1985, and 10% in 1986) and (2) the elimination of the government budget deficit by a balanced program of tax and public sector price increases and spending reductions.[3]

Compared to other countries, Colombia relied more on raising tax revenues than on spending reductions, and it was more successful than

Table 5-2. Macroeconomic Data on Employment and Wages, Colombia, 1980–1990

Year	Employment (thousands)	Unemployment Rate (%)	Participation Rate (%)	Real Wage Indexes Minimum	Real Wage Indexes Average
1980	7,217	9.6	5.4	100	100
1981	7,549	8.2	5.2	98	101
1982	7,702	9.2	5.3	103	105
1983	7,695	11.8	5.5	108	110
1984	7,755	13.5	5.6	113	118
1985	7,899	13.9	5.7	109	115
1986	8,133	13.5	5.7	114	120
1987	8,533	11.8	5.8	113	119
1988	8,802	11.3	5.9	108	118
1989	9,149	9.9	5.8	110	119
1990	9,323	10.2	5.8		116

Source: IADB, Economic and Social Data Base.

most in maintaining social sector programs and government investment (PREALC, 1990a, 1:19). In addition, the government temporarily raised tariffs even while it was eliminating some nontariff barriers to imports. The rise in tariffs coupled with real devaluation was an old-fashioned remedy to balance of payments deficits. But it worked. Domestic output increased and imports declined. Furthermore, the rise in tariff revenue contributed more than one-fourth of the total increase in government tax receipts between 1983 and 1986. On the wage side, as the reader can see in table 5-2, the rise in real wages came to a halt, but again this may be as much the result of a rise in the inflation rate as deliberate government policy.

In the labor market, one of the notable characteristics was a sharp rise in both employment and unemployment. For most of the years between 1980 and 1986, employment growth exceeded output growth, quite an unusual pattern. Since that took place along with a rise in the real wage, there had to have been a significant increase in the labor share in national income. That more progress was not made in reducing unemployment is not due to a lack of employment opportunities but rather to a sharp increase in the participation rate. Whether that represents favorable pull factors in the job market or unfavorable push factors caused by lower incomes is difficult to judge at the aggregate level.

Growth continued under the new Barco government (1986–90) but under external conditions somewhat less favorable than in the coffee boom of 1986. The terms of trade fell by 25 percent in 1987, and a poor crop year in agriculture caused a resurgence of inflation. The government responded with a fairly contractionary monetary policy, which drove up real interest rates and caused a slowdown in the overall growth rate in 1988 and 1989. In the foreign sector the government continued the policy of significant real devaluations. At the same time, it took steps to lower tariff and nontariff trade barriers, all of which led to a billion-dollar increase in imports between 1986 and 1989. Exports also went up, but at a slower rate.

In the labor market there appears to have been a switch from the previous pattern of high rates of growth in real wages and slow growth in employment to exactly the reverse. Real wages remained at the high level they reached in 1986 but did not continue the rising trend that had been the rule for the previous ten years. At the same time, rising employment coupled with a leveling in the participation rate caused open unemployment to decline toward the levels observed in 1980 and before.

Table 5-3 displays several estimates of the proportion of the population below a poverty line. Note that there were significant differences among the poverty lines used in the several studies as well as in their treatment of underreporting of income; such differences affect poverty estimates and explain why there seem to be such large differences between the studies. But the data are useful as indicators of trends or changes in poverty over time; from that perspective, it is evident that poverty in Colombia was substantially reduced during the long period of uninterrupted growth from 1964 to 1980. There is no disagreement among the three sources that cover all or part of that period. About the 1980s, however, there is less agreement. PREALC, Londoño, and Psacharapoulos find that poverty continued to decline, whereas ECLAC shows no further progress being made between 1980 and 1986, the last date for which it made poverty estimates.

Table 5-4 gives data for the year 1980, before the entire debt crisis was felt in Colombia; table 5-5 covers 1986, at the end of the stabilization, when the economy was in a strong recovery helped by a boom in the coffee sector. Data from the subperiod 1980–82 allow us to compare the level of urban poverty before the whole debt crisis started with the level reached after the first three years of adjustment. Unfortunately, there is no observation of 1983 or 1984, so the effect of the adjustment program per se cannot be examined. Table 5-6 covers 1989; it is evident that in 1986–89 the economy continued to grow but at a much slower rate than before.

During the 1970s, Colombia enjoyed both rapid growth and declining levels of income inequality. Rural wages rose relative to national income,

Table 5-3.   Poverty Population, Colombia, 1964–1989 (various years)

Year	World Bank (1990b)	Psachar-opoulos et al. (1993)	PREALC (1990a)	ECLAC (1990b)					Londoño (1990)
				Metro	Urban	Rural	Total for Indi-viduals	Total for House-holds	
1964									50
1970							45		
1971	41								39
1972									
1973									
1974									
1975									
1976									
1977									
1978	24								29
1979									
1980		13		34	40	48	39	42	
1981									
1982			44						
1983									
1984			38						
1985									
1986				35	40	45	38	42	
1987									
1988	25		38						25
1989		8							

Note: Figures are for households except as noted.

and within the urban sector, wage differentials narrowed.[4] Colombia is one of the rare countries in the region in which those favorable trends continued in the 1980s. There is some disagreement about the magnitude and timing of the decline, with World Bank estimates apparently somewhat larger than those of Altimir (1993).[5] Also, according to the World Bank, the reduction was greater at the beginning than at the end of the decade, a pattern that seems consistent with the coffee boom and the rapid reduction in poverty between 1980 and 1986.[6]

Changes in Poverty During the 1980s

Urban poverty continued to decline in Colombia during the 1980s, the entire reduction coming in the 1980–86 period, during which both the

Table 5-4. Decomposition of the P^i Class of Poverty Measures, by Head of Household Characteristics, Colombia, 1980

Characteristic	P^0	P^1	P^2	Share of Population	Contribution to National Poverty P^0	P^1	P^2
Educational level							
Illiterate	.690	.350	.227	.073	.126	.134	.140
Grade school	.515	.247	.154	.527	.680	.685	.685
High school	.251	.112	.067	.289	.182	.170	.164
University	.043	.019	.013	.111	.012	.011	.012
Total	.399	.190	.119				
Age in years							
16–20	.476	.234	.143	.006	.007	.007	.007
21–25	.323	.150	.095	.048	.038	.038	.038
26–30	.395	.187	.118	.104	.103	.102	.104
31–35	.366	.182	.113	.117	.107	.112	.112
36–40	.417	.198	.121	.151	.158	.157	.153
41–45	.435	.210	.132	.129	.141	.143	.143
46–50	.401	.190	.118	.135	.136	.135	.134
51–55	.392	.185	.118	.114	.112	.111	.113
56–60	.388	.180	.113	.088	.086	.083	.084
61–65	.420	.198	.121	.051	.054	.053	.052
66 and older	.406	.194	.121	.058	.059	.059	.059
Total	.399	.190	.119				
Gender							
Women	.456	.230	.147	.158	.180	.191	.196
Men	.388	.183	.113	.842	.820	.809	.804
Total	.399	.190	.119				
Employment							
Unemployed	.529	.262	.171	.148	.197	.204	.214
Employee, private sector	.424	.219	.144	.406	.431	.468	.494
Employee, public sector	.254	.102	.055	.108	.069	.058	.050
Employer	.134	.060	.034	.063	.021	.020	.018
Self-employed	.408	.171	.095	.274	.280	.247	.221
Nonsalaried	.643	.431	.321	.001	.002	.003	.003
Total	.399	.190	.119				
Occupation							
Professional	.060	.024	.014	.082	.012	.010	.010
Public	.063	.038	.026	.030	.005	.006	.007
Administrative	.240	.095	.053	.065	.039	.033	.029
Sales	.331	.147	.088	.173	.143	.134	.128
Service	.461	.216	.133	.112	.130	.128	.126
Agriculture	.410	.205	.133	.020	.020	.021	.022
Operative	.489	.238	.149	.370	.453	.464	.465
Total	.399	.190	.119				

Table 5-4—Continued

Characteristic	P^0	P^1	P^2	Share of Population	Contribution to National Poverty		
					P^0	P^1	P^2
Economic sector							
Agriculture	.347	.184	.120	.018	.016	.017	.018
Mining	.241	.132	.092	.005	.003	.003	.004
Industry	.411	.204	.130	.209	.216	.225	.229
Basic services	.472	.251	.160	.011	.013	.014	.015
Construction	.536	.264	.170	.090	.121	.126	.130
Commerce	.358	.167	.102	.209	.188	.183	.180
Transportation	.371	.170	.102	.081	.075	.072	.069
Finance	.167	.070	.041	.056	.023	.021	.019
Services	.343	.147	.083	.172	.148	.134	.121
Total	.399	.190	.119				

Source: Author calculations from government household survey data tapes.
Note: Three right-hand columns may not sum to 1.0 due to rounding.

adjustment and the coffee boom took place. This pattern confirms the evidence from table 5-3 that poverty did indeed decline in the 1980s, a pattern very different from what happened throughout most of Latin America. But the data tell us even more. Like the PREALC series in table 5-3, these estimates show that the decline happened in the first half of the decade, just when Colombia was successfully adjusting to its debt crisis. This was a period with a relatively low growth rate of per capita income but rapid increases in real wages and labor share.[7] In the subsequent period, the poverty ratio did not decline further, despite the faster rate of growth of output and employment.

The estimates in the tables, if anything, understate the downward trend in poverty between 1980 and 1986. Also, the surveys covered only the urban sector. The 1980 survey covered only the seven largest cities; the 1986 and 1989 surveys expanded urban coverage to twenty-two cities and towns. Since level of poverty generally varies inversely with size of city, this change in the sample should bias the poverty estimates for 1986 and 1989 upward relative to those for 1980—or equivalently, bias downward the estimate of reductions in poverty between 1980 and the two later dates.[8]

The poverty picture is somewhat different if severe poverty is measured by P^1 or P^2 rather than P^0. Both of the former declined in both subperiods, and both declined by greater percentage amounts than P^0,

Table 5-5. Decomposition of the P^i Class of Poverty Measures, by Head of Household Characteristics, Colombia, 1986

Characteristic	P^0	P^1	P^2	Share of Population	Contribution to National Poverty P^0	P^1	P^2
Educational level							
Illiterate	.547	.270	.176	.057	.095	.106	.113
Grade school	.429	.194	.119	.473	.616	.627	.631
High school	.252	.103	.061	.349	.267	.247	.238
University	.061	.024	.011	.121	.022	.020	.018
Total	.329	.146	.089				
Age in years							
16–20	.290	.147	.089	.006	.005	.006	.006
21–25	.323	.144	.091	.047	.046	.047	.048
26–30	.345	.151	.091	.099	.103	.102	.100
31–35	.350	.163	.099	.116	.126	.129	.129
36–40	.350	.158	.099	.147	.156	.159	.163
41–45	.354	.162	.100	.119	.128	.132	.133
46–50	.313	.139	.085	.128	.122	.122	.123
51–55	.307	.127	.075	.111	.104	.097	.093
56–60	.318	.143	.088	.089	.086	.087	.087
61–65	.287	.126	.076	.057	.049	.049	.048
66 and older	.313	.130	.077	.081	.077	.072	.070
Total	.329	.146	.089				
Gender							
Women	.346	.152	.092	.202	.212	.211	.209
Men	.325	.145	.089	.798	.788	.789	.791
Total	.329	.146	.089				
Employment							
Unemployed	.369	.166	.102	.215	.241	.243	.244
Employee, private sector	.372	.171	.108	.380	.429	.445	.457
Employee, public sector	.180	.066	.036	.098	.054	.044	.040
Employer	.175	.071	.041	.048	.025	.023	.022
Self-employed	.319	.138	.081	.259	.251	.244	.236
Nonsalaried	.261	.169	.111	.001	.000	.001	.001
Total	.329	.146	.089				
Occupation							
Professional	.073	.028	.016	.077	.017	.015	.014
Public	.035	.014	.007	.011	.001	.001	.001
Administrative	.176	.069	.037	.060	.032	.028	.025
Sales	.279	.121	.073	.173	.147	.143	.142
Service	.371	.156	.092	.105	.119	.112	.109
Agriculture	.376	.183	.115	.019	.021	.023	.024
Operative	.409	.187	.116	.340	.422	.433	.442
Total	.329	.146	.089				

Table 5-5—*Continued*

Characteristic	P^0	P^1	P^2	Share of Population	Contribution to National Poverty		
					P^0	P^1	P^2
Economic sector							
Agriculture	.360	.180	.115	.017	.019	.021	.022
Mining	.396	.195	.130	.006	.007	.008	.009
Industry	.352	.162	.101	.165	.177	.182	.186
Basic services	.221	.092	.057	.007	.005	.005	.005
Construction	.455	.215	.131	.069	.096	.102	.101
Commerce	.300	.132	.080	.203	.185	.182	.182
Transportation	.336	.155	.101	.079	.080	.083	.089
Finance	.181	.065	.034	.047	.026	.021	.018
Services	.283	.116	.067	.192	.165	.152	.144
Total	.329	.146	.089				

Source: Author calculations from government household survey data tapes.
Note: Three right-hand columns may not sum to 1.0 due to rounding.

which implies that Colombia's record in combating severe poverty was even better than its record in moving people out of poverty. Furthermore, progress continued to be made on that front under the Barco government, even though the poverty ratio increased slightly.[9]

Comparisons over time are always problematic because of changes in sampling, measurement error, and so on; to get a sense of how significant such errors might be, frequency distributions for the sample for the each of the three years were constructed. It was found that 1989 lay entirely below 1980, which means that poverty unambiguously decreased, regardless of how different parts of the poverty population were weighted or where the poverty line was set. Furthermore, the shift in the frequency distribution between 1981 and 1989 was so large that any measurement error in income of the poor would have to have been at least 23 percent to reverse the finding that poverty declined. Measurement errors of this magnitude are unlikely.

Data in table 5-6 give some idea of who the poor were in 1989 and the incidence of poverty that year in various subgroups of the population. The columns on the left-hand side show the incidence of poverty or the probability of being poor for any member of a subgroup; the columns on the right-hand side show who the poor were. For example, 55 percent of illiterates were poor and composed 8.6 percent of the overall poverty population in 1989. One clear and unsurprising pattern was the high

Table 5-6. Decomposition of the P^i Class of Poverty Measures, by Head of Household Characteristics, Colombia, 1989

Characteristic	P^0	P^1	P^2	Share of Population	Contribution to National Poverty P^0	P^1	P^2
Educational level							
Illiterate	.555	.237	.138	.053	.086	.094	.097
Grade school	.441	.178	.100	.440	.571	.586	.589
High school	.291	.109	.060	.370	.317	.301	.297
University	.064	.019	.009	.137	.026	.019	.017
Total	.340	.133	.075				
Age in years							
16–20	.443	.202	.125	.006	.008	.004	.004
21–25	.390	.154	.089	.044	.050	.028	.026
26–30	.381	.154	.088	.100	.112	.078	.071
31–35	.410	.164	.094	.119	.143	.122	.119
36–40	.387	.157	.089	.143	.163	.179	.182
41–45	.361	.139	.077	.124	.132	.169	.176
46–50	.310	.122	.070	.120	.110	.122	.121
51–55	.294	.111	.061	.097	.084	.101	.098
56–60	.265	.094	.051	.092	.072	.076	.079
61–65	.242	.097	.055	.064	.045	.051	.053
66 and older	.303	.115	.062	.091	.081	.068	.072
Total	.340	.133	.075				
Gender							
Women	.345	.140	.080	.206	.209	.209	.220
Men	.339	.132	.074	.794	.791	.785	.780
Total	.340	.133	.075				
Employment							
Unemployed	.350	.143	.083	.219	.225	.235	.241
Employee, private sector	.401	.167	.097	.365	.431	.456	.472
Employee, public sector	.175	.056	.028	.094	.049	.039	.035
Employer	.145	.048	.026	.075	.032	.027	.025
Self-employed	.364	.131	.069	.246	.264	.242	.226
Nonsalaried	.346	.142	.092	.001	.001	.001	.001
Total	.340	.133	.075				
Occupation							
Professional	.058	.019	.011	.086	.015	.012	.012
Public	.035	.011	.006	.019	.002	.002	.002
Administrative	.211	.071	.035	.057	.035	.030	.027
Sales	.310	.109	.057	.164	.150	.135	.126
Service	.424	.163	.091	.105	.132	.129	.128
Agriculture	.289	.140	.086	.016	.014	.017	.019
Operative	.437	.177	.101	.332	.427	.440	.446
Total	.340	.133	.075				

Table 5-6—*Continued*

Characteristic	P^0	P^1	P^2	Share of Population	Contribution to National Poverty		
					P^0	P^1	P^2
Economic sector							
Agriculture	.295	.142	.086	.014	.012	.015	.016
Mining	.187	.071	.038	.006	.004	.003	.003
Industry	.354	.133	.072	.176	.183	.176	.168
Basic services	.248	.089	.045	.009	.006	.006	.005
Construction	.479	.207	.123	.061	.085	.094	.099
Commerce	.340	.126	.068	.186	.186	.175	.168
Transportation	.344	.151	.094	.076	.077	.086	.095
Finance	.193	.070	.036	.059	.034	.031	.029
Services	.329	.123	.068	.194	.188	.179	.175
Total	.340	.133	.075				

Source: Author calculations from government household survey data tapes.
Note: Three right-hand columns may not sum to 1.0 due to rounding.

correlation between poverty and education. Two-thirds of the poor had a grade school education or less, even though the group composed less than one-half of the population. Even in Colombia's relatively equitable environment, a low level of education increased dramatically one's chances of being poor.

Data in table 5-6 also suggest that the incidence of poverty was higher in younger households, a pattern also found in Argentina, and that poverty was not concentrated among the old or the retired. Indeed, while the incidence of poverty in households with a head more than sixty-six years old was greater than for those headed by someone more than fifty years old, it was lower than the average for the population as a whole. One of the striking findings in the survey was the high proportion of female-headed households, a proportion three times that of any other country in the study. Perhaps even more surprising, there was virtually no difference in poverty incidence between the households headed by each sex. Thus, although the proportion of the poor living in female-headed households was much higher in Colombia than elsewhere, that is solely due to the large proportion of such households in the country, not differences in P^0 across gender.

Finally, table 5-6 data show that about one-fourth of the poor were self-employed, undoubtedly primarily in the informal sector, while about one-half were employees and the remainder either unemployed or inactive. Cross-classifying workers by membership in the formal or informal sector was not possible, because the survey did not specify size of firm for employees in the private sector.

PREALC (1990a) estimates, however, do shed light on this question. This survey shows that the informal sector grew rapidly during the 1980s, increasing its participation in the urban labor market from 52 percent in 1980 to 56 percent in 1988 (1:25). This expansion does not imply rising levels of poverty, because most of the new jobs created were in the relatively productive microenterprise part of the sector. That must explain why, overall, estimates show a fall in the incidence of poverty in the informal sector, from 34.8 percent in 1984 to 33.1 percent in 1988 (ibid., 1:114; Lopez, 1990, p. 13).

The decomposability formula developed in chapter 4 can be used to divide aggregate changes in the poverty indexes into reductions in poverty within sectors, as opposed to movements of the population between sectors. Table 5-7 displays the decompositions of changes in P^0, P^1, and P^2 between 1980 and 1989 for various groupings of heads of households. The overall change in the poverty index gives a reference point by which to evaluate the importance of changes in each cell.

The education data tell us that all of the reduction in poverty came from the group with no more than a grade school education. The negative signs for the within-group and between-group entries mean that poverty incidence and the size of the group were both declining. Thus, poverty reduction came both from improvements in the average educational level of the labor force and from rising wages for those unable to move up and out of the two lowest educational classes. Perhaps more surprising, the positive entries for the within-group cell for the two top educational classes imply that poverty incidence rose during the 1980s for the better educated. While this may be to some extent the result of expanding the survey in 1986 and 1989 to smaller cities with higher levels of poverty, it must also reflect the progressive style of development in Colombia, particularly between 1980 and 1986.

Decomposing the changes in poverty by occupation, we find that most new prosperity was accounted for by private employees and the self-employed: in both groups, poverty incidence and group size shrank. Since a large fraction of the self-employed were in the informal sector, a significant part of poverty reduction must have come in that sector, which is what PREALC found in its study of the period between 1984 and 1988 (1990a, 1:114). The other pattern is the sharp reduction in poverty inci-

Table 5-7. Changes in Poverty Level, by Head of Household Characteristics, Colombia, 1980–1989

Characteristic	P^0 Between Groups	P^0 Within Groups	P^0 Cross-Product	P^1 Between Groups	P^1 Within Groups	P^1 Cross-Product	P^2 Between Groups	P^2 Within Groups	P^2 Cross-Product
Educational level									
Illiterate	-.0138	-.0098	.0027	-.0070	-.0082	.0023	-.0046	-.0065	.0018
Grade school	-.0446	-.0390	.0064	-.0214	-.0366	.0060	-.0133	-.0283	.0047
High school	.0203	.0117	.0033	.0090	-.0009	-.0002	.0054	-.0020	-.0006
University	.0011	.0023	.0005	.0005	-.0001	.0000	.0003	-.0004	-.0001
Total	-.0371	-.0348	.0129	-.0189	-.0458	.0080	-.0121	-.0372	.0058
Change			-.0589			-.0567			-.0436
Age in years									
16–20	.0000	-.0002	.0000	.0000	-.0002	.0000	.0000	-.0001	.0000
21–25	-.0011	.0032	-.0002	-.0005	.0002	.0000	-.0003	-.0003	.0000
26–30	-.0016	-.0015	.0001	-.0008	-.0035	.0001	-.0005	-.0032	.0001
31–35	.0006	.0052	.0001	.0003	-.0021	.0000	.0002	-.0023	.0000
36–40	-.0034	-.0046	.0002	-.0016	-.0061	.0003	-.0010	-.0047	.0003
41–45	-.0022	-.0095	.0004	-.0010	-.0092	.0004	-.0007	-.0071	.0003
46–50	-.0059	-.0122	.0013	-.0028	-.0091	.0010	-.0017	-.0065	.0007
51–55	-.0066	-.0112	.0016	-.0031	-.0084	.0012	-.0020	-.0065	.0009
56–60	.0014	-.0108	-.0004	.0006	-.0075	-.0003	.0004	-.0054	-.0002
61–65	.0055	-.0091	-.0023	.0026	-.0051	-.0013	.0016	-.0034	-.0009
66 and older	.0136	-.0060	-.0035	.0065	-.0045	-.0026	.0041	-.0034	-.0020
Total	.0004	-.0567	-.0027	.0002	.0557	.0013	.0001	-.0429	-.0007
Change			-.0590			-.0567			-.0436

Continued next page

Table 5-7—Continued

Characteristic	P^0			P^1			P^2		
	Between Groups	Within Groups	Cross-Product	Between Groups	Within Groups	Cross-Product	Between Groups	Within Groups	Cross-Product
Gender									
Women	.0218	-.0175	-.0053	.0110	-.1420	-.0043	.0070	-.0106	-.0032
Men	-.0186	-.0418	.0024	-.0087	-.0429	.0024	-.0054	-.0333	.0019
Total	.0032	-.0593	-.0029	.0022	-.0571	-.0019	.0016	-.0439	-.0013
Change			-.0589			-.0567			-.0436
Employment									
Unemployed	.0375	-.0266	-.0127	.0185	-.0176	-.0084	.0121	-.0131	-.0063
Employee, private	-.0172	-.0094	.0009	.0089	-.0214	.0021	-.0059	-.0193	.0019
Employee, public	-.0034	-.0085	.0011	-.0013	-.0050	.0006	-.0007	-.0029	.0004
Employer	.0016	.0007	.0001	.0007	-.0008	-.0001	.0004	-.0005	-.0001
Self-employed	-.0116	-.0120	.0012	-.0049	-.0109	.0011	-.0027	-.0073	.0008
Nonsalaried	-.0003	-.0004	.0001	-.0002	-.0003	.0001	-.0001	-.0003	.0001
Total	.0067	-.0563	-.0092	.0040	-.0560	-.0045	.0031	-.0433	-.0032
Change			-.0588			-.0566			-.0435

Source: Author calculations from government household survey data tapes.

dence among the unemployed and the large increase in the size of that group (due to a rise in the number of retirees). Overall, the three poverty components for this group just about cancel each other out, which means that the net reduction in poverty over the period came almost entirely from households headed by members of the labor force. Further, most of the reduction in poverty was in older households, particularly those still in the labor force; 72.5 percent of the decline in poverty came from households with heads between the ages of forty-six and sixty.

Earnings Differentials

Another dimension of the adjustment and growth process is the change in the differential between workers' earnings, by such characteristics as educational level, age, and gender. In tables 5-8 and 5-9, the indexes of total real earned income for various categories of workers are shown. Note that all earnings were deflated by the same cost-of-living index and no adjustment was made for underreporting, since our interest here is in changes in relative position across the labor force rather than in levels of income relative to a poverty line.

The key feature of earnings movements over the decade is their progressivity. However one chooses to cross-classify the labor market, there was a significant narrowing of differentials. Indexes of total and earned

Table 5-8.   Indexes of Real Household Income, by Decile,
Colombia, 1986 and 1989 (1980 = 1.0)

Income Decile	1986	1989
1	1.02	1.41
2	1.02	1.17
3	1.06	1.15
4	1.03	1.13
5	1.04	1.11
6	1.01	1.06
7	0.99	1.04
8	0.97	1.02
9	0.90	0.99
10	0.84	0.89

Source: Author calculations from government household survey data tapes.

Table 5-9.   Indexes of Real Wages by Employment and
Education, Colombia, 1986 and 1989
(1980 = 1.0)

Characteristic	1986	1989
Employment		
Private employee	1.00	0.99
Public employee	1.02	1.04
Employer	0.82	0.62
Self-employed	0.99	0.94
Educational level		
Illiterate	1.04	1.01
Grade school	1.05	1.01
High school	0.93	0.87
University	0.78	0.77

Source: Author calculations from government household
survey data tapes.

income for 1986 and 1989 relative to 1980 have the same pattern—a sharp
rise in the bottom relative to the top. The educational differential narrowed by almost one-fourth over the decade. Operatives, the worst-paid
class of urban worker, gained relative to all other members of the urban
labor market.[10] These results are consistent with the big decline in inequality shown in the World Bank Gini coefficients reported in table 2-1.
Thus the 1980s in Colombia was a period of relatively equitable growth,
an experience in sharp contrast to other Latin American countries—first
in there having been positive growth and second in the narrowing of
wage differentials.[11]

Lessons from Colombia

Colombia in the 1980s was unusual in at least two respects. First, it
avoided a recession during its stabilization and adjustment period;
second, even though its growth was not as rapid as in previous decades, it
reduced both poverty and inequality. These results stand in stark contrast
to the experience of almost every other country in Latin America. The
question we should therefore be asking ourselves is, What was so different about either the policies or the economic conditions in Colombia that
permitted so benign a passage through the turbulent 1980s? I argue that a
mixture of sound policies and favorable structural preconditions explain

this good performance, primarily because they made it possible to actually increase the growth rate during the stabilization period and because they led to a significant increase in both real wages and employment. No other country in Latin America avoided a recession during its adjustment to the debt crisis.

What made Colombia different in this regard is, first, that its debt was not nearly so large when the debt crisis started. Thus, while it did have a significant current account deficit to eliminate, it did not have to produce a large trade surplus to pay the interest on a large debt when capital inflows stopped in 1984–85. Second, Colombia in 1981–83 was in a growth recession; output was stagnant because the country was running current account deficits at the expense of domestic production. Capital inflows were permitted to appreciate the exchange rate and crowd out domestic production both of exports and import substitutes.

Thus, to a significant extent, Colombia's trade deficit was low because of excess demand rather than because the overvalued exchange rate discouraged domestic production—exactly the same pattern in Argentina and Chile at the time of the Tablita experiment. Correcting this problem was relatively easy, because the real devaluation necessary to help the balance of payments did not need to be offset by a contractionary domestic policy. The real devaluation and the surcharge on imports led to rising production of exports and import substitutes, and because all this happened in an economy with excess capacity, it was not inflationary. Indeed, the inflation rate fell during stabilization; it is highly unlikely that this would have occurred had Colombia been in a boom when the adjustment process started.

An important structural feature of the Colombian economy is the nature of its traded goods sector and the relation of the poor to that sector. A significant real devaluation is the key policy required to eliminate a current account deficit. Devaluation helps producers in the traded goods sector and hurts those whose consumption is heavily weighted with traded goods, in both instances because of the rise in their relative prices. From the point of view of poverty reduction, the most favorable case is to be a country in which the poor are the producers, but not the consumers, of traded goods. The least favorable situation is one in which the poor consume but do not produce traded goods.

Clearly, no country is a perfect example of either case, but Colombia has a relatively favorable structure compared to either Venezuela or Argentina. Colombia is essentially self-sufficient in food and other wage goods, which can mean that domestic prices of such goods will not rise much when there is a devaluation.[12] For example, in Colombia the exchange rate affects only 8 percent of the goods in the consumer price index, either directly or indirectly (Perry and Arbelaez, 1990). One can see from table 1-8 that domestic prices did not respond to devaluation. Between 1983 and 1986, Colombia devalued by more than 50 percent, and the inflation rate actually declined. Yet at the same time the production of traded goods was highly responsive to real devaluation: both exports and the domestic production of import substitutes increased. This was a major stimulus to employment and raised the real wages of both the poor and the nonpoor.[13]

Average real wages rose and the skill differential narrowed, both of which must have had a favorable impact on poverty, but to what extent was this the result of government policies and to what extent other factors? One could argue that the narrowing of the skill differential was the result of the rise in the minimum wage (table 5-2), but, while that may be a factor, the evidence from the agricultural sector suggests that other reasons may have been more important.

Real-wage series all show a significant narrowing of the rural-urban wage differential after 1984 (PREALC, 1990a, 1:76, 2:72–76; Perry and Arbelaez, 1990, p. 29). This pattern fits exactly with the distinction between traded and nontraded goods. For the most part, commercial agriculture in Colombia produces traded goods; it is not surprising, therefore, to find the real wage reflecting movements in the real exchange rate, falling when the real exchange rate appreciated and then rising throughout the period after 1984, when the real exchange rate was devalued by 80 percent. Also, there was a strong positive relation between the rural wage and coffee prices during the coffee boom of 1986 (Londoño, 1990, p. 35). In the poorer part of the agricultural sector, the picture was even more progressive. In traditional agriculture, real wages rose throughout the decade (PREALC, 1990a, 1:26). So did the rural minimum wage.[14] While there is no hard evidence on the coverage of that minimum wage, we do know that these wage trends, combined with rising employment, produced a dramatic decline in rural poverty.[15] The point here is that improvements in agriculture appear to have pulled up the wages of the unskilled. To the extent that the urban and rural sectors are linked by migration, the rise in rural real wages was likely to have had a favorable impact on real wages at the bottom of the urban labor pyramid as well.

Another factor leading to a narrowing of skill differentials is education.

Colombia has invested heavily in education, and that has quite dramatically reduced the share of uneducated labor, which fell from 40 percent in the 1950s to only 16 percent in 1980. That trend continued in the 1980s, with the share of illiterates falling from 4 percent to 2 percent of the labor force and those with less than a grade school education shrinking from 45 percent in 1980 to 32 percent nine years later. This implies an absolute shrinkage in the number of these workers in the urban labor force. Thus fewer unskilled workers entered the urban labor market during the 1980s, first, because of the educational system and, second, because of the reduced size of rural-to-urban migration. At the same time, rising real wages in agriculture undoubtedly raised the reservation wage at which this migration took place. All of this would have tended to raise wages at the bottom of the urban labor market and to narrow the urban skill differential, even had the government not raised the real minimum wage.

An important characteristic of the Colombian labor market during the adjustment was rising average real wages. There is a debate in the literature about the cause of this trend, although there is no doubt about its significance or its effect on poverty. The PREALC study (1990a) gives minimum wage policy a large share of the credit for the result. Perry and Arbelaez (1990), however, argue that the increase in wages was more the result of commercial policy than wage policy, reasoning that nominal wages are set with an inflation component that reflects actual past inflation. Thus when inflation accelerates, the real wage tends to decline, and vice versa. The implied inverse relation is clearly observable in Colombia, where most of the increase in real wages occurred in the 1981–84 period, when inflation fell from almost 30 percent to less than 20 percent per year. Similarly, after 1986, as inflation accelerated, the real wage fell. The link of all this to commercial policy is that capital inflows prior to 1984 permitted a rise in imports and limited the rise in the exchange rate and domestic prices. As a result, the real exchange rate appreciated, and the real wage increased. Subsequently, real devaluation and rising domestic production raised the inflation rate back toward 30 percent and stopped any further increase in either the average or the minimum real wage rate.

On the fiscal side, several features of the Colombian stabilization program made it both progressive and successful. First, it eliminated the government deficit in a fairly balanced way, which avoided really large reductions in social expenditure. About one-half of the reduction came from higher tax revenues, and a significant part of that came from import duties, the one tax that increases the demand for domestic output in addition to helping eliminate the deficit. That meant smaller reductions in social spending than were observed in other countries during the stabiliz-ation process. Per capita social expenditures were 7.8 percent of GDP in 1980. They rose to 9.2 percent in 1984 and then fell back to 7.6 percent in 1988. But since GDP was increasing throughout the period, overall per capita spending in this category fell only 0.3 percent per year (PREALC, 1990a, 1:19). Second, public sector investment is not large in Colombia. Therefore, fiscal adjustment did not come as much at the expense of capital formation as in other countries, which had positive implications in the long run for future growth. In the short run, it helped support internal demand, as did imposing surcharges on imports and maintaining the real value of the minimum wage.

Eliminating the balance of payments deficit in other adjusting coun-tries required contractionary policy on the demand side, because they were using all their productive capacity when the adjustment occurred. In Colombia, the situation was different and a good deal easier, because the country was in a growth recession. It had the idle capacity with which to increase the production of tradables and improve the balance of pay-ments. The problem was to change the real exchange rate and eliminate the government deficit in a way that did not reduce aggregate demand. The policy mix of surcharges on imports, minimal reductions in social expenditure, and maintenance of the real wage did just that. Thanks in part to a particularly favorable economic structure and this policy mix, Colombia then enjoyed the unusual combination of an adjustment or stabilization in which the growth rate of both the economy and employ-ment increased while poverty fell.

COSTA RICA

When the debt crisis hit Costa Rica in 1981–82, it hit with extraordinary force. The terms of trade, dependent largely on coffee and bananas, fell by 25 percent between 1980 and 1982, and the interest bill (assuming the country had continued to service its debt, which it did not) rose from 18 percent to 36 percent of exports. The ensuing balance of payments pres-sure forced the country into one of the severest and sharpest adjustments in Latin America during the period. Tables 5-10 and 5-11 give some of the key macroeconomic indicators. Cut off from external finance, the public

Table 5-10. Indicators of Economic Performance, Costa Rica, 1980–1989

Year	GDP per Capita (1980 = 100)	Investment (% of GDP)	Current Account Deficit (% of GDP)	Terms of Trade (1980 = 100)
1980	100	30.2	10.4	100
1981	95	19.3	–2.4	85
1982	85	15.5	–6.2	84
1983	85	20.1	–1.9	86
1984	89	20.7	–2.1	90
1985	87	22.1	0.8	88
1986	90	27.5	4.8	106
1987	91	27.2	4.4	88
1988	91	24.5	1.6	88
1989	94	25.6	2.6	84

Source: IADB, Economic and Social Data Base.

sector was forced to reduce its deficit from 8 percent to 2 percent of GDP. A combination of tight money and unindexed wages caused real wages to fall by 27 percent and led to a severe recession, in which per capita income fell by 14 percent between 1980 and 1982. To make matters worse, inflation jumped to over 90 percent, thanks in part to a significant devaluation and a forced reduction in total absorption. This severe adjustment process had a big impact on the poor, raising the fraction below the poverty line by about 60 percent.

Such depressing statistics are common in Latin America. What is not common is the record of Costa Rica's recovery after 1982. Real wages, national saving, and investment were pushed back to prerecession levels, while a real devaluation and a shift of production toward tradable goods led to a 30 percent rise in export earnings between 1980 and 1989. At the same time, inflation was brought down to 20 percent, the government deficit was brought under control, and the burden of the foreign debt was gradually reduced to manageable levels, thanks partly to the growth in exports and partly to the Brady Plan signed in 1989.

Of particular interest here is the impact of this economic cycle on poverty and inequality. As noted, poverty rose sharply during the recession phase of the adjustment process. What is unusual about Costa Rica is its dramatic reduction in poverty during the recovery. By 1989 poverty was far less than it had been in 1981, even though per capita income was actually lower in the former year than in the latter. Costa Rica's growth

Table 5-11. Macroeconomic Data on Employment,
Costa Rica, 1980–1990

Year	Employment (thousands)	Unemployment Rate (%)
1980	724.7	5.9
1981	726.2	8.7
1982	759.9	9.4
1983	767.6	9.0
1984	797.0	7.9
1985	826.7	6.9
1986	854.2	6.2
1987	922.7	5.6
1988	951.0	5.5
1989	987.0	3.8
1990	1,017.0	4.6

Source: ECLAC, various years, Economic Survey.

strategy and adjustment program favorably shifted the entire relation between poverty and per capita income.

Changes in Poverty During the Adjustment

Poverty and inequality in Costa Rica are both highly sensitive to level of economic activity (see table 5-12). It is obvious that there are problems of comparability between the several studies in the table, mainly in their handling of underreporting of salary income. All the studies but Gindling and Berry make an adjustment for the difference between total salaries as reported in the household surveys and total salary income from the national accounts. Despite these problems of comparability, the patterns are broadly similar: poverty declined significantly as per capita income rose in the 1970s, jumped dramatically during the adjustment period 1980–82, and as the economy recovered after 1982, fell sharply. According to all of the table's sources but ECLAC, these gains by the poor more than offset losses during the 1980–82 recession, so that poverty fell below the levels of the late 1970s—probably by 1986 and certainly by 1987.[16]

Wages and real incomes fell across the board during the adjustment period (1980–82), with the decline reaching 37 percent for salaried employees (Altimir, 1984, p. 270). Not surprisingly, the effect of this reduction was most keenly felt by those at the bottom of the distribution: poverty rose from 34 percent to 53 percent for agricultural workers and

Table 5-12. Population in Poverty, Five Estimates, Costa Rica, 1971–1990 (percent)

Year	World Bank (1990b)	ECLAC (1990a)[1]	Gindling and Berry (1992)[2]	IADB (1992a)	Programa Ruta Social (1994)[3]
1971	45				39
1972					
1973					
1974					
1975					
1976					
1977	29				25
1978					
1979					
1980			48	32	
1981		22	62		
1982			78	47	
1983	36		69	40	34
1984			58		
1985			63		
1986	24		52	29	25
1987					21[4]
1988		25			22
1989				25	22
1990				25	21

[1] Based on total household income per capita, adjusted for underreporting.
[2] Based on earned household income per capita.
[3] Percent of households with average income below poverty line.
[4] Adjusted for changes in the real value of the poverty line in 1987 (see Trejos, 1994).

from 15 percent to 27 percent for manual laborers (ibid., p. 268). Overall, as the reader can see from the Programa Ruta Social series, poverty incidence rose by almost 50 percent.

What is striking about the Costa Rican case is the rapidity with which the poverty level returned to its precrisis level (Programa Ruta Social).[17] This decline is all the more remarkable in an economy in which per capita income rose by only 7 percent during the recovery period and never reached its 1980 level over the balance of the decade. In other words, Costa Rica managed to reduce poverty in spite of having no net increase in per capita income. Few if any other countries in Latin America have had a similar experience. The remainder of this chapter is devoted to a discussion of the measurement of poverty and a closer investigation of the factors explaining how Costa Rica managed to reduce poverty with so little overall growth.

By Latin American standards, Costa Rica had an equitable distribution of income (see table 2-1).[18] During the 1980s, Gini estimates follow roughly the same pattern as poverty indexes. Inequality rose during the 1980–82 recession, and then declined during the succeeding recovery. There is some question about just how much it declined and just when because of a comparability problem with the surveys before and after 1987, but it would appear that some reduction in inequality must have occurred during the recovery that started in 1982.

Tables 5-13, 5-14, and 5-15 present the three poverty measures and decompositions for the years 1981, 1986, and 1989. Since 1981 was a recession year (though not the trough) and 1989 was at the end of a seven-year period of gradual recovery, the data are ideal to measure changes in poverty during the recovery. The results confirm those of other studies (see table 6-1) in showing a very large reduction in poverty after 1982. The ratio of people in poverty fell from 25.4 percent in 1981 to only 10.2 percent in 1989. P^1 and P^2 show even steeper declines, implying that recovery was particularly helpful to those at the very bottom of the poverty population. Thus, by any measure the benefits of the recovery reached the poor, enabling Costa Rica to recoup all the losses in poverty alleviation suffered during the downturn of 1981–82.

One test of the robustness of findings about trends in poverty is a comparison of frequency distributions of the years in question. In this case, the frequency distribution for 1989 lies entirely below the distribution for 1981, meaning that poverty unambiguously decreased regardless of how the different parts of the distribution are weighted or where the poverty line is set. Of course, that test does not correct for errors in measurement. But for this sample, errors in income measurement at the poverty line would have had to have been at least 42 percent in 1989 to reverse the poverty reduction finding. Errors that large seem unlikely.

Tables 5-13, 5-14, and 5-15 can give us a better idea of who the poor were and which groups had the highest incidence of poverty. In table 5-13, as in the comparable table for Colombia, columns 1 through 3 give the poverty measures for different subgroups of the population, while columns 5 through 7 tell us the contribution of each such group to the aggregate poverty measure. As might be expected, in 1981 poverty was largely rural and was concentrated in households with poorly educated primary earners. Overall, 55 percent of the population was in rural house-

Table 5-13. Decomposition of the P^i Class of Poverty Measures, by Head of Household Characteristics, Costa Rica, 1981

Characteristic	P^0	P^1	P^2	Share of Population	Contribution to National Poverty P^0	P^1	P^2
Educational level							
Illiterate	.419	.206	.129	.121	.200	.227	.239
Grade school	.293	.123	.073	.646	.745	.726	.720
High school	.072	.026	.014	.164	.046	.039	.035
University	.034	.012	.006	.069	.009	.008	.006
Total	.254	.109	.066				
Age in years							
16–20	.042	.005	.001	.006	.001	.000	.000
21–25	.149	.061	.034	.060	.035	.034	.031
26–30	.115	.042	.022	.113	.051	.043	.037
31–35	.200	.071	.038	.123	.097	.079	.072
36–40	.234	.079	.040	.133	.123	.096	.082
41–45	.266	.113	.067	.135	.142	.140	.139
46–50	.290	.129	.078	.111	.127	.131	.133
51–55	.273	.127	.080	.110	.118	.128	.135
56–60	.319	.150	.093	.075	.095	.103	.135
61–65	.342	.166	.104	.050	.068	.077	.107
66 and older	.444	.225	.146	.083	.144	.169	.080
Total	.254	.109	.066				
Gender							
Women	.488	.249	.161	.106	.204	.204	.261
Men	.226	.093	.054	.894	.796	.759	.739
Total	.254	.109	.066				
Employment (urban)							
Formal labor market (private)	.115	.028	.010	.294	.170	.100	.062
Formal labor market (public)	.072	.022	.009	.230	.082	.060	.041
Informal labor market	.209	.072	.036	.290	.304	.250	.211
Unemployed	.595	.355	.246	.022	.067	.095	.111
Inactive	.463	.255	.175	.163	.378	.496	.575
Total	.200	.084	.050				
Geographical area							
Metropolitan	.195	.081	.048	.217	.167	.161	.158
Urban	.204	.087	.052	.231	.186	.183	.182
Rural	.298	.130	.078	.552	.647	.657	.660
Total	.254	.109	.066				

Source: Author calculations from government household survey data tapes.

Table 5-14. Decomposition of the P^i Class of Poverty Measures, by Head of Household
          Characteristics, Costa Rica, 1986

Characteristic	P^0	P^1	P^2	Share of Population	Contribution to National Poverty P^0	P^1	P^2
Age in years							
16–20	.132	.072	.049	.006	.003	.004	.005
21–25	.177	.070	.042	.058	.038	.037	.037
26–30	.282	.125	.076	.112	.117	.126	.130
31–35	.322	.136	.082	.143	.172	.175	.180
36–40	.321	.142	.085	.132	.159	.169	.172
41–45	.299	.120	.067	.118	.132	.129	.121
46–50	.246	.097	.056	.113	.104	.099	.098
51–55	.210	.077	.045	.101	.079	.071	.069
56–60	.214	.077	.042	.086	.069	.060	.055
61–65	.246	.110	.070	.055	.051	.055	.060
66 and older	.270	.109	.063	.075	.076	.074	.074
Total	.268	.111	.065				
Gender							
Women	.274	.101	.058	.130	.133	.119	.116
Men	.267	.112	.066	.870	.867	.881	.884
Total	.268	.111	.065				
Geographical area							
Metropolitan	.377	.162	.098	.215	.303	.316	.325
Urban	.257	.107	.065	.239	.229	.232	.237
Rural	.229	.092	.052	.545	.467	.452	.438
Total	.268	.111	.065				

Source: Author calculations from government household survey data tapes.

holds, but those same families had two-thirds of the poor and an even
slightly higher proportion of severe poverty. Ninety-five percent of the
poor were in families whose head had no more than a grade school
education. Age and retirement status also appear to be important poverty
factors: the older the family head, the greater the incidence of poverty or
the chance of being poor. Forty percent of the poor were in families whose
head was fifty years old or older, even though such families composed
only 30 percent of the population.[19] (That poverty seems to have been a
particular problem for those who were retired or over sixty-five years of
age is somewhat misleading, since only earned income was reported.
Excluding income from savings and pensions obviously biased upward
the estimated 38 percent of the poverty population coming from families
of retired persons.)

Table 5-15. Decomposition of the P^i Class of Poverty Measures, by Head of Household
Characteristics, Costa Rica, 1989

Characteristic	P^0	P^1	P^2	Share of Population	Contribution to National Poverty		
					P^0	P^1	P^2
Educational level							
Illiterate	.184	.075	.042	.102	.184	.196	.196
Grade school	.115	.042	.023	.606	.679	.648	.631
High school	.057	.023	.014	.201	.111	.118	.128
University	.028	.016	.011	.091	.025	.038	.045
Total	.102	.039					
Age in years							
16–20	.019	.012	.008	.004	.001	.001	.001
21–25	.045	.019	.012	.052	.023	.025	.029
26–30	.097	.036	.018	.112	.107	.102	.095
31–35	.080	.030	.016	.145	.114	.111	.110
36–40	.088	.030	.016	.157	.135	.119	.114
41–45	.109	.042	.023	.123	.131	.131	.132
46–50	.078	.028	.014	.112	.086	.078	.074
51–55	.104	.042	.024	.088	.090	.095	.097
56–60	.095	.048	.033	.074	.069	.091	.113
61–65	.177	.072	.038	.057	.099	.104	.098
66 and older	.197	.074	.039	.076	.146	.142	.135
Total	.102	.039	.022				
Gender							
Women	.177	.072	.043	.143	.247	.259	.281
Men	.090	.034	.018	.857	.753	.741	.719
Total	.102	.039	.022				
Employment (urban)							
Formal labor market (private)	.055	.022	.013	.306	.181	.183	.188
Formal labor market (public)	.024	.012	.008	.229	.059	.077	.090
Informal labor market	.135	.053	.029	.324	.466	.470	.457
Unemployed	.469	.262	.158	.009	.047	.067	.072
Inactive	.176	.057	.030	.131	.247	.203	.194
Total	.094	.037	.020				
Geographical area							
Metropolitan	.100	.038	.021	.223	.218	.214	.216
Urban	.088	.036	.020	.269	.232	.243	.249
Rural	.110	.042	.023	.508	.550	.543	.535
Total	.102	.039	.022				

Source: Author calculations from government household survey data tapes.

Poverty in urban households was two to three times as high for families in the informal employment sector, compared with those in the formal sector. If retirees are excluded (for the reasons noted above), about one-half of urban poverty came from families in the informal sector, even though they made up only one-third of the urban population. Unemployment was not a big cause of poverty during the recession, since there were very few unemployed heads of households. Those who were unemployed did have a very high probability of being poor, but they composed only 6.7 percent of the total poverty population. Furthermore, all non-earned income was excluded in the calculation of total family income, so to the extent that the unemployed had other sources of support, both poverty incidence and contribution to poverty is overstated.

Poverty dropped sharply during the recovery, particularly among those in the rural sector and those with low levels of education—precisely the groups with the highest incidence of poverty in 1981. By 1989 rural poverty was cut by almost two-thirds. So was poverty among less-educated households. In both cases, the reduction exceeded improvement in the national poverty indexes, with a resulting fall in the share of the poor coming from these two groups. Consistent with this relatively progressive pattern, poverty fell in female-headed households faster and further than it did in male-headed households.[20] The only area in which the progressive pattern of poverty reduction seems to have been reversed was in the urban informal employment sector, where, although the incidence of poverty did fall, it fell more slowly than in the formal employment sector. In 1989, as a result, almost three-fourths of urban poverty among the employed came from families in the informal sector, up from about one-half in 1981.

Decomposing Changes in Poverty, 1981–1989

To answer the question, What caused the massive reduction in poverty shown in tables 5-13 through 5-15? the FGT indexes can be decomposed to reflect changes in poverty within and between groups (table 5-16). The table gives us two messages: the first is that the bulk of poverty reduction was due to reductions within different population groups rather than a movement of people between groups; the second, more significant, message is that the recovery was highly progressive, bringing particularly strong benefits to the poorest households. In particular, rural and poorly educated households had the highest incidence of poverty in 1981; the

Table 5-16. Changes in Poverty Level, by Head of Household Characteristics, Costa Rica, 1980–1989

	P^0			P^1			P^2		
Characteristic	Between Groups	Within Groups	Cross-Product	Between Groups	Within Groups	Cross-Product	Between Groups	Within Groups	Cross-Product
Educational level									
Illiterate	-.0077	-.0285	.0044	-.0038	-.0158	.0024	-.0024	-.0106	.0016
Grade school	-.0119	-.1153	.0072	-.0050	-.0522	.0033	-.0030	-.0326	.0020
High school	.0026	-.0025	-.0006	.0010	-.0005	-.0001	.0005	-.0001	.0000
University	.0008	-.0004	-.0001	.0003	.0003	.0001	.0001	.0003	.0001
Total	-.0162	-.1467	.0109	-.0076	.0682	.0057	-.0047	-.0429	.0037
Change			-.1520			-.0700			-.0439
Age in years									
16–20	-.0001	-.0001	.0001	.0000	.0000	.0000	.0000	.0000	.0000
21–25	-.0012	-.0062	.0008	-.0005	-.0025	.0003	-.0003	-.0013	.0002
26–30	.0000	-.0020	.0000	.0000	-.0007	.0000	.0000	-.0004	.0000
31–35	.0045	-.0148	-.0027	.0016	-.0050	-.0009	.0009	-.0027	-.0005
36–40	.0055	-.0195	-.0034	.0018	-.0065	-.0011	.0009	-.0033	-.0006
41–45	-.0034	-.0213	.0020	-.0014	-.0096	.0009	-.0008	-.0060	.0006
46–50	.0001	-.0235	-.0001	.0001	-.0113	.0000	.0000	-.0071	.0000
51–55	-.0058	-.0186	.0036	-.0027	-.0093	.0018	-.0017	-.0062	-.0012
56–60	-.0003	-.0169	.0002	-.0002	-.0077	.0001	-.0001	-.0045	.0001
61–65	.0022	-.0083	-.0010	.0011	-.0047	-.0006	.0007	-.0034	-.0004
66 and older	-.0030	-.0204	.0017	-.0015	-.0124	.0010	-.0010	-.0088	.0007
Total	-.0016	-.1515	.0012	-.0018	-.0697	.0015	-.0014	-.0436	.0012
Change			-.1520			-.0700			-.0439

Continued next page

Table 5-16—Continued

Characteristic	P^0			P^1			P^2		
	Between Groups	Within Groups	Cross-Product	Between Groups	Within Groups	Cross-Product	Between Groups	Within Groups	Cross-Product
Gender									
Women	.0177	-.0330	-.0113	.0090	-.0188	-.0064	.0059	-.0126	-.0043
Men	-.0082	-.1221	.0050	-.0034	-.0526	.0021	-.0020	-.0322	.0013
Total	.0095	-.1552	-.0063	.0057	-.0714	-.0043	.0039	-.0448	-.0030
Change			-.1520			-.0700			-.0439
Employment									
Unemployed	-.0078	-.0028	.0016	-.0046	-.0021	.0012	-.0032	-.0020	.0011
Inactive	-.0149	-.0468	.0092	-.0082	-.0323	.0064	-.0056	-.0236	.0046
Private formal sector	.0014	-.0176	-.0007	.0003	-.0019	-.0001	.0001	.0006	.0000
Public formal sector	-.0001	-.0110	.0000	.0000	-.0021	.0000	.0000	-.0002	.0000
Informal sector	.0071	-.0217	-.0025	.0024	-.0055	-.0006	.0012	-.0021	-.0002
Total	-.0142	-.0998	.0076	-.0100	-.0440	.0069	-.0075	-.0273	.0056
Change			-.1064			-.0472			-.0292

Geographical area

Metropolitan	.0011	-.0206	-.0005	.0004	-.0094	-.0002	.0003	-.0058	-.0001
Urban	.0078	-.0269	-.0045	.0033	-.0118	-.0020	.0020	-.0073	-.0012
Rural	-.0130	-.1036	.0082	-.0057	-.0486	.0039	-.0034	-.0307	.0024
Total	-.0041	-.1511	.0032	-.0019	-.0698	.0017	-.0012	-.0437	.0011
Change			-.1520			-.0700			-.0439

Economic sector

Not applicable	-.0216	-.0718	.0153	-.0122	-.0458	.0097	-.0083	-.0325	.0069
Agriculture	-.0138	-.0525	.0076	-.0048	-.0174	.0025	.0025	-.0089	.0013
Industry	.0021	-.0047	-.0007	.0007	-.0009	-.0001	.0003	-.0003	.0000
Construction	-.0016	-.0069	.0013	-.0006	-.0024	.0005	-.0003	-.0012	.0002
Basic services	-.0011	-.0052	.0007	-.0004	-.0020	.0003	-.0002	-.0011	.0001
Commerce	.0015	-.0044	-.0005	.0004	-.0007	-.0001	.0002	-.0002	.0000
Services	.0072	-.0006	-.0004	.0026	.0008	.0005	.0013	-.0009	.0005
Not specified	-.0001	-.0019	.0001	.0000	-.0007	.0000	.0000	-.0003	.0000
Total	-.0275	-.1479	.0234	-.0143	-.0690	.0133	-.0094	-.0435	.0091
Change			-.1520			-.0700			-.0439

Source: Author calculations from government household survey data tapes.

improvement in their income during the recovery is the main reason why overall poverty fell so far.

Two-thirds of the decline in the poverty ratio came from the decline in P^0 for rural families: 95 percent came from those with a grade school education or less. At the same time, the sign on the cross-product terms for these two groups indicates that not only was poverty declining for both but the groups were shrinking as well. Recovery generated big salary increases for those who remained in the rural sector and also provided a substantial amount of upward mobility out of the sector. Educationally, Costa Rica continued to make progress in upgrading the educational level of its labor force, significantly shrinking the fraction at the two lowest levels.

All age cohorts contributed to the sharp reduction in poverty, but unlike the situation in 1981, improvements appear to have been distributed quite equally across all age groups. Under the employment characteristic, poverty reduction took place among agricultural workers, the unemployed, and the inactives. Almost half of the within-group reduction in P^0 and an even larger fraction of the change in P^1 and P^2 come from the fall in the poverty measures. Furthermore, there was a significant shrinkage in the size of the group itself, leading to a very high between-groups contribution to poverty reduction.

It is somewhat difficult to interpret the significance of poverty reduction among the inactives. On the one hand, because unearned income was not included in the questionnaires, the degree of poverty and poverty reduction for this particular group must be overstated. But on the other hand, the survey does not adequately reflect rising employment opportunities either. A cross-tabulation disclosed that in 1981 44 percent of all household heads and 17 percent of the total population were inactive or unemployed. That number fell to 22.7 percent of household heads and 13 percent of the population in 1989, suggesting that in 1981 a very large number of household heads simply stopped looking for work. When the economy recovered, many reentered the labor market and found jobs. The full impact of the recovery on job availability is not adequately reflected in the drop from 16.8 percent to 13.3 percent in the share of inactives, because that share includes all household members rather than only workers.

For the urban labor market, the progressive pattern is less clear than it is for the economy as a whole. First, the inactive group played a large role in the reduction of poverty, just as it did in occupational breakdown—

undoubtedly for the same reasons. Beyond that, the informal sector apparently did not benefit as much from the recovery as agriculture did. As we know, the incidence of poverty was relatively high in the informal sector, and in 1981 it contained roughly 40 percent of the working poor. Yet in the recovery it contributed only 20 percent to the reduction in poverty. Furthermore, there was an increase in the share of the urban population in the informal sector. Thus it appears that the recovery was not uniformly beneficial to those at the bottom; it favored the poor in the rural sector but not in the urban sector. We will return to the implications of this pattern further on.[21]

Earnings Differentials

We now look at the labor market for further evidence on how and why poverty was so strikingly reduced in Costa Rica between 1981 and 1989. What we find is, first, a substantial rise in average real earnings, second, a progressive narrowing of skill differentials, and third, an impressive increase in employment.

Consider first the behavior of real earnings (see tables 5-17 and 5-18). All the series confirm the strongly progressive nature of the recovery: real earnings went up for every group, but they went up fastest for those at the bottom of the earnings pyramid. Any way one divides the labor market,

Table 5-17. Nominal Income, by Household Income Decile, Costa Rica, 1986 and 1989 (1981 = 1.0)

Income Decile	1986	1989
1	3.83	11.72
2	3.49	9.93
3	3.48	9.00
4	3.35	8.48
5	3.33	8.38
6	3.17	8.32
7	3.00	8.47
8	2.96	8.42
9	2.81	8.13
10	2.54	8.57

Source: Author calculations from government household survey data tapes.

Table 5-18. Nominal Wages, by Worker Characteristics,
Costa Rica, 1986 and 1989 (1981 = 1.0)

Characteristic	1986	1989
Age in years		
Less than 15	12.80	19.28
16–20	6.94	13.22
21–25	3.32	8.21
26–30	2.19	7.25
31–35	2.08	7.95
36–40	2.06	8.36
41–45	2.14	8.41
46–50	2.07	7.51
51–55	2.45	8.97
56–60	2.46	8.49
61–65	2.65	6.64
66 and older	2.79	6.33
Economic sector		
Agriculture	4.20	10.04
Industry	3.45	9.94
Construction	2.85	8.31
Basic services	2.27	9.81
Commerce	2.47	7.57
Services	1.70	8.17
Not specified	2.76	8.52
Educational level		
Illiterate	na	7.91
Grade school	na	8.90
High school	na	8.05
University	na	7.70

Source: Author calculations from government household
survey data tapes.

there was a significant narrowing of wage differentials: those in the bottom deciles in both the rural and urban sectors gained on the rest of the
labor force, the young gained on the old, and of special significance,
agriculture gained on all other sectors (see also table 5-15). The Costa
Rican government, unlike most others in the region, followed an explicit
policy of limiting the impact of recession on the poor. One element of this
policy was to moderate the decline in the minimum wage during the crisis
and to raise it rapidly during the recovery (IADB, 1992a, p. 119).[22] Thus
even as early as 1984, the minimum wage reached and surpassed its 1980

level, and for the decade as a whole it rose by 10 percent, while average wages were declining.

Between 1981 and 1989 employment increased rapidly—by at least 4 percent per year, or 42 percent compared to 24 percent growth in GDP (see table 5-11). These numbers help explain how average real earnings rose by over 40 percent even though average real wages rose by only 5 percent. All of this implies that the recovery was both progressive and labor-intensive, a fact confirmed by the national accounts, which show that labor income as a share of GDP rose from 49 percent in 1981 to 57 percent in 1989 (ECLAC, *Statistical Yearbook 1991*).

Lessons from Costa Rica

The key to understanding how Costa Rica's recovery was so progressive seems to be that it was led by agriculture, the income source of most of the nation's poor. Between 1981 and 1989 agriculture increased its share of GDP in all but three years. Thanks to rapid export growth, real agricultural wages went up during 1980—88, and employment expanded at 2.8 percent per year at the same time (Gindling and Berry, 1992, table 2). Agriculture-led growth is almost exactly the opposite of the trickle-down growth strategy. Here, the sector employing the bulk of the poor led the recovery, which had highly positive and beneficial effects on poverty.

One can hypothesize that the reason Costa Rica's recovery was led by agriculture is that its agricultural sector produced mainly traded goods. Costa Rica's adjustment was brought on by a balance of payments crisis, which required a shift of productive resources into the traded goods sector—generally through a real devaluation. The real exchange rate was devalued by 40 percent between 1980 and 1982 and by an additional 20 percent over the rest of the decade (see table 1-3). One would expect that the wages and incomes of those factors of production used intensively in the traded goods sector would rise in response to the change in the real exchange rate, and so they did.

Two measures confirm the rising relative wage in agriculture: the indexes of earnings per worker (table 5-17) and that derived from Gindling and Berry (1992). The latter calculate a number of real-wage series, which show that all real wages increased between 1980 and 1989 and that real wages in the exportable sector rose 10 percent relative to wages in the nontradable sector—and even to wages in the public sector (ibid., table 3).

Two-thirds of all Costa Rican exports came from agriculture, and exports compose roughly the same percentage of agricultural output. Thus agriculture in Costa Rica can be considered a traded good, for which the real devaluation after 1980 could be expected to have a powerful positive effect. By all accounts, it did. The traditional exports—of coffee, bananas, and sugar—dominated the recovery, but there was also rapid growth in nontraditional crops such as tropical flowers, fruit, and nuts (World Bank, 1988, iii). This growth made it possible for both the real wage and the demand for labor in agriculture to go up at the same time. All this goes a long way toward explaining the country's labor-intensive and progressive pattern of growth during the recovery after 1982.

Costa Rica was fortunate enough to have its poor heavily concentrated in a traded goods sector. Real devaluation and other export-promoting policies then permitted an economically justifiable increase of both wages and demand for the type of labor that could be supplied by the poor. These favorable conditions were aided by the relatively equal distribution of agricultural land and by the government's decision to raise the minimum wage. When prices and export prospects improved as a result of the balance of payments adjustment, these initial conditions and policy decisions helped the poor share in the benefits of the export-led recovery that followed.

Chapter Six

Determinants of
Changes in Poverty

The evidence on poverty and inequality over the 1980s in Latin America is based on household surveys taken at the beginning and the end of the decade. Now we combine this evidence with evidence from other sources to answer two questions: First, what were the main causes of the rise in poverty? Second, what factors explain why some countries did so much better than others, either in growth or in alleviating poverty.

POVERTY AND INCOME

Data from household surveys at the beginning and end of the decade are helpful if one wants to establish what happened over the decade as a whole, but they are not very useful for understanding the macroeconomic forces that affect poverty, because pairs of observations may not represent turning points in the economic cycle.[1] For example, the surveys for Brazil are for 1979 and 1989, the first prior to the crisis, the second after an entire recession-recovery cycle that started in 1981 and peaked in 1986. If one wants to understand the effect of recession and recovery on poverty in Brazil, one needs observations in 1983 and 1986, the first being the bottom of the cycle, the second being at or near the top of the cycle. Likewise, in Costa Rica the first observation was in 1981, when the adjustment and recession were already under way, and the second was in 1989, far into the recovery. We need observations for 1979 or 1980, prior to the entire adjustment, and for 1982, at the bottom of the adjustment. There are similar problems for most other countries.

To give more perspective on the relation between macroconditions and poverty, and because they are interesting in their own right, poverty estimates from studies done at various times were examined. Many of these studies allow one to more clearly see the connection between economic conditions and poverty. We present some of these estimates in table 6-1.

One has to use some care in interpreting the table. Generally, there are wide differences in the poverty estimates by different researchers at any point in time, because they generally use different poverty lines and different methods of correcting for underreporting. Since a great many people have incomes close to poverty, poverty indexes are very sensitive to both the chosen poverty line and the treatment of underreporting. But this sensitivity appears to be much less for changes in poverty over time.[2] This feature of the poverty index suggests that, while it is inappropriate to compare different estimates of poverty at a point in time, one can compare trends over time, provided that the estimates being compared use the same methodology. This idea was applied in constructing table 6-1; each line represents a series of internally consistent estimates of poverty over time. Taking the various series together, a fairly consistent picture of what happened to poverty over various different subperiods of the decade is evident. In particular, for some countries the series allow us to link cycles in poverty and income.

Where there are observations at the appropriate points in the cycle, the evidence strongly supports the hypothesis that poverty is countercyclical. It rises, often sharply, in recession and falls, usually less sharply, in recovery. As an example, consider the cases of Brazil, Costa Rica, and Uruguay. In Brazil, the series labeled IADB closely follows the economic cycle, rising from 1981 to 1983 during the recession, then falling as the economy recovers to 1986, and finally rising to a new peak in 1989 during the second round of stabilization and inflation.

This same correspondence can be seen in the Gindling and Berry and Programa Ruta Social series for Costa Rica, where the adjustment took place during 1981–82. The recession bottomed and poverty peaked in 1982. Subsequently, the economy recovered and poverty indexes declined. By either 1986 or 1987 the absolute level of poverty appears to have fallen below its 1979, preadjustment, level, despite the fact that per capita

Table 6-1. Poverty in the 1980s: Estimates for Twelve Countries, 1978–1992

Country and Source	1978	1979	1980	1981	1982	1983	1984	1985	1986	1987	1988	1989	1990	1991	1992
Argentina															
INDEC (1990), Buenos Aires			0.101		0.28			0.206		0.252	0.279	0.346	0.352	0.226	0.173
Morley and Alvarez (1992c), Buenos Aires			0.063						0.109			0.215			
ECLAC (1990a), total			0.10						0.16						
Psacharopoulos et al. (1993), Buenos Aires			0.030									0.064			
Brazil (total)															
Fox and Morley (1993)				0.25		0.31		0.254	0.161	0.233	0.269				
IADB (1993a)				0.22		0.28			0.12			0.19			
Psacharopoulos et al. (1993)		0.341										0.409			
Colombia (total)															
ECLAC (1990a)			0.42						0.42						
Londoño (1990)	0.29										0.25				
Morley (1992b), urban			0.39						0.33			0.34			
Psacharopoulos et al. (1993), urban			0.130									0.080			
Anzola (1993)									0.38			0.41	0.41	0.41	0.44
Costa Rica															
Gindling and Berry (1992)			0.48	0.62	0.78	0.69	0.58	0.63	0.52	0.45					
Morley and Alvarez (1992a)				0.254					0.27			0.10			
IADB (1992a)			0.32		0.47	0.40			0.29			0.25	0.25		
Programa Ruta Social (1994)						0.34			0.25	0.21	0.22	0.22	0.21	0.24	0.22
Psacharopoulos et al. (1993), urban				0.099								0.035			
Psacharopoulos et al. (1993), rural				0.167								0.032			

Continued next page

Table 6-1—Continued

Country and Source	1978	1979	1980	1981	1982	1983	1984	1985	1986	1987	1988	1989	1990	1991	1992
Chile															
PREALC (1990b), metro		0.36	0.403		0.312		0.485	0.454	0.509	0.486					
ECLAC (1990a), total										0.38			0.35		
ECLAC (1990a), urban										0.37			0.34		
Racyzinski and Romaguera (1992)										0.445			0.40		0.33
Guatemala															
ECLAC (1990a), urban			0.47						0.60						
ECLAC (1990a), rural			0.84						0.80						
Psacharopoulos et al. (1993), urban									0.494			0.548			
Psacharopoulos et al. (1993), rural									0.724			0.794			
Mexico (total)															
ECLAC (1990a)	0.40[1]						0.37								
Psacharopoulos et al. (1993)							0.166					0.177			
Panama															
ECLAC (1990a), urban		0.36							0.36						
ECLAC (1990a), rural		0.50							0.52						
Psacharopoulos et al. (1993), urban		0.260										0.269			
Psacharopoulos et al. (1993), rural		0.330										0.368			

Paraguay

Psacharopoulos et al. (1993), Asuncion				0.076

Peru

ECLAC (1990a), total	0.53	0.131	0.60	

Uruguay

Altimir (1993), urban households	0.09		0.14	0.10
Altimir (1993), rural households	0.21		0.23	0.23
Psacharopoulos et al. (1993), urban	0.062			0.053

Venezuela

ECLAC (1990a), total	0.25		0.32	0.482
Morley and Alvarez (1992b), total	0.24		0.29	0.413
Marquez et al. (1993), total	0.18	0.284	0.318	0.346
Psacharopoulos et al. (1993), urban	0.025			0.108
Psacharopoulos et al. (1993), rural	0.090			0.235

Note: Psacharopoulos et al. (1993) use a uniform poverty line of $60 in 1985 PPP dollars per month per household member. Other poverty lines are country-specific and are based on the cost of a minimum subsistence basket of food. The ECLAC estimate of poverty for the entire country of Argentina is based on a best-guess estimate of rural poverty.

[1] 1977.

income was lower throughout the decade than it was in 1980. This suggests that, in at least this case, the poor may have come out ahead after the adjustment was completed.

The picture is similar in Uruguay. There, the early 1980s were a period of adjustment and recession, with a trough in 1985. The Altimir (1993) observations do not exactly match this period but are close enough to suggest that, here too, recession caused an increase in poverty. Subsequently, between 1986 and 1989, the economy recovered with per capita income growing by 10 percent. According to Altimir, urban poverty fell 30 percent during the same three-year period.[3] Just as earlier (in the cross-section regression in chapter 3), there was a significant correlation between poverty and per capita income, the poverty indexes in table 6-1 suggest quite a strong relation between changes in poverty and changes in per capita income. That is, poverty typically rises in recession and declines in recovery.

As a check on the validity of that statement, all available information was collected for both rural and urban sectors for the intervals during which an economy was in either recession or recovery (beginning around 1980). Table 6-1 contains a subset of all these observations. Recession was defined as at least two years of falling per capita income; all other observations were classified as recoveries. In all, fifty-eight observations of recession periods were used (some countries having multiple observations for the same interval). In fifty-five of the fifty-eight cases, poverty increased. There were thirty-two recovery observations; of these, twenty-two fell, in three cases there was no change, and in the remaining seven, poverty increased.[4] Thus the evidence supports the proposition that poverty is sensitive to income level. While it is theoretically possible for improvements in the distribution of income to offset falling average income, in practice that almost never happened. Adjustment recessions raised the level of poverty in almost every case, and recoveries reduced it.

To estimate more precisely the relation between income and poverty, the poverty data underlying table 6-1 was used as the basis of a cross-section regression of changes in the level of poverty on changes in income and other variables, such as the minimum wage, inflation, and educational structure (Morley, 1992c). Separate regressions were run for the recession and recovery observations as well as one single regression with all the observations. Findings confirm the patterns in table 6-1: poverty is highly sensitive to level of income and has an elasticity of around −2, similar to that found in other studies. That implies that a 1 percent reduction in the growth rate of income reduces the decline in the growth rate of poverty by around 2 percent. Clearly, poverty is highly sensitive to the state of the economy.

The regressions suggest another important thing about the role of income, and that is that poverty seems to be particularly sensitive to income losses during the recession phase of structural adjustment. In all the recession regressions, the income coefficient was larger than for the other regressions. This was confirmed as well by a significant negative-slope dummy for recession in the regressions for all the observations, which suggests that recessions impose an especially heavy burden on the poor. This is consistent with the finding that inequality typically increased during the recessions of the 1980s.

POVERTY AND INFLATION

Inflation affects the welfare of the poor though two main channels. First, since inflation is a tax on money balances, and since the poor hold most of their assets in the form of currency rather than inflation-protected assets, inflation could have a disequalizing effect on the real value of wealth. Second, inflation can have an effect on the real wage. Of these two impacts, the wage effect is by far the most important (see Cardoso, 1992a) for an extended discussion). The reason is that money holdings of the truly poor are a small fraction of their income, not large enough to make the inflation tax a significant burden. Furthermore, when there is an acceleration of inflation to levels at which the tax might become important, there may be a speedup of wage payments, which reduces the need to hold cash balances.[5]

Wages are another matter. Virtually all the income of the poor comes from labor. Thus anything that affects either the average real wage or employment opportunities has a big impact on absolute poverty. What is the relation between inflation and the real wage of the poor? In answering that question, it is important to distinguish between the steady state and transitions between steady states. In the steady state, there may be little relation at all between the real wage and the inflation rate, because all participants in the labor market have time to adjust their behavior and expectations to the inflation rate. Transitions to either a higher or a lower inflation rate are very different because of lags in adjustment. Even with 100 percent indexing, inflation lowers the ex post average wage. It is possible to adjust target wage demands to take account of this, and that is undoubtedly what would happen in the steady state. But in practice, this is generally not done during transitions, with the result that periods when inflation was increasing in Latin America were also periods when the average and the minimum real wage were decreasing.

This is very clear in the period 1985–89, a period of drastic acceleration in inflation in Peru, Brazil, Argentina, and to a lesser extent, Mexico and Venezuela (see table 1-8). In all 5 of these countries, the acceleration of inflation caused or was accompanied by a big reduction in the real wage over the same period (see table 1-3). The same process occurred in Costa Rica in 1982 (Gindling and Berry, 1992). That year, nominal adjustments in the nominal minimum wage lagged behind the rapidly rising inflation rate. As a result, real wages fell sharply. Cardoso (1992a, p. 16) confirms this negative relation between the real wage and inflation more formally in a regression for seven countries for the period 1977–89. (Argentina, Colombia, Costa Rica, Chile, Mexico, and Peru). She estimates that a doubling of the inflation rate will on average reduce real wages by 14 percent.

There seems to be a clear connection between all of this and poverty. The transition to a much higher rate of inflation during 1985–90 in Peru, Brazil, Argentina, Mexico, and Venezuela not only lowered the real value of the minimum wage, it also raised the level of poverty and inequality. Matching poverty evidence with the dates of the acceleration of inflation, one finds that the average poverty level rose by 47 percent, a big jump.[6] The Ginis all rose, too, but by a somewhat smaller amount.

Ironically, transitions from a high to a low rate of inflation are also likely to hurt the poor. Inflation is generally controlled through some sort of austerity program, and such programs typically feature falling demand, rising unemployment, and perhaps a lowering of the minimum wage. The poor can be expected to pay a heavy price for all of this; not only will their ex post wage fall further than it would have due to inflation alone, but the austerity program will reduce their employment opportunities as well. Whether the long-run benefits to the poor of a lower rate of inflation exceed the short-run costs of reaching that lower rate depends on how long it takes to bring inflation down—which in turn depends on economic rigidities and lags (which differ across countries). The experience of Argentina and Bolivia suggest, somewhat paradoxically, that when a country reaches hyperinflation, the costs of adjustment are fairly low because of a speedup of inflation corrections on wages.

Another lesson of this period is that heterodox adjustment programs generally failed. Given the severity of the adjustment that was required, there was an understandable desire to find some combination of policies that would lead to balance of payments equilibrium without either a lengthy recession or a big rise in inflation. It was evident what the orthodox adjustment package did in the short run in places like Chile, Argentina, and Peru. But the alternatives turned out to be worse, particularly for the poor. The typical heterodox program tended to rely on incomes policies to control inflationary pressure rather than on contractionary fiscal and monetary retrenchment, which are the heart of the orthodox approach. There were three such cases during the 1980s: Peru under Garcia between 1985 and 1990, Brazil under Sarney (1985–89), and Argentina under Alfonsín (1983–89). Both Brazil and Argentina introduced novel and complex incomes policies (the Cruzado and Austral plans) intended to control what they called inertial inflation without eliminating government budget deficits and without lengthy recessions. Both attempts were disastrous failures. After short recoveries marked by rising real wages and repressed inflation, both countries suffered through a period of very high inflation accompanied by severe recession. Peru went through a similar experience under Alan Garcia.[7]

Tables 2-1 and 6-1 show just how costly these heterodox programs were for poverty and social equity. In Lima poverty rose from 31 percent to 40.5 percent, and the Gini rose from 0.39 to 0.44.[8] In Buenos Aires, the Gini rose from 0.40 to 0.45 between 1985 and 1988, and by one estimate poverty doubled between 1986 and 1989 (Morley and Alvarez, 1992c). The picture for Brazil is similar, with poverty rising by 58 percent (from 12 percent to 19 percent) and with a severe rise in inequality.[9]

Venezuela had a quite similar experience between 1986 and 1988, during the regime of Lusinchi. The country had gone through an orthodox adjustment between 1982 and 1985 in which the government had successfully eliminated a very large deficit and had endured a 19 percent decline in per capita income (1980–85). But then, despite the collapse of oil prices in 1986 and a decline in oil revenues of $7 billion, the government embarked on a round of public sector spending and tax cuts in which the government deficit rose to over 10 percent of GDP. The predictable result was a sharp jump in inflation, a new adjustment program, and another recession (per capita income fell 11 percent in 1989). And, as the reader can verify from tables 2-1 and 6-1, poverty jumped sharply over the period. Inequality is somewhat more ambiguous, but it appears also to have risen.[10]

The point of all this is that, for the poor, the populist or heterodox desire to avoid fiscal contraction, in order to spare both the poor and the rest of the voting public the pain of an adjustment recession, always seems to backfire; such schemes typically lead to a sharp increase in inflation. Not only will the poor be hurt as inflation accelerates, they are sure to be hurt even more when the rest of society demands that inflation be brought back down to previous levels.

POVERTY AND THE MINIMUM WAGE

Those interested in equity have long argued that maintaining or raising the minimum wage is progressive, that it will improve the distribution of income and alleviate poverty. To accept that argument requires three significant assumptions: first, that the poor work in minimum wage jobs; second, that these jobs are insensitive to the minimum wage in real terms; and third, that the government can affect the real value of the minimum wage by manipulating its nominal value. None of these conditions necessarily hold in Latin America. Many people work either in the urban informal sector or in agriculture at wages well below the minimum. Such people could be helped, not hurt, if a decline in the minimum wage expanded formal sector job opportunities. However, if the decline in the minimum wage took place in a recession setting, in which the number of formal sector jobs was declining as well, then the cost to workers in the formal sector would not be offset by gains to the newly employed. Furthermore, by affecting the distribution of income, the minimum wage could also affect the demand for formal sector output by shrinking the market for goods intended for the mass market, thus amplifying the reduction in labor income and worsening the adjustment recession. With respect to the relation between the nominal and real value of the minimum wage, the government controls only the former, not the latter. If the government sets a nominal wage inconsistent with the level of profits desired by the private sector or with the marginal product of labor, either inflation or unemployment will ensue. In either case, the desire to raise the incomes of the unskilled will backfire.

These dilemmas cannot be resolved theoretically. Rather, they require an appeal to experience, and in this regard Latin America offers a rich laboratory of alternative patterns of real wages, adjustment, inflation, and poverty. In the previous section, it was shown that high inflation drove down the real wage in many countries in the second half of the 1980s. That, along with recession, caused a big jump in poverty and in income inequality. We now look more closely at the record of the rest of the decade to see what further lessons it suggests.

There are three sorts of evidence, none of which is definitive but all of which is suggestive. The first comes from a simple linking of the real wage series shown in table 1-3 and what we know about poverty trends over the decade. The real wage increased in only three countries: Colombia, Costa Rica, and Paraguay, which are also three of the four countries that showed a decline in poverty over the decade.

Second, consider the changes in the distribution during the contractionary phase of adjustment episodes in the 1980s (see table 2-2). In the southwest quadrant of table 2-2, which shows a combination of recession and rising inequality, real wages fell in twelve cases and were essentially constant in the other three. What is perhaps more interesting is that all the cases (both of recession and recovery) in which the real wage increased were also ones in which income distribution improved. In Brazil, Uruguay, and Chile the real wage fell and the distribution became more equal; in all three cases, recovery was accompanied by a substantial increase in employment and a rise in the average wage relative to the minimum wage.[11]

Another piece of evidence is a comparison of actual and hypothetical distributions in 1989 and their relation to changes in the minimum wage. Recall that in chapter 3, for those countries where household surveys of the distribution of income for both 1980 and 1989 are available, the hypothetical level of poverty in 1989 was calculated assuming that each member of the 1980 population had received the same increase or reduction in income (see table 2-7). Let us now relate this calculation to the minimum wage.

In seven countries, poverty was lower than predicted on the basis of income growth, and in five it was higher. Of the seven better-than-expected countries, five had an increase in minimum wage, whereas all five of the worse-than-expected countries had a decline in the minimum wage. The two exceptions were Mexico and Uruguay, both of which did better than expected despite a fall in the minimum wage. In both countries, unemployment was cut sharply in the recoveries after 1983.[12] Thus the fall in their minimum wages wage must have been offset by rising employment opportunities. In Mexico there was also an increasing divergence between the minimum and the average wage. The latter was essentially constant between 1984 and 1989, even though the former fell by 30 percent. None of this evidence is conclusive, but it is suggestive that, of the four countries with improvements in poverty over the decade (Colombia, Costa Rica, Paraguay, and Uruguay), three had rising real minimum wages. Note further than in none of these three did it rise at the expense of either the balance of payments or inflation.

All of the foregoing evidence, while suggestive, is ad hoc in the sense that all other factors that may affect the poverty level were not held constant. Thus the observations may be picking up the influence of factors other than the minimum wage. To attempt to get a more accurate estimate of the independent influence of the minimum wage, the minimum wage was included in the regressions reported earlier for changes in the level of poverty (Morley, 1992c). The regression results support, though somewhat ambiguously, the negative relation between the real minimum wage and poverty. It is a highly significant variable both in the overall regressions, where all observations are lumped together, and in a separate regression for only recovery observations. It is not significant in regressions limited to only recession observations. The reason for that may have something to do with the wide variations in the minimum wage due to hyperinflation in several countries. On average, the real wage fell by 13 percent in this sample, but the individual observations run all the way from a 51 percent reduction in Argentina between 1980 and 1989 to a 42 percent gain in Venezuela between 1982 and 1987, a time when poverty was increasing.[13] In a slightly smaller set of recession observations, which excluded several 1980–89 observations for Brazil, Uruguay, and Venezuela, the minimum wage was a highly significant variable and had the expected negative sign.

What all of this suggests is that there is a clear link between macroeconomic conditions and inequality. Inequality is countercyclical, and real minimum wages appear to have an equalizing effect on the distribution. In most cases it is probably true that the real wage is also related to the cycle, falling during recession and rising in recovery. Thus in most cases it is not an additional variable, but is itself driven by economic conditions. But there are cases where the two do not move together (in Argentina, 1980–82 and 1982–85; in Brazil, 1983–86; and in Chile, 1983–87). In the Argentine cases, the improvement in the real wage may help explain why distribution improved despite the severe recession of those years. Brazil's experience between 1979 and 1983 is also instructive in this regard: per capita income fell 12.3 percent, yet by policy design the real minimum wage was held virtually constant. This may have tempered the rise in inequality, which was relatively moderate compared to the experience of other countries suffering comparable recessions.

Even if one is able to establish a clear link between the minimum wage and the level of poverty, it does not follow that raising the nominal minimum wage is a sensible antipoverty policy, for the real minimum wage is not fully under the control of the government. If one raises it under the wrong conditions, one runs the risk of exacerbating either inflation or unemployment. One particularly disastrous policy combination is the one followed under all the heterodox inflation control programs in the 1985–90 period in Argentina, Brazil, Peru, and Venezuela. In each of these programs the government attempted to control nominal wages and prices with incomes programs while failing to control aggregate demand at the same time. The result was virulent inflation, falling real wages, recession, and a big increase in poverty, certainly not the result desired by policymakers.

Clearly, government wage policy has to depend on conditions in the economy. The countries that maintained their minimum wages— Colombia, Costa Rica, Paraguay, Brazil prior to 1985, Uruguay, and Panama—for the most part went into the decade with fairly competitive economies, with large traded goods sectors, and with real wages in line with local labor market conditions. These factors permitted these countries to come through the adjustment without an extended recession or a long and massive contraction in real wages. If a country is in that situation, there is no reason why its stabilization has to start with a sharp cut in the minimum wage. Experience shows that, if the traded goods sector is large, such cuts are not necessary either for the balance of payments or for successful stabilization.

THE ROLE OF ECONOMIC STRUCTURE

Granted that falling income was a major cause of the increase in poverty that took place in Latin America during the 1980s, one still must wonder why the adjustment process was so much more severe in some countries than in others. What is it about Costa Rica, Colombia, Paraguay, and Uruguay that permitted significant reductions in poverty in spite of slow or even negative income growth? Why did Argentina, Venezuela, and Brazil have such a rapid increase in poverty? What do the experiences of these countries have to teach us about the effect of differences in economic structure and their effect on the relation between poverty and growth.

To show the sharp difference in performance of different countries in response to structural adjustment, I hypothesize that a key distinction is the size and role of the traded goods sector and the relationship of the poor to that sector. Traded goods are those commodities whose price moves in lockstep with the exchange rate; exports and import substitutes are the main examples. Nominal devaluation, a key element in a structural adjustment to a balance of payments deficit, should help the traded goods sector and hurt the nontraded goods sector, assuming the government does not neutralize the devaluation with expansionary policy. By definition, the price of traded goods rises by the full amount of the devaluation, while the price of nontraded goods rises by a lesser amount, thus raising the relative price of traded goods. Here again, I am assuming complementary demand management by the government. Under these conditions, a nominal devaluation leads to a real devaluation, which will help the producers of traded goods but, at the same time, will hurt both the producers of nontraded goods and the consumers of traded goods. Furthermore, the size of the traded goods sector plays a big part in determining how large the real devaluation has to be. Generally speaking, the bigger the sector, the easier the adjustment and the smaller the necessary real devaluation.

From the point of view of poverty, the most favorable situation is to be in a country where the poor are producers but not consumers of traded goods, because real devaluation will raise their wages by more than it will raise their cost of living. The least favorable situation is one in which the poor consume but do not produce traded goods. Clearly, no country is a perfect example of either polar case, but it appears that countries like Costa Rica, Paraguay, and Colombia have a relatively favorable structure compared to Venezuela and Argentina.

Colombia is essentially self-sufficient in food and other wage goods, which seems to explain why domestic prices are relatively insensitive to movements in the real exchange rate.[14] At the same time, in the 1980s the production of tradable goods was highly responsive to real devaluation, and that was a stimulus to real wages and employment for both the poor and the nonpoor. In Costa Rica, agriculture predominantly produces traded goods and employs a significant fraction of the poor. Real devaluation after 1980 had a powerful positive impact on agricultural production, exports, and wages. Morley and Alvarez (1992a) show that real wages in the exportable sector, which is primarily agricultural, rose 10 percent relative to wages in the nontradables sector between 1980 and 1989. In addition, the urban-rural average income differential fell from 1.94 in 1981 to 1.81 in 1989. Thus Costa Rica was in the fortunate situation of having a relatively large traded goods sector, which in expansion was able to push up wages and incomes for the rural poor. This had a dramatic effect on rural poverty, which fell from 17.2 percent to 3.8 percent between 1981 and 1989.

Paraguay's large agricultural sector enjoyed a period of export-led growth during the 1980s.[15] The data are, unfortunately, urban, but it is reasonable to suppose that the rising wages in the rural sector would tend to put upward pressure on the wage of the urban unskilled. That would explain the impressive reduction in urban inequality and poverty between 1983 and 1990.

Argentina and Venezuela are in a completely different situation. In Argentina the two main traded exports are wheat and beef, but clearly, these two are also important wage goods. Because real devaluation drives up the price of these two commodities, it can be expected to hurt the poor as consumers, particularly those in the urban sector. But does it help them as producers? The answer appears to be, not much. Argentina has a substantial manufacturing sector, but it is highly protected. That means that, while it produces potentially tradable goods, those goods are not traded. Economists call such products nontraded tradables. More important, the sector as a whole is hurt more than it is helped by real devaluation, because prices are determined internally, not by the real exchange rate. For Argentine manufacturing, real devaluation drives up the price of essential imported intermediates and capital more than it raises the prices of its own output. Hence the sector is likely to contract in response to real devaluation just as if it were producing nontraded goods. This is why real devaluation is likely to hurt the urban poor, both as producers and as consumers. Because of high levels of protection, the traded goods sector appears to be relatively small in Argentina, which reduces the flexibility of the economy to respond to changes in the real exchange rate and means that structural adjustments are likely to be long and difficult.

Venezuela has a slightly different problem than Argentina. Its traded good is oil, but real devaluation does not have much effect on the production of oil, which is controlled by quotas. The rest of the potential traded goods sector in manufacturing and agriculture is abnormally small. The poor are, therefore, not helped much in Venezuela as producers, but they are hurt as consumers. Some food is imported, and its price has risen with the exchange rate. In addition, the elimination of food subsidies, an important part of the adjustment program, further increased the price of food. (The relative price of food rose 83 percent between 1980 and 1989 (ECLAC, *Statistical Yearbook 1992*).) Thus, as in Argentina, in Venezuela devaluation is likely to hurt the poor as consumers but not help them as producers. Under these unfortunate structural conditions, adjustments to balance of payments deficits will be long, will require extended periods of recession, and will generate bitter disputes over real wage reductions.

Brazil had relatively high levels and rates of growth of poverty over the decade. However, this was not because it had a small traded goods sector; instead, the Brazilian case represents a failure of macroeconomic policy, in particular fiscal policy. In effect, Brazil had two adjustments. During the one between 1980 ad 1985, it imposed a large real devaluation and improved its current account deficit by $12 billion, all at a relatively low cost in terms of poverty or output forgone. But, as successful as this adjustment was on these grounds, it failed to deal with either the government deficit or inflation, forcing the country into a second adjustment period after 1986. These two episodes are quite distinct, and from the point of view of the discussion about the relevance of economic structure to the adjustment process, the first period is more relevant than the second. Thus Brazil's record between 1981 and 1985 shows a far more favorable adjustment to the balance of payments deficit then does the second adjustment.

Between 1981 and 1985 Brazil essentially corrected its balance of payments deficit and went through a typical adjustment cycle of recession and recovery. Between 1981 and 1983, GDP per capita fell by around 9 percent, but then, during the next two years it recovered all the ground it had lost. This is a relatively mild and short adjustment compared to the experience of most other Latin countries. In the traded goods sector there was an expansion of both exports and import substitutes in response to a real devaluation of about 20 percent. Between 1981 and 1985 the value of exports rose by 9 percent despite a 20 percent decline in export prices. Imports of goods and services fell by $9 billion, which implies a substantial switch to import substitutes, given that GDP rose by 14 percent. Manufacturing employment and output increased, and real wages in manufacturing either fell or rose by a small amount, depending on which wage series one uses.[16]

What happened to poverty during this period? In contrast to what came later in the decade, the evidence suggests that Brazil's performance was quite good, like the other traded goods economies. Fox and Morley (1991) give poverty indexes based on the Brazilian minimum wage for the period in question. Poverty incidence rose from 0.248 in 1981 to 0.309 in 1983, at the depth of the recession. Subsequently, poverty declined as the economy recovered, with the ratio reaching 0.254 in 1985, 0.161 in the boom year 1986, and 0.233 in 1987 (see table 6-1). This does not permit a comparison of poverty prior to the entire adjustment episode; however, one estimate (ECLAC, 1990a) permits a comparison of 1979 and 1987, a year when the economy was already beginning to decline in the second stage of the adjustment process. Rural poverty fell from 68 percent to 66 percent, while urban poverty rose from 34 percent to 38 percent. Overall, poverty was constant at 45 percent, which compares well with the experience of other adjusting countries (ibid., table 13).

Brazil managed to complete its adjustment with a relatively modest short-run decline in per capita income, followed by a recovery that more than gained back all the ground that had been lost (per capita GDP in constant cruzados rose 8 percent between 1979 and 1987). As in other countries, poverty was countercyclical, rising from 1979 to 1983 and falling thereafter. Even though it cannot be directly confirmed with a time series of poverty ratios, it is almost certainly that by 1986 poverty was below its preadjustment level. And we do know that in 1987 poverty overall was just where it had been when the crisis started (see ibid.). In other words, Brazil resolved its balance of payments deficit, recovered from recession, and reduced poverty, a record that looks very good compared with what happened in other countries. Subsequent events were far more difficult for both Brazil and its poor, but that should not obscure its relatively good performance during the early period, when it made a successful balance of payments adjustment.

This performance was possible because both agricultural and manufacturing sectors had a significant proportion of tradable goods, whose production expanded when there was a real devaluation. Brazil's relatively benign adjustment during the first half of the decade is consistent with the hypothesis that tradability affects the speed and severity of adjustment as well as its impact on the poor. Note also that the relative performance of the rural sector, where poverty declined, is consistent with the experience of agriculture in Costa Rica and Paraguay.

TRADED GOODS IN LATIN ECONOMIES

Theory tells us that, when there is a real devaluation, traded goods should expand and nontraded goods should contract. While that is clear, what is not clear is which goods are traded goods. Generally, one thinks of agriculture and industry as the principal candidates, even though some components of services, such as travel, education, and insurance, may also be important. But within both industry and agriculture there may be subsectors that, although tradable, do not act like traded goods in response to devaluation; either their production for exports is subject to quotas, as is the case with oil, coffee, and textiles, or domestic protection is so high that the domestic price is lower than what the foreign good would have to sell for to pay the tariff.

In Latin America, agriculture acts like a traded good but industry does not. As shown earlier, agriculture did much better than industry and the rest of the urban sector during the 1980s in most Latin American countries. Farm output grew in absolute terms in every country but Uruguay, and its share of GDP grew in all but three countries (Colombia, Mexico, and Uruguay). Almost the opposite pattern is seen for industry: its share fell in all but three countries—Chile, Colombia, and Honduras—all of which have relatively low levels of protection.

The relation between these relative growth patterns and the real exchange rates is shown in table 6-2. Since one expects traded goods to grow faster than income (or to fall by less than income), the traded goods share should rise with real devaluation, and vice versa. One would therefore expect traded goods to be found in either the northwest or the southeast quadrant, and nontraded goods in the southwest or northeast. Agriculture tends to follow that pattern, while industry does not. This is not to say that some industry subsectors are not competitive but rather that, in the aggregate, such subsectors are too small to outweigh those industry subsectors that depend on imported inputs and serve only the internal market. For these subsectors, the combination of real devaluation and a contraction of domestic demand caused a downturn in production. Unfortunately, that was the typical response, and it meant that, for the urban labor force, there was a severe shrinkage of both real wages and job opportunities during the adjustment.

When this evidence is combined with the cross-country patterns of growth, one begins to see more clearly the importance of openness and

Table 6-2.   Relation of Real Exchange Rates and Sectoral Behavior

Sector Share Behavior	Real Exchange Rate Rises	Real Exchange Rate Falls
Agricultural share rises	10^1	2^2
Agricultural share falls	3^3	0
Industry share rises	2^4	1^5
Industry share falls	11^6	1^7

[1] Argentina, Bolivia, Brazil, Chile, Costa Rica, Ecuador, Guatemala, Panama, Paraguay, Venezuela.
[2] Honduras, Peru.
[3] Colombia, Mexico, Uruguay.
[4] Chile, Colombia.
[5] Honduras.
[6] Argentina, Bolivia, Brazil, Costa Rica, Ecuador, Guatemala, Mexico, Panama, Paraguay, Uruguay, Venezuela.
[7] Peru.

the nature of the export sector. Among the fifteen countries on table 6-2, four had short and relatively easy stabilizations, with recovery by 1985: Paraguay, Costa Rica, Colombia, and Uruguay. Agriculture was the key sector in Paraguay and Costa Rica; it was big, it produced exportable traded goods, and it expanded rapidly in response to real devaluation. This helped to offset the contractionary part of the adjustment program. In Colombia, industry was the leading traded goods sector. Not only did it expand rapidly in response to real devaluation, but it also made a big contribution to the expansion of exports. Uruguay is something of a special case in that its recovery was led by services rather than by either industry or agriculture.

A second group of economies was heavily dependent on mineral exports: Ecuador, Venezuela, and Mexico live on oil. Each had long and extended adjustments due to their dependence on a sector producing a traded good that could not respond to devaluation and that, in addition, suffered from a sharp decline in price over the decade. Chile was still in this group in 1980 because of its heavy dependence on copper, a commodity whose price fell sharply until 1987. (Chilean terms of trade fell by 27 percent between 1980 and 1985.) Like the other three countries in the group, it had a very severe adjustment in 1982–86, though it seems to have been as much the result of a financial crisis and mismanagement of the exchange rate as the result of terms of trade or the tradability of its manufacturing and agricultural sector. By the late 1980s a determined effort by the government to privatize the economy and reduce the level of protection began to pay off. Manufacturing had been changed from a highly protected sector, producing nontraded tradables for the domestic market, to one that helped lead the drive to a new growth model based on exports other than copper.

Three other nonoil economies—Argentina, Brazil, and Peru—had two adjustments over the decade. The first attempted to deal with the balance of payments problem, while the second was primarily an attempt to control hyperinflation. One could also put Venezuela in this group of double-adjustment economies. Because they all had to adjust twice (with the exception of Brazil, which we have discussed earlier), their growth record is the worst of the fifteen countries. Brazil and Peru did not have a real devaluation. Argentina and Venezuela did, but their industries were either too small or too protected to counteract the severe effects of domestic contraction. In all four, their governments were unable to sustain the adjustment process, which degenerated into a round of rapidly rising inflation in the second half of the decade. That probably would not have happened had the export sectors in these economies been able to offer expanding employment in response to the real devaluations that all of these economies achieved before 1985 (see table 1-8).

The remaining three economies are small; Bolivia, Honduras, and Guatemala each specialized in the production and export of a natural-resource-based commodity that was not expanding in the 1980s. These economies had no domestic production base to take advantage of real devaluation, and as a result their stabilizations were long. Even in 1994 their recoveries are uncertain.[17]

Chapter Seven

Emerging from the Crisis: Adjustment and Reform After 1990

After 1990 more and more Latin American countries began to experience the positive benefits of the arduous process of adjustment and structural reform they had endured during the eighties. Chile, Argentina, Panama, and Costa Rica, especially, had very rapid growth, declining inflation rates, and impressive reductions in their debt burdens (see table 7-1). Uruguay and Venezuela also grew rapidly for several years but had setbacks in 1993. While the rest of the countries grew more slowly, the important thing is that all but two of them (Brazil and Paraguay) did grow. Furthermore, Peru (along with war-torn Nicaragua), the most severely affected of all the countries in the region, was growing rapidly by 1993. Even Brazil, despite its accelerating inflation, grew by 5 percent, or 3.3 percent per capita, in 1993.

I do not fully analyze the post-1990 period here. Rather, I look at several key parameters to get a notion of the vigorousness and sustainability of the new round of growth. The data in table 7-1 provide grounds for both optimism and pessimism. On the positive side are the much higher growth rates of per capita income and the dramatic reduction in both inflation and the burden of the debt in most countries. With the glaring exception of Brazil, inflation was under control everywhere, and debt burdens were sharply reduced relative to their peaks in 1982, in most cases back to the levels of the late 1970s. More to the point, all of the countries that gloomy prognosticators forecast would never work their

Table 7-1.   Macroeconomic Indicators, Fifteen Countries, 1990–1993

Country	Average Annual GDP Growth per Capita, 1990–1993 (%)	Export Growth, 1990–1993[1] (%)	Yearly Inflation, 1993 (%)	Real Exchange Rate ,1993 (1990 = 100) (%)	Ratio of Interest to Exports, 1993
Argentina	6.6	6	11	59	.23
Bolivia	1.2	–15	9	101	.21
Brazil	–0.1	23	214	124	.22
Chile	5.3	11	13	91	.10
Colombia	1.8	7	22	84	.12
Costa Rica	2.6	44	10	106	.07
Ecuador	1.0	7	45	85	.20[2]
Guatemala	1.2	12	13	79	.06
Honduras	1.1	–5	11	115	.22
Mexico	0.1	12	10	81	.17
Panama	5.8	17	0	103	.13
Paraguay	–0.2	–14	18	91	.05
Peru	0.3	6	49	87	.25
Uruguay	3.3	–2	54	70	.18[2]
Venezuela	3.0	–18	38	87	.21[2]

Source: IADB, Economic and Social Data Base.
[1] Exports of goods in nominal dollars.
[2] 1992.

way out from under their debt burdens did so, thanks in part to debt write-downs, lower interest rates, and export growth.[1] All of this led to a revival of international confidence in Latin America and a surge of capital inflows and repatriation. In 1993 alone net capital inflows were over $69 billion, enabling the region to accumulate the highest level of international reserves in its history. Capital formation returned to almost precrisis levels, and thanks to fiscal reforms, domestic saving increased and could be devoted to financing investment rather than government deficits or interest payments on the external debt.

All of these were positive developments. But there were some indications of trouble ahead as well. First, despite appearances, most countries in the region had yet to establish a successful export sector by 1993, one capable of sustained growth. There were some striking export success stories, particularly Chile, Costa Rica, Panama, Mexico, and Brazil (see table 7-1). But the overall record was disappointing. Five of the countries had negative export growth, and the overall average was only 6 percent over three years. That was not enough to keep up with the rise in the price of imports or the rise in GDP per capita. Despite a decade of attempts to change to a more outward-looking growth strategy, exports in most countries had not responded very vigorously by 1993.

One obvious culprit for this weak export performance was terms of trade; all the oil economies faced a severe reduction in their terms of trade between 1990 and 1993, as did other exporters of natural resource products, such as Bolivia and Peru. Another reason for the weak export performance was a real appreciation of the exchange rate. As one can see from table 7-1, ten of the fifteen countries had a real appreciation over the period—several, including Uruguay and Argentina, by a very large amount. One cannot expect to develop and sustain viable export industries with such sharp fluctuations in their relative prices.

The use of the exchange rate to help control inflation and capital inflows seems to have been responsible for the real appreciation. After Bolivia and Argentina used the nominal exchange rate as a nominal anchor in their successful battle against hyperinflation, that strategy became popular in many other countries, all of which were battling either inertial inflation or active inflationary pressure. The theoretical justification for this policy is that, if one freezes the nominal exchange rate, inflationary expectations will subside and other prices will quite quickly fall into line. There may be a transitory real appreciation while that is happening, but if other macroeconomic conditions are in balance, inflation should decline. That at least is the theory. But it has not worked out that way in practice. According to the data, real appreciations were not temporary, largely because of capital inflows. They were what made it possible for countries to have a real appreciation that was not self-correcting. And real appreciation should be self-correcting, because it causes a fall in net exports. That is contractionary in its own right; and it also causes an outflow of money, which should be deflationary. But that does not happen when there are capital inflows. Receipts in the capital account substitute for export earnings and provide additional money to the economy, which stops the downward pressure on domestic prices and permits a continuation of the overvaluation for as long as there are capital inflows.

There is surely nothing wrong with external borrowing in moderation. But when capital inflows reach $25 billion in one year, as they did in Mexico in 1993, the situation becomes dangerous and unsustainable. There is no reason to believe that inflows of such a magnitude are permanent, and when they stop, imports are again determined by export capacity rather than borrowing capacity. But if that export capacity has not been created or if it has been damaged during a long period of overvaluation, one is likely to stumble into another balance of payments crisis.

What is perhaps worse, governments will be tempted to use high domestic real interest rates to attract foreign capital and so to put off the day of reckoning, when they have to face the unpleasant realities of the world export market. There is a good deal of evidence that this was happening in many countries. High real interest rates have several very unfortunate side effects other than their effect on the real exchange rate and exports: they discourage real investment, they exacerbate government deficits in countries with internal bond markets, and they are regressive.

To return to the main theme, the Latin American balance of payments in the early 1990s was heavily influenced by and dependent on foreign capital inflows, as it was in the last several years before the debt crisis began in 1982. This is dangerous and unsustainable. It is critical that Latin governments find a way to live with fluctuating capital movements without making their export sectors hostage to unstable real exchange rates. In the long run, it is export capacity that determines how fast economies can grow and how much they can import. Export markets, if anything, are going to get more competitive, so there is no more pressing task facing the region than to make sure that exports do not lose out. And on this score, the most recent export results are not particularly promising.

POVERTY AND INCOME DISTRIBUTION SINCE 1990

In Chile, Argentina, Venezuela, and Costa Rica, recovery has had a dramatic effect on the level of poverty (see table 7-1 and the poverty data in table 6-1). Argentine per capita income grew by 6.6 percent per year between 1990 and 1993; poverty in Buenos Aires was cut in half. Chile grew slightly slower over the same period, and its national poverty level fell from 40 percent to 33 percent. Venezuela, before its collapse in 1993, enjoyed the same sort of poverty-reducing growth as Argentina and Chile. Costa Rica's is a slightly different story since 1990, because it had a short downturn in 1991. In the following two years (1991–93), its per capita income grew by 4.4 percent per year and its poverty level fell by 29 percent (from 24.4 percent of households to 17.4 percent). The only case for which we have data that appear to be different is Colombia: income per capita grew slowly in Colombia since 1990, but according to table 6-1 poverty increased at the same time. However, a poverty assessment by the World Bank indicates no such increase; indeed, it shows poverty falling by over 5 percent between 1990 and 1992.[2]

Thus the post-1990 data strongly confirm the relation between poverty and growth discussed in chapter 6. While it is unlikely that the poor made up all the ground they lost during the 1980s, the experience of the nineties has shown once again that economic recovery is the most powerful and surest antidote to poverty that policymakers can find. The big question for the future—and for the poor—is whether these recoveries are temporary or permanent.

THE EFFECT OF STRUCTURAL REFORM

The process of adjustment and reform in Latin America has gone through several distinct stages. The first corrected the balance of payments deficit by means of large real devaluations, contractions in the government deficit, mainly through reduced government investment, and a contractionary monetary policy. This stage generally resulted in severe recession, mainly in the early to mid 1980s, and by now it has been pretty much completed. The second stage came in the second half of the decade in most countries and was still, in 1994, being implemented. The main elements of this stage were the streamlining and downsizing of the state, the privatization of government enterprises, the elimination of price controls and government subsidies, and trade liberalization through the reduction of tariff and nontariff protection of domestic industry.[3] For most countries, these changes were so recent that it is too early to tell what the likely long-run effects will be, but for some countries the postreform pattern is more predictable. It is to those cases that we now turn.

Mexico, Chile, and Bolivia were the three earliest adopters of trade liberalization reforms (see World Bank, 1993, p. 59). Costa Rica started later, but very recent data permit a preliminary evaluation of the results of its reforms. The evidence from these four countries shows a very big difference between what the reforms achieved in Chile and Costa Rica relative to the other two countries.

By 1992 Chile was profiting very handsomely from the change of growth strategy adopted between 1973 and 1985. Export growth stimulated the entire economy and eliminated the external debt as a pressing problem. By 1992 unemployment fell to the lowest level in thirty years, and there was a significant increase in income equality, as well. Costa Rica had the same favorable response to its reforms as Chile did. Exports, led by tourism and other nontraditional products, expanded by 59 percent between 1983 and 1993. That, along with a big inflow of foreign capital, sparked a strong recovery, in which the economy grew by 15 percent in 1992–93. As in Chile, that growth created a large number of jobs, which drove up the real wage and caused both the unemployment and poverty rates to fall sharply.

The situation was far less positive in Bolivia. Its reforms came in the year 1985, when the new government of Paz Estenssoro eliminated hyperinflation, opened up the economy, and reduced the government deficit to practically zero. But unlike Chile, there was little response from either the export sector or aggregate growth. The dollar volume of exports was lower in 1992 than it was in the years before the 1985 reforms, and GDP per capita showed the same pattern, lower in 1992 than it was before the reforms started.[4]

No other country started structural reform earlier or carried it further than Chile, so it is appropriate that we look first at the country. Having done that, we look at Bolivia and Mexico, two other countries that liberalized early, but with much less success than Chile. We conclude with an examination of events in Costa Rica since 1989.

Chile

One of the main thrusts of the Pinochet government in Chile was trade liberalization. Prior to 1973 Chile had been a high-tariff economy that depended on import substitution for domestic growth and on its foreign-owned copper industry for foreign exchange and tax revenues. At that time, copper accounted for 80 percent of total exports, and the average tariff rate was 105 percent (Meller, 1992b, p. 3 and table 5.4). But in effect, total protection was higher than the tariff rate, because Chile also had a host of nontariff barriers, such as advance deposits for imports, quotas, multiple exchange rates, and cumbersome licensing procedures (ibid., p. 3). Virtually all of these instruments of protection for domestic production were swept away between 1973 and 1979. The first to go were nontariff barriers, eliminated in 1973–74. Next, the average tariff was reduced in steps, from an average of 105 percent in 1973, 36 percent in 1976, and 10 percent in 1979 (ibid., p. 5).

In 1979 the government freed the capital account and froze the exchange rate in an attempt to reduce inflation. The result was a dramatic inflow of foreign capital, an appreciation of the real exchange rate, a balance of payments crisis, and a severe domestic recession. In response, the government reimposed capital controls and permitted a 50 percent real devaluation. Over the remainder of the eighties, so great was the real depreciation of the exchange rate that the level of real protection in 1990 was only 15 percent less than it had been in 1973, despite the elimination of tariff and nontariff barriers. In effect, the government had eliminated the anti-export bias of the previous import-substitution strategy.[5] Exports and import substitutes could compete on a level playing field whenever the balance of payments required a real devaluation to increase the production of tradables.

The initial result of these trade reforms is difficult to assess because of the financial crisis and severe recession that followed the fixed exchange rate experiment in 1982. But in the longer run, trade liberalization worked exactly as the trade optimists had hoped: total exports rose from $2 billion in 1973 to $8.5 billion in 1990, and the economy became significantly more open, with exports rising as a share of GDP from less than 10 percent in 1973 to 25 percent in 1982 and 33 percent in 1990. Furthermore, there was a very significant diversification of exports, the major new products being fish, fresh fruit, wine, minerals other than copper, lumber, and logs. Export revenues from copper, which provided more than 80 percent of the total in 1973, fell to only 45 percent of the total in 1990. Other exports rose from less than $300 million in 1973 to $4.7 billion in 1990 (Meller, 1992b, table 5.4). This diversification significantly reduced Chile's sensitivity to fluctuations in the price of copper and was a major gain in its own right.

But successful as these new exports were, they did not change the essential nature of Chile's export activities. Almost none of the new exports were manufactures. Rather, almost all were based on natural resources, such as lumber and the products of agriculture and fishing. In natural-resource-dependent economies, trade liberalization is likely to work against domestic manufacturing. That is what happened in Chile. Manufacturing played only a small role in the export boom; it was not even a leading sector internally. Over the period 1974–90, the share of manufacturing in GDP fell from 25 percent to around 21 percent, and its share of employment fell by about the same amount (ibid., p. 41).

To summarize, trade liberalization permitted a big increase in both copper and noncopper exports, but at least 90 percent of these exports were based on natural resources. Manufacturing grew too, but at a lower rate than the rest of the economy. By the end of the decade, thanks to the low across-the-board tariff, those manufacturing activities that survived were far more likely than they had been in 1973 to be competitive.

In a previous section, I hypothesized that growth based on the export of tradables based on natural resources might be unable to create a sufficient number of good jobs for the emergent middle class, which could lead to featherbedding in the government or to pressure for greater protection of domestic manufacturing. None of this happened in Chile. First of all, growth was so rapid after 1985 that all parts of the labor pyramid benefited. Overall, employment grew an average of 6.1 percent per year from 1985 to 1992, and unemployment fell from 21 percent of the labor force to 4.9 percent (see table 7-2 for several key macroeconomic indicators).

What kind of jobs were created in this expansion? It turns out that, in Chile's case, natural-resource-based exports did create many good jobs as well as work for unskilled labor. There are a number of instructive reasons why. First, many of the new export activities became profitable: these exports were almost all Chilean-owned, so that all the income they earned stayed in Chile—to be invested, paid out in wages, or consumed as profits, thus increasing aggregate demand and employment across the board. Second, the notion that natural-resource-based activities use only unskilled labor or limited amounts of labor is too narrow. In the Chilean case, many of the new exports did require skilled labor. Exporting fresh fruit, fish, or shrimp, for example, required a complex distribution and storage capacity. The emergent wine industry required skilled workers, new technology, and marketing (see Meller, 1992a, p. 15). Thus the new activities stimulated expansion in supporting service sector activities through both backward and forward linkages. When one adds the direct and indirect employment effects of the new products that Chile developed, the employment effects can be seen at all levels of skill.

The effects of the new growth strategy on poverty and distribution can be seen quite clearly, and the results are impressive, particularly after 1990 (see table 7-2). Overall, rapid economic growth translated into big gains in employment, hours worked, and salaries, particularly at the bottom of the income pyramid. Improvements were spread equally all across the country, thanks to the widespread dispersion of natural resource activities. As a result, poverty fell from 44.6 percent of the population in 1987

Table 7-2.   Macroeconomic Indicators, Chile, 1980–1993, Various Years

Indicator	1980	1985	1987	1990	1992	1993[6]
Gini[1]			.522	.526	.466	
Minimum wage[2]	136	87	79	100	114	120
Average wage[2]	95	90	90	100	112	116
Poverty index (percent)[3]			44.6	40.1	32.7	
Unemployment rate (percent)[4]	15.7	21.4	12.2	6.0	4.9	4.9
Industrial employment						
(1980 = 100)[4]	100	86.6	100.3	116.9	131.6	
GDP/capita (1988 US$)[5]	100	90.2	98.1	113.7	128.8	134

[1] Pardo et al., 1993. The 1992 Gini is an estimate, but direction is confirmed by IADB, 1994b.
[2] Minimum and average wages for 1987, 1990, 1992 from ECLAC, *Economic Survey 1992*; previous years from Cox Edwards, 1991, converted to a 1990 base.
[3] Raczynski, 1993.
[4] ECLAC, *Economic Survey 1992*.
[5] IADB, 1994b.
[6] 1993 data from IADB, 1994b.

to 32.7 percent in 1992. And thanks to a narrowing of wage differentials, there seems to have been a substantial reduction in inequality as well. The 1992 Gini coefficient is based on growth in salaries; it may overstate the magnitude of the decline in inequality, but the direction of change is confirmed by the data in table 7-3. The gain in real income in the poorest economic quintile between 1990 and 1992 was the highest of any group; also, part of the increase in equality was due to the shrinkage of subsidies, particular for upper-income households.

In the typical recovery in Latin America during the 1980s, there was a reduction in both wage dispersion and inequality. That happened as well in Chile between 1987 and 1990. But what is more significant is that this trend continued beyond 1990, when Chile had emerged from its recovery phase and was on a new long-run growth trajectory. Thus the picture after 1990 is important for the light it can shed on what one might be able to expect in the long run from the new export-based growth strategy. And here, the clear implication of the data seems to be that the growth strategy was equitable; it generated rapid growth, which was shared across the board and particularly at the bottom. Obviously, with overall growth as rapid as that in Chile, there was bound to be some reduction in poverty. Of more importance is that in this period of rapid growth, unlike what happened in Brazil during its boom (1967–80), inequality fell at the same

Table 7-3.   Changes in Components of Household Income, Chile, by Income Quintile
(percent)

Income	1987–1990			1990–1992		
Quintile	Income	Subsidies	Total	Income	Subsidies	Total
1	12.6	−34.7	4.6	28.3	7.7	26.1
2	19.6	−26.1	16.7	18.8	10.3	18.4
3	19.5	−32.1	17.6	16.8	8.4	16.6
4	15.3	−36.9	14.3	16.9	2.7	16.7
5	11.0	−42.4	10.7	12.9	−20.3	17.8
Total	13.6	−33.6	12.5	18.0	4.7	17.8

Source: Raczynski, 1993.

time (see table 7-3), the main reason being reduction in wage inequality. The minimum wage rose faster than average wages, even while employment was also growing rapidly. Whether the minimum wage was following the market or leading it one cannot say. But one can say that the increase in demand for unskilled labor permitted an impressive gain in real wages across the board, particularly for unskilled labor.

Chile's process of adjustment, ending in its later happy state of affairs was long and painful. Output per capita fell by 15 percent between 1982 and 1985, real minimum wages fell by one-third, and there were very large increases in both poverty and inequality. But the country appears to have found a successful formula for rapid, equitable growth. It is instructive to ask what elements made that possible. I argue that there two principle reasons. First and most important, growth was so rapid that it pushed up the demand for unskilled labor to a point where the market itself either caused or permitted a significant narrowing of wage differentials. That was helped by the nature of the growth strategy, based as it was on natural-resource-intensive activities, in which the poor and the unskilled could do productive work.

Second is Chile's complementary strategy of investing in education; during the 1980s, Chile achieved almost complete coverage of both primary and secondary school-age children. Secondary school enrollment rate rose from 80 percent in 1980 to 91 percent in 1990 (ECLAC, Statistical Yearbook 1993), which was the highest rate in all of Latin America. This figure means that new entrants to the labor force were virtually sure to have at least a high school education. Over time, these improvements showed up in the average educational level of the Chilean labor force. In 1970 only one-third of workers had more than a primary level of education. Twenty years later, that figure had jumped to 57 percent (Chile, 1970, 1992). Thus, Chile's educational policy reduced the relative supply of unskilled labor at the same time that its demand policy was creating a large number of jobs at all levels. The net effect of the two was to guarantee that the better educated would have good jobs while, at the same time, demand was putting upward pressure on wages in the unskilled segments of the labor market. As the model predicted, there was a slight reduction in the wage share of the middle class. However, the overall rate of growth of real incomes was so rapid that this relative loss caused no political problems or pressure to change the export-based growth strategy.

Bolivia and Mexico

What happened in Bolivia? Why did its reform efforts turn out so much less favorably than those of Chile? First and foremost, there was no growth in export earnings in Chile. The volume of exports went up, but that was offset by a sharp drop in the terms of trade. Between 1984 and 1991 the quantum of exports rose by 45 percent, but the terms of trade fell by 49 percent. Thus, even though there was some diversification and output growth, there was no increase in export earnings at all. Domestic production mirrors this somber picture. GDP per capita fell from 1985 through 1989, before finally beginning a modest recovery until 1992. But even in that year, the level of per capita income was no greater than it had been in 1985, a year of recession and hyperinflation. Sectorally, one does not find much of a domestic production response in any sector. Between 1984 and 1991, manufacturing grew at only 2.4 percent per year, while mining and agriculture grew at 2.8 percent and 1.9 percent, respectively.

Bolivia's record on wages, employment, poverty, and income distribution is equally dispiriting. The urban minimum wage was cut by 60 percent in real terms in the hyperinflation year 1985. During the following five years it remained at that low level, rising slightly in 1991. Even in that year it was still only 60 percent of its value in 1984 and only one-fourth of its value at the beginning of the decade (ECLAC, *Economic Survey 1993*, table 5-5). Employment statistics for Bolivia are not available, but from urban unemployment figures it would appear that employment must have fallen along with production from 1985 through 1989. In the following three years, employment appears to have risen, thanks particularly to a construction boom in 1992 (ibid.).

The latest poverty and income distribution figures for Bolivia are for 1989, a year when the economy was still in a severe postadjustment recession. Not surprisingly, this recession caused an increase in both poverty and income inequality. Data from urban household income surveys for 1986 and 1989 show that urban poverty rose from .511 to .540 and that the Gini coefficient rose from .515 to .525 between those two years (Psacharopoulos et al., 1993). Keep in mind that the base year in this comparison is 1986, when the postadjustment recession was already under way. If one had an observation from any year before 1985, undoubtedly the effects of the adjustment on poverty and distribution would be far greater.[6] There are no poverty or distribution data after 1989. However, judging by the very modest growth and the behavior of wages since that time, it is unlikely that the situation has changed very much.

Why were the results of the Bolivian reform so much less satisfactory than those in Chile? The primary and most obvious reason is that there was not much internal production response in Bolivia, as there was in Chile—but that answer only leads to the further question of why that was the case. The reason may have to do with comparative advantage and economic structure. Both economies prior to their reforms were heavily dependent on extractive mining. However, with economic reform, Chile was able to develop a wide range of alternatives, which rapidly expanded as markets were freed and relative prices changed. Most of the new activities were also natural resource based rather than manufacturing, but they were dynamic enough to support an economic boom led by nontraditional exports. That nothing like that happened in Bolivia is a matter of availability of natural resources; Bolivia does not have the land or the climate necessary to develop fruit and wine exports, nor does it have a coastline to develop a fishing industry or forests to develop a lumber industry. Unfortunately neither did it have a well-educated labor force or a domestic manufacturing base with which to expand into industrial exports. For all of these reasons, a reform process relying on the price mechanism and the private sector takes a much longer time in a country like Bolivia than in a country like Chile. Indeed, each countries' nature or structure may dictate a different strategy for the two cases. At the very least, it should dictate different expectations about how long and how difficult the adjustment to a reform growth strategy would be.

The third early trade liberalizer was Mexico, which began in 1983 with a lowering of some tariff rates and continued with a removal of nontariff barriers and export controls. Even as early as 1985 the average tariff level had been reduced to 34 percent (World Bank, 1993a, p. 59). The process accelerated after 1985 with the removal of nontariff barriers to imports and export controls. By 1992 the average tariff rate had fallen to only 4 percent, and the bias against exports had been significantly reduced (IADB, 1992b, pp. 65–70; World Bank 1993b, p. 59). Privatization and downsizing the government, two other key components of the reform package, started in earnest under Salinas after 1989, so it is too early to ascertain their effects.[7]

Unfortunately, it is difficult to say what the long-run effect of Mexico's trade liberalization will be. There is little doubt that the reform dramatically increased imports: in 1992 they were four times what they were in 1986. But there was much less response in exports, which rose $9 billion over the 1986 amount. But even so, 1992 total exports were still only 23 percent higher than they were in 1983. In other words, trade liberalization did not unleash an export boom as it did in Chile; rather, it permitted a dramatic increase in imports. Overall, it would appear that the production of tradables might well have fallen. Consider what happened in manufacturing and agriculture, the source of most traded goods. Since 1985 manufacturing grew by 23 percent, or 2.9 percent per year through 1992 (IADB, *Economic and social Progress Report 1993*). That is undoubtedly one reason why industrial employment in 1992 was 10 percent lower than it was in 1980.[8] Furthermore, the real value of agricultural output was roughly constant over the same time period. Whatever the contractionary effects of this real appreciation were, they were surely exacerbated by the highly contractionary fiscal policy carried out by Salinas at the same time. His government increased government saving by almost 10 percent of GDP.

In Chile, trade liberalization sparked a boom in nontraditional but natural-resource-based activities, most of them not manufactures. One would have expected Mexico to be different, because unlike Chile, it already had a large and fairly modern manufacturing sector when the process began. Why didn't it respond more positively? Ironically, from the macroeconomic evidence it seems that the reform process, particularly under Salinas, so increased international confidence in Mexico that there was a tremendous inflow of foreign capital. This inflow permitted a sharp 22 percent revaluation of the exchange rate after Salinas took office, which of course made imports cheaper and Mexican exports more expensive. The result was that Mexico once again began to run large trade deficits.[9] Trade liberalization plus capital inflows had the unintended consequence of crowding out the production of competitive import substitutes and discouraging the development of new export activities, which make it difficult to know if the reform strategy would promote rapid export-led growth in the long run. A hopeful sign is that a good deal of the capital inflow did finance new investment, which was over 25 percent of GDP in 1993.

It is unlikely that the large capital inflows that Mexico experienced in the early 1990s will continue. Rather, they were a part of the adjustment process, a result of rising confidence in the Mexican development model and the ability of the government to carry it out. That being the case, it is too early to evaluate what the long-run characteristics of the new growth strategy will be, but there is little doubt about the distributional impact. The most recent data on distribution and poverty, from 1989, show that, during the first phase of the trade liberalization and stabilization process, wage differentials increased and both the distribution of income and the level of poverty got worse (tables 2-1 and 6-1). Statistics paint a somewhat ambiguous picture about what might have happened subsequently: per capita income rose modestly (1.5 percent per year), and average real industrial wages rose by 6.6 percent. But at the same time industrial employment, agricultural output, and the real value of the minimum wage stagnated (ECLAC, *Statistical Yearbook 1992;* IADB, *Economic and Social Progress Report 1993*).[10] On balance, given these indicators, it is unlikely there were any dramatic changes in either distribution or poverty between 1989 and 1992.

Costa Rica

Costa Rica also liberalized the economy and downsized the state after 1988. Despite Costa Rica's relatively late start in the second stage of the adjustment process, the positive effects of reform were visible by 1992. Trade liberalization was begun in 1986 with the elimination of all import quotas. Subsequently, a program of tariff reductions reduced the maximum tariff to 20 percent, a goal it reached in 1993. At the same time, the government made a major effort to reduce its deficit, which fell by over 3.5 percentage points between 1989 and 1993, thanks mainly to tax increases rather than reductions in government spending.[11]

Table 7-4. Index of Real Wages, by Occupation and Economic Sector, Costa Rica, 1989–1993 (1991 = 100)

Category	1989	1991	1992	1993
Occupation				
High-level white collar	105.4	100	108.4	120.8
Routine white collar	111.9	100	104.5	117.2
Skilled blue collar	109.6	100	104.7	116.7
Other blue collar	100.4	100	101.3	114.9
Agricultural labor	110.3	100	105.9	118.6
Economic sector				
Agriculture	108.7	100	106.4	119.1
Industry	104.2	100	104.6	113.2
Construction	104.3	100	99.2	114.2
Services	113.0	100	104.7	118.9

Source: Costa Rica, 1993, table 17.

As is generally the case, these adjustment efforts led first to a slow-down in the growth rate (over the period 1990–91). However, unlike the case of Bolivia and Mexico, in Costa Rica the recession was shallow and the recovery was rapid. By 1992 the country was growing strongly again, and by the end of 1993 real GDP was 15 percent higher than in 1991. The recovery was led by nontraditional exports, particularly tourism, which by 1993 replaced coffee and bananas as the country's leading earner of foreign exchange. All of this had two very favorable implications. First, growth in exports dramatically reduced the ratio of debt service to exports, increasing foreign confidence in the Costa Rican economy. That in turn led to a big increase in foreign capital inflows.

Second, renewed growth in 1992–93 supported a big increase in employment and real wages, both of which had a favorable impact on poverty (table 7-4). Poverty rose sharply in 1991 as the economy went through its adjustment recession (table 7-5), which was to be expected. Poverty then fell even more sharply in response to renewed growth in the following two years, since there was a strong relation between level of economic activity and poverty in all countries in the study. That relation was particularly true in Costa Rica.

Growth in Costa Rica was so progressive and had such a powerful effect on poverty in Costa Rica because a good deal of it was based in sectors, particularly agriculture, that employed a large number of the poor. That was true not only in the 1980s, when real devaluation helped

Table 7-5. Incidence of Poverty, by Urban/Rural Dichotomy, Costa Rica, 1988–1993
(percent)

Category	1988	1989	1990	1991	1992	1993
Family						
Total	.216	.219	.205	.244	.222	.174
Rural	.303	.312	.294	.333	.301	.252
Urban	.108	.108	.102	.135	.127	.080
Individual						
Total	.249	.248	.234	.279	.256	.202

Source: Trejos, 1994, table 1; IADB, 1994a.

agriculture lead the country out of its balance of payments crisis, but also in the period since 1989. The data in table 7-4 show that, since 1991 (the trough of the most recent adjustment) real wages in agriculture rose faster than wages in any of the three urban sectors and for all but the highest white-collar occupation. Thus there was a narrowing of the rural-urban wage differential, continuing a trend that goes back to at least 1981, if not before (Morley and Alvarez, 1992a). That trend is the result of growth, and it obviously had a big effect on rural poverty.

Within the urban sector, growth led to some widening of the skill differential. That is, the high-skilled white-collar occupations had a higher rate of real wage growth than did the blue-collar or even routine white-collar occupations. Growth led by tourism and other service sector activities put a premium on skills, which raised the skill differential. But at the same time, real wages were rising rapidly at all levels, which reduced urban poverty even if the urban income distribution became more unequal at the same time.

The surest way to reduce poverty is to eliminate the pool of workers so unskilled or so unsuited to the sort of labor demanded in an economy that they are incapable of earning an above-poverty wage. That is what the combination of education and growth have done in Costa Rica. Costa Rica has a long tradition of investment in education, and this tradition continued in the 1980s despite the long adjustment and contraction that took place. Absolute expenditures per pupil in education declined, but even so there were significant reductions in the share of families headed by people with no more than a primary school education. In 1981 three-fourths of Costa Rica's families were headed by someone with no more than primary education, but thanks to the entry of better educated young people into the labor force, that percentage fell to 65 percent by 1992 (table

Table 7-6. Educational Level of Household Heads, Costa
Rica, 1981, 1989, 1992 (percent)

Educational Level	1981	1989	1992
Illiterate	12.1	10.2	8.3
Primary school	64.6	60.6	56.6
Secondary school	16.4	20.1	24.1
University	6.9	9.1	11.1

Source: Morley and Alvarez, 1992a; Trejos, 1994.

7-6). New entrants entered the labor market with far more education than
their parents, which tended to shrink, at least relatively if not absolutely,
the supply of unskilled labor.

Growth did the rest, creating a relative shortage on the demand side.
Growth, based as it is on tourism, nontraditional agricultural exports, and
supporting urban service activities such as construction, was so rapid that
it pulled labor out of low-wage agriculture and into higher paying urban
occupations. At the same time, real wages went up across the board, but
particularly for the lowest component of the labor force, unskilled agricultural labor.

The data in table 7-7 show the changes in the occupational and sectoral
structure of the labor force between 1989 and 1993. One can see a sharp

Table 7-7. Percentage of Labor Force, by Occupation and Economic Sector, Costa Rica,
1989–1993

Category	1989	1991	1992	1993
Occupation				
Skilled white collar	12.8	13.2	13.0	13.5
Other white collar	31.8	32.0	33.6	34.4
Skilled blue collar	22.6	22.9	22.7	23.2
Other blue collar	7.6	7.5	7.4	7.1
Agriculture	25.3	24.3	23.2	21.7
Total (thousands)	986.8	1,006.6	1,043.0	1,096.4
Economic sector				
Agriculture and mining	26.4	25.6	24.2	22.7
Industry	19.9	19.8	20.1	19.4
Construction	6.2	6.3	5.9	6.1
Services	47.5	48.3	49.8	51.8

Source: Costa Rica, 1993, table 8.

reduction in the share of agriculture and an equivalent rise in the share of services. Many claim that agricultural jobs were increasingly filled by Nicaraguan immigrants, while Costa Rican agricultural workers migrated to better-paying jobs in nontraditional agriculture or the urban sector. Whatever the case, the Costa Rican labor force moved toward the more lucrative urban sector, particularly services. Since all this occurred at the same time that real wages were increasing rapidly, it cannot have been caused by the eviction or displacement of rural workers. Rather, rural workers were pulled into the urban sector by the expansion of better-paying employment opportunities. Overall urban employment grew by more than 10 percent between 1991 and 1993, and the open unemployment rate fell to 4.1 percent. These are the classic signs of an economic boom, which created employment opportunities fast enough to draw down the available stock of unskilled labor across the entire economy. The result was a rise in real wages for those at the bottom of the labor pyramid and an impressive reduction in poverty.[12]

Conclusion

Events in the 1980s pushed many Latin American countries back to income levels they had not seen since the 1960s. Economic adjustment, while necessary in some form after the excessive borrowing of the previous decade, caused severe and extended recession, which in turn caused a severe increase in poverty and inequality everywhere. Between 1980 and 1989 there was an increase of almost 40 million in the number of Latin Americans living on less than $2 per day. Poverty rose from just over one-fourth to just under one-third of the population. Recession had a particularly severe impact on the cities; urban poverty rose by 31 percent and, by the end of the decade, for the first time composed over the one-half of the poverty population.

If there is anything to be salvaged from this grim period, it is the lessons that were learned and the basis that was laid for future progress. And here the signs are more encouraging: all countries recovered from their severe balance of payments crises, debt burdens were reduced to supportable levels, many government enterprises were privatized, and there was a significant effort to reduce government deficits. Overall, the region once again enjoyed fairly rapid growth, with Argentina, Chile, and Costa Rica being particularly successful—with rising exports, rapid economic expansion, and moderate inflation. This growth benefited the poor: in every country where there was recovery there was a significant reduction in poverty.

Unfortunately, data also show the fragility of the recovery in many countries. Venezuela, Mexico, and Ecuador, which were growing rapidly in 1990, were all in recession by 1993. Bolivia, Honduras, and Guatemala continued to have slow economic growth. Particularly troublesome is the failure of most of the countries in the region to establish a successful export sector, one capable of sustained growth. There are some striking success stories, particularly in Chile, Costa Rica, Mexico, Brazil, and Panama, but the overall record is disappointing, with nominal exports for the region as a whole growing by less than 2 percent per year since 1990.

At the end of the decade, the poverty problem was highly localized in a subset of countries that were not successful in their adjustments. Quantitatively, Brazil was the biggest problem. It has always had a highly inequitable style of development, but its adjustment early in the eighties was one of the most progressive and successful. Tragically, it failed to use this opportunity and succumbed to populist pressure after 1985. Like Peru, by 1989 it was caught in a vicious stagflationary trap, largely of its own making, that dramatically increased poverty and inequality. As a result, Brazil had 45 percent of the continent's poor in that year, even though it had only 33 percent of the continent's population.

Nine percent of the poor were in Peru, a country whose adjustment was made more difficult by its having a very small nonminerals traded goods sector, a serious revolution in the countryside, and some very unfortunate populist policy choices under Garcia. Under Fujimori there was a small recovery in 1993, but it is too soon to know whether it will be sustainable. Finally, a large fraction of the remainder of the poor (19%) were in small, relatively poor, countries: Bolivia, Haiti, Guatemala, and Honduras. Their problem was that they specialized in export commodities with stagnant demand. Altogether, Brazil, Peru, and this group of countries accounted for almost 75 percent of the poverty in 1989, even though they composed only 48 percent of the population. What is more serious is that, as of 1992, none of them had resumed a stable growth path, so the poverty problem has undoubtedly worsened since 1989.[1]

What lessons can we learn from a study of poverty in Latin America during the 1980s? The first and foremost lesson is that change in per capita income is the key determinant of change in the poverty level. Anything that slows down the growth rate or that causes a recession will hurt the poor. Indeed, since inequality typically rises during recession, recessions hurt the poor more than they hurt other groups. No social emergency program or special antipoverty social policy can completely offset the effect on the poor of a macroeconomic downturn. Maintaining the minimum wage, as many countries tried to do when they went into recession, did moderate the rise in poverty somewhat, but this policy and emergency employment programs are mere palliatives, bandaids. The only truly effective policy is to get the economy growing again—and in a sustainable way.

Variations in income have an overwhelming influence on poverty; thus it would appear to follow that most of the rise in poverty during the 1980s was caused by recession and the adjustment that followed. In a purely technical sense, that is undoubtedly true: if the South American economies had continued growing as they had during the 1970s, poverty no doubt would have continued declining. But the point is that Latin American countries could not have continued as they were going in 1980; most of them had severe balance of payments and fiscal deficits, which they were temporarily financing with capital inflows. This remedy could not have continued indefinitely; some adjustment to reduce dependence on external borrowing had to take place. Part of the relative prosperity in 1980 was in a real sense borrowed from the future. Think of Colombia in comparison to Brazil or Argentina: Colombia did not grow as fast or reduce poverty as much in the 1970s as it could have had it borrowed more, but that meant that in the 1980s it had a very mild adjustment and was able to continue reducing its poverty level. Thus, for the continent as a whole, to blame all the increase in poverty during the 1980s on the adjustment process is unfair. It would be as reasonable to blame it on the unwise policies and excessive borrowing that made that adjustment necessary.

Having agreed that some adjustment was inevitable and that it was bound to cause a contraction in income and a rise in poverty, one can still ask whether the adjustment was excessive. That is, were these countries forced into a longer period of recession than necessary? Or, to put the question in a different way, were they forced to generate too high a trade surplus in order to meet debt and interest payments? The continent went from receiving an average of 4 percent of GDP from external resources to transferring about the same amount to its creditors—primarily because the source of its previous loans were commercial banks. Their loans carried flexible interest rates, which dramatically increased the burden of the debt after 1982. But perhaps even more serious, the banks were not a dependable source of continued financing; when the crisis exploded in 1982, the banks were either unwilling or unable to continue lending.

When no alternative source of funds was available, there was no offset to the drain of foreign exchange from rising interest payments on the existing debt.

A significant part of those increased interest rates reflected inflation, contractionary monetary policy, and fiscal deficits in the United States. As is now recognized, a rise in inflation, which is incorporated into the interest rate, effectively forces the borrower to pay back loans in real terms faster than planned. The solution is to make new loans at a rate just sufficient to keep the real amortization schedule constant. That was never done in Latin America, either by the commercial banks or by the international monetary institutions. The inevitable result was that these countries were forced to generate very large trade surpluses, which they did more through recession than through the expansion of tradables.

Every actor shares some blame for what happened. One can fault Latin American borrowers for their unwise decisions (and choice of lenders) in the 1970s. Banks were intransigent in their demands that interest payments be met. The international agencies were unimaginative in dealing with the crisis and in finding alternative sources of new funds. The U.S. government failed to make the changes in banking regulations that would have permitted U.S. banks to increase their nominal loan balances enough to cover at least the inflation component of interest payments. The net result of all of this was an unprecedented transfer of resources from developing countries to industrial countries. While one expects borrowers to pay back loans, one does not expect new capital flows to stop as suddenly. Nor does one expect world capital markets to transfer savings from poorer to richer countries. That is what happened in Latin America in the 1980s, and it was possible only because these countries endured long recessions—for which the poor paid a very heavy price.

Aside from paying back debt, another reason that adjustment was long is because of the desire to control inflation. Several countries, such as Brazil and Argentina, corrected their balance of payments problem but only at the cost of a serious rise in inflation. Their second adjustment after 1985 was caused by a desire to bring the inflation rate down, not by a desire to further increase the trade surplus.

Many people argue that an adjustment to reduce inflation will help the poor, because inflation is a tax on money holdings, that is, since the poor hold most of their assets in the form of money, cutting inflation should help them. I find little justification for such an argument. Because there are no data on wealth holdings, one cannot be sure how important this effect is, but it is likely that a far bigger impact of inflation on the poor comes through its effect on the real wage. Since virtually all of the income of the poor comes from labor earnings, anything that affects either the average real wage or employment opportunities will have a big impact.

Here, it is important to distinguish between the steady state (the long run), and transitions (the short run). Wages tend to adjust to inflation with a lag; when there is a rise in the inflation rate, the real wage tends to fall. That was very clear during the latter half of the eighties, a period of rapidly increasing inflation in Brazil, Peru, Venezuela, and Argentina, all of which suffered large declines in the real value of their minimum wages. Perversely, when there is a decline in the inflation rate, those same lags tend to raise the real wage but to shrink employment. Thus it is not so much the level of inflation but changes in the level that hurt workers and the poor.

Latin America had three different sorts of adjustment during the 1980s: one to correct the balance of payments deficit, a second to control inflation, and a third to introduce structural reforms like privatization and trade liberalization. When thinking about the effect of these adjustments on the poor, one must distinguish between the short and the long run. Each of these adjustments causes a recession in the short run, hurting the poor along with everyone else. It is this transitional recession that is costly to the poor in the typical adjustment program, not the long-run changes that the recession helps to bring about. In Costa Rica and Colombia, after the adjustment to the new real exchange rate was complete, the poor were better off than they had been when the adjustment started. However, if the transition recession is long and severe, the cumulative losses it causes may never be offset by long-term gains.

Privatization, downsizing the government, and trade liberalization are much less likely to help the poor, even in the long run, unless these policies significantly increase the growth rate of the economy. This is because many of the reforms take away entitlements, subsidies, and government jobs, all of which directly benefit the poor. Fiscal reform in countries such as Mexico and Venezuela included the elimination of substantial subsidies of food and public services, which is regressive. Similarly, trade liberalization is likely to reduce employment opportunities for all people, at least in the short run. Such policies may help the poor in the long run, but only if efficiency and growth are increased by enough to offset the direct, negative impact of these policies.

Even though falling income was a major cause of the increase in poverty in Latin America during the 1980s, one must still wonder why the adjustment process was so much more severe in some countries than in others. I argue that a major part was played by differences in structural conditions: economies with small traded goods sectors or with rigid production structures tended to have long and difficult balance of payments adjustments, for which the poor paid a heavy price. Growth performance was positively correlated with the ability to expand exports. Countries with large traded goods sectors that were able to respond to real devaluation by increasing production tended to have short adjustments, because the expansion in traded goods offset the reduction in absorption required by the balance of payments adjustment. Where the traded goods sector was also a large employer of the poor, as was the case for agriculture in Paraguay, Colombia, and Costa Rica, the results were especially progressive.

Another factor that influenced performance was comprehensive inflation indexing. Countries with rigid indexing systems are likely to have a difficult time reducing inflation; they will be tempted to try heterodox alternatives to orthodox contraction because that is likely to cause an extended recession. This happened in three cases (Brazil, Argentina, and Peru). Each was a failure, and each required a second stabilization program in the second half of the decade, which had a very severe impact on the poor.

All of these structural factors help us understand differences in performance across the economies we have been following.[2] One group had short and relatively easy stabilization, with recovery by 1985: Chile, Costa Rica, Colombia, Paraguay, and Uruguay. Agriculture was the key sector in Paraguay and Costa Rica; it was big, produced exportable traded goods, and expanded rapidly in response to real devaluation, helping to offset the contractionary part of the adjustment program. In Chile and Colombia industry was the leading traded goods sector. Not only did it expand rapidly in response to real devaluation, it also made a big contribution to the expansion of exports. Uruguay is something of a special case in that its recovery was led by services rather than by industry or agriculture.

A second group comprises the three oil economies, Ecuador, Venezuela, and Mexico. These had long and extended adjustments due to their dependence on a sector producing a traded good that could not respond to devaluation and that, in addition, suffered from a sharp price decline over the decade.

A third group, non-oil-producing economies, had two adjustments over the decade: Argentina, Brazil, and Peru. The first adjustment attempted to deal with the balance of payments problem, while the second was primarily an attempt to control hyperinflation brought on by the failure of a heterodox stabilization. (One could put Venezuela into this group of double adjustment economies, as well.) Because these countries had to adjust twice, their growth record (with the exception of Brazil's) was the worst of all fifteen countries. Brazil and Peru did not have a real devaluation. Argentina and Venezuela did, but their industries were either too small or too protected to counteract the severe effects of domestic contraction. In all four cases, governments were unable to sustain the adjustment process, which degenerated into a round of rapid inflation in the second half of the decade. Inflation probably would not have happened had the export sectors of these economies expanded employment in response to the real devaluations that all of these economies achieved before 1985.

The remaining group is composed of the small economies of Bolivia, Honduras, and Guatemala, each of which specialized in the production and export of a natural-resource-based commodity that did not expand in the 1980s. These economies had no domestic production base to take advantage of real devaluation, and as a result their stabilizations were long. As of 1994 their recoveries are still uncertain.

In general, in twelve of the countries studied, agriculture responded like a traded good while industry did not, in that the former expanded and the latter contracted in response to real devaluation. This is consistent with the finding that, over the decade, the rise in poverty was far larger in urban areas than in the countryside. It also underlines the importance to the urban poor of having an internationally competitive industrial sector.

The Latin American economic adjustment of the 1980s was long and difficult but not, for the most part, because these countries did not follow the orthodox policy prescriptions of their international advisers. In most countries, there were substantial real devaluations, falling minimum wages, and a big rise in exports. There was also a concerted effort to gain control of government finances and an unprecedented shift in trade deficits, from an average 4 percent deficit in 1980 to an average 4.6 percent surplus in 1989. A drastic reduction in absorption took a long time because of the size of the shift required by changed international financial conditions and the fact that, at the beginning of the decade, the traded goods sector of most countries was small and unprepared to offset the contractionary shock. As a result, poverty rose rapidly while the economies adjusted their production structures, shrank their government sectors, and expanded their exports.

As the 1990s unfold, the positive results of these efforts can be seen in most countries. But the transition to an equitable and sustainable growth path is still fragile and uncertain. The 1980s left a backlog of unmet needs in education, health, infrastructure, and private investment. It added 40 million to the poverty rolls. Latin American governments face the daunting task of consolidating their progress while reducing poverty and attending to the unmet social needs left by the 1980s. This will not be an easy task.

Notes

Introduction

1. Poverty lines were converted into local currency, using purchasing power parity exchange rates to control for differences in the cost of living not reflected in official rates.
2. In Mexico, average tariffs were reduced from 34 percent in 1985 to 4 percent in 1991–92, in Chile from 36 percent to 11 percent, and in Costa Rica from 92 percent to 16 percent. See World Bank (1993a).

Chapter One   A Comparison of Macroeconomic Performance and Policy

1. Chile, Brazil, Paraguay, Uruguay, Costa Rica, and Ecuador were highest in income growth. Ecuador is the only one of this group that did not rank high in exports, thanks to the decline in oil prices. Mexico was a top exporter but ranked ninth in income growth.
2. Had we used the average real wage series collected by Cox Edwards (1991) for urban blue-collar and manufacturing workers, the pattern would have been substantially the same. There is no information for Ecuador, Honduras, and Bolivia. For the other twelve, there are ten depreciations, in six of which the real wage goes down and four where it increases, thus again making the point that real devaluation did not necessitate a fall in real wages.
3. The government budget identity states that the government deficit is financed through the sum of changes in high-powered money plus the sale of domestic and foreign bonds. Cutting the latter means that deficits are either monetized or financed through the domestic sale of bonds.

4. The Tanzi-Oliveira effect refers to the negative effect of inflation on real tax revenues because of collection lags. See Tanzi (1978).
5. This estimate comes from Guillermo Perry's unpublished worksheets.
6. In Mexico there was rapid GDP growth in 1990 and constant growth in government, while in Honduras there was a sharp decline in the government.
7. I do not have data on government employment; instead, I used real product indexes for the government sector and the economy as a whole. If the index of government services is deflated by the government wage index, it would be a good proxy for what happened to government employment.
8. Information on average wages for Ecuador, Bolivia, and Honduras are not available.
9. In five cases, the real wage of government workers rose (table 1-7). Two (Costa Rica and Panama) are questionable, leaving three (Bolivia, Brazil, and Colombia) where it went up and another seven where it rose relative to the minimum wage.

Chapter Two   Changes in Income Distribution and Poverty

Parts of this chapter and chapters 6 and 7 draw heavily on Morley (1994).
1. The Gini coefficient is a measure of inequality. It goes from zero for perfect equality, in which each person has the same income, to one for maximum inequality, in which one individual has all the income. The household survey data on which this discussion is based are of varying quality. In all cases, total income was substantially underreported. To make matters worse for those interested in income distribution, the underreporting of profits and interest income was larger than the underreporting of wages. The Economic Commission for Latin America and the Caribbean (ECLAC) made an attempt to correct for underreporting by comparing average profit and wage income with national accounts figures. The World Bank used the ECLAC adjustments in their estimates. Given this high degree of underreporting, one should take the Gini coefficients as broad indicators of trends rather than as exact estimates of the degree of inequality.
2. In developed countries, the profit share goes up in booms because there is a tendency to stockpile labor during recessions that are expected to be temporary, and wages do not reflect cyclical changes in productivity.
3. For further evidence on the age-wage differential during the 1980s, see Morley and Alvarez (1992a, 1992b, 1992c); and Morley (1992a).
4. For this calculation, the real minimum wages displayed in table 1-3 were used.
5. The one exception is Chile between 1987 and 1990, where there is some ambiguity about what happened to the distribution. Altimir (1993) claims that the Gini fell, while Pardo et al. (1993) claim that it increased.
6. In Chile unemployment fell from 22 percent to 12 percent between 1983 and 1987; in Venezuela between 1989 and 1991 it fell from 9.7 percent to 8.5 percent

(Marquez, 1992); and in Uruguay it was cut almost in half between 1983 and 1989. Furthermore, in contrast to the minimum wage, the average real wage rose in Uruguay and was roughly constant in Venezuela and Chile. See Cox Edwards (1991, table 1) for average real wage data; ECLAC, *Economic Survey 1990*, for unemployment rates; and Marquez (1992) for unemployment and the real wage in Venezuela.

7. It is possible to calculate the labor share for twelve countries in Latin America using data from the ECLAC *Statistical Yearbook*. It rose in three countries and fell in eight; it undoubtedly fell in Brazil as well, but we do not have data beyond 1985. The three countries where the share rose slightly are Costa Rica, Uruguay, and Panama, all of which protected the real value of the minimum wage. See Morley (1994, table 3).

8. Real interest rates diverge widely across countries in Latin America. The country that comes closest to the hypothetical case described in the text is Brazil, where the real rate rose to over 65 percent for a short period in 1988. The real rate also rose in Mexico, Costa Rica, and Bolivia, because of both internal government deficits and capital outflows. Countries such as Argentina, Uruguay, and Venezuela never had a significant positive real interest rate—at least, according to the interest rate series reported over the decade.

9. Argentina, Panama, Peru, and Venezuela all had sharp declines in income in 1989.

10. A full description of the surveys and the methods used in making the poverty estimates can be found in Psacharopoulos et al. (1993). The poverty estimates shown also are drawn from that report and are based on my work for the World Bank during summer 1992.

11. The multiple is 3 in the United States, and the line is adjusted for family composition, reflecting the notion that there are economies of scale in both food and shelter.

12. The World Bank did a national LSMS (living standards measurement survey) for Peru in 1985 and a metropolitan LSMS for Lima in 1990. Peru's poverty estimate was based on the 1985 LSMS, adjusted for change in income between 1985 and 1989 by the poverty-income elasticity obtained from the 1989 poverty regression:

$$P^0 = C - .116Y + .00003Y^2 - 18.8UD + 36.3BD,$$

$$(-3.15) \quad (2.54) \quad (-2.67) \quad (2.79)$$

where

Y = income,
UD = urban dummy,
BD = Brazil dummy,
the adjusted R^2 = .52, and
df = 25.

13. For a more extended discussion of the rural and urban components of poverty and rural to urban migration, see Altimir (n.d., and 1992b).

14. A Brazil dummy, which was positive and highly significant, was included in the poverty regression. The coefficient on the dummy was 36.3, implying that, other things equal, Brazil would have a poverty ration 36 percent higher than the average country.

15. This group includes Dominican Republic, Haiti, Bolivia, and all the Central American countries except Mexico, Panama, and Costa Rica.

16. Good data for 1980 and 1986 for a large number of countries is available in ECLAC (1990a). Altimir (1992a, 1992b) gives a deeper analysis of the 1980–86 period; for several of the countries, he extends his period of observation to the 1989 surveys. Morley and Alvarez analyze the 1980–89 period for Colombia, Venezuela, Costa Rica, and Argentina (1992a, 1992b, 1992c; Morley, 1992a). The 1980 regression was as follows:

$$lnP^0 = 15.2 - 1.60lnY - .76UD + .89BD,$$

$$(-7.22) \qquad (3.37) \qquad (2.47)$$

where

adjusted $R^2 = .77$, and
$df = 19$.

See n.12 for definitions.

18. Those cases were Bolivia, Honduras, and Guatemala, for which 1986 observations were available; Peru, with a 1985 observation; and Mexico with a 1984 observation.

19. Brazil, 46.8 percent; Peru, 14.5 percent; Dominican Republic, 1.4 percent; El Salvador, 1.7 percent; Guatemala, 7.9 percent; Haiti, 3.2 percent; Honduras, 3.4 percent; Bolivia, 3.2 percent; and Nicaragua, 3.5 percent.

20. For evidence on education-wage differentials during the 1980s see Morley (1992a) and Morley and Alvarez (1992a, 1992b, 1992c).

21. World Bank surveys classify workers as in the informal sector if they meet one of the following criteria: (a) either owned or was employed by a business with fewer than five employees, (b) is self-employed but not a professional, (c) is in an occupation such as domestic servant or work without pay as a family member (Psacharopoulos et al., 1993).

Chapter Three Social Indicators and Social Expenditures

1. Only Uruguay and Venezuela had significant rises in the student-teacher ratio at either the primary or the secondary level. In Venezuela, the rise occurred in 1987 and was so large (it doubled) that it casts doubt on the validity of the data. Another possibility (noted by Queisser et al., 1993, p. 381) is that teach-

er's unions forced a rise in the number of teachers; however, many of them did not really work as teachers.

2. The two exceptions were Uruguay and Venezuela for secondary school.

3. Grosh (1990, app. table 7). The university share of the government education budget also increased during the 1980s, according to Friedman, Lustig, and Legovini (1992, p. 7).

4. The PEM required participants to be of working age and to work more than thirty-five hours per week. Much of the work was in very low-skilled jobs, such as street cleaning. Given the low salary, much of the PEM labor force was female. For a good description and discussion of Chilean employment programs see Graham (1991a) and Grosh (1994).

5. For a fuller description of the PAIT program, see Graham (1991).

6. The PAIT program was part of the Keynesian pump-priming fiscal stimulus policy of the first several years of the Garcia government. The policy caused a boom in Peru, during which per capita income rose by 17 percent between 1985 and 1987. How big a part the PAIT played in the stimulus and recovery is impossible to say.

7. According to Graham (1991a, p. 101), in the third quarter of 1986 the PAIT spent 630 million intis and created 150,000 jobs.

8. Graham (1994, p. 74), reports that after three years of operation 68 percent of resources were channeled through state institutions and 32 percent were channeled through nongovernmental organizations, primarily social assistance oriented.

9. Jorgensen et al. (1992, p. 41) estimates that the least poor area in Bolivia received almost three times as much ESF funds per capita as the poorest.

10. FIS attracted $240 million during its four-year existence (Graham, 1994, p. 60).

11. Simply measuring the income level of program participants biases downward the percentage at the bottom part of the income distribution, because of the influence of the income received on total family income. This may explain why early World Bank estimates of the targeting of the ESF say that less than one-half of workers came from the bottom 40 percent of households (World Bank, 1990b, p. 119).

12. Jorgensen et al. (1992, p. 42) estimate that $56 million went to the richest area and only $22.5 to the two poorest areas, even though both contained roughly the same number of people.

13. The index was called Ficha CAS and was a social stratification measurement system that established a person's position in the bottom five deciles based on a number of characteristics, including ownership of durables, education, and employment (see Graham, 1991a, p. 9).

14. For a complete description of this effort, see World Bank (1990a).

15. The employment program was discontinued in 1990 (Cline, 1991, p. 100).

16. Cline (ibid., p. 99), using a different methodology, estimates that the vouchers

plus the other PEP food programs must have been worth about 40 percent of the minimum wage for an average-size family. While one can argue with his method of measurement, his general point is valid that these subsidies were large relative to the income of the average poor family.

17. Navarro, however (1994, p. 19), has another breakdown of the costs of various PEP programs, and his data diverge fairly dramatically from IADB (1993b).

18. These were the *tortibonos* and *liconsa* milk programs. As of March 1991 the *tortibono* program was replaced by a program whereby one kilo of tortilla flour per day is distributed to any family earning less than twice the minimum wage (Levy, 1991, p. 73).

19. Friedman et al. (1992) arrive at a higher estimate of the effect of these programs, but it is not inconsistent with the calculation here. They calculate the value of the two subsidies for the average family at $197 per year ($50 greater than Levy's estimate), and they then compare this with the average family income of those earning less than 1.5 times the minimum wage. Assuming that the average urban family size was around four, the average income level of this group would have been around $30 per month.

20. Solidarity is first and foremost an organization to develop the earning power of the poor rather than an income transfer agency. Nonetheless, it also coordinates the targeted subsidies.

21. In 1986 it is estimated that PAN reached 1.3 million families and that there were about 1.6 million with unmet basic needs. While the number of families in poverty grew between 1986 and 1989, this statement is probably defensible. See Queisser et al. (1993, pp. 91–92).

22. The source for this and the other factual statements in this paragraph is UNICAMP (1994, pp. 36–37), which also provides excellent descriptions of the programs and their coverage.

23. The ECLAC poverty line for Brazil converted to comparable 1985 dollars was $79. See Psacharopoulos et al. (1993, annex 11). Under Sarney, the program that expanded the fastest was the free milk program for children in families with less than twice the minimum wage (PNLCC). In 1990 it spent $579 million on 7.8 million children, each of which got 148 liters of milk per year at an average cost of $0.50 per liter. This program absorbed a lot of resources, mainly because of the high cost of milk (UNICAMP, 1994, p. 44).

24. In 1992, federal expenditure in these programs fell by almost $400 million, or 0.1 percent of GDP (ibid., p. 37).

25. Useful descriptions of the Solidarity program are in Levy (1991), Lustig (1992), and Sahota (1991). The description of the program in text is drawn from these three sources.

26. One survey reports a 75 percent approval rate for the program (Sahota, 1991, p. 38).

27. For a description of FOSIS, see Graham (1994, chap. 2); and Raczynski (1993).

Chapter Four   Case Studies: Poverty and Adjustment in Argentina and Venezuela

1. The section on Argentina draws heavily from Morley and Alvarez (1992c).
2. For further evidence on real wages, see Beccaria (1991).
3. It is also likely that the distribution became more equal under Menem. According to Beccaria (ibid., fig. 1, table 2), the income share of the top quintile dropped by 5 percentage points between 1989 and 1990 and the real wage rose by approximately 6 percent. This equalizing trend is likely to have continued after 1990.
4. A simple ordinary least squares regression of the poverty index was run on per capita income using the census bureau poverty indexes. From that regression, the predicted value for 1989 was used to predict the percentage increase in poverty from 1980 to 1989.
5. There is a vast literature on the measurement of poverty. See in particular Atkinson (1987); Foster (1984); Foster et al. (1984); Kanbur (1987); Ravallion (1992); and Sen (1976).
6. See Kanbur (1987) and Ravallion and Huppi (1991) for applications of the technique.
7. By construction, these estimates of overall poverty for 1980 and 1986 are identical to those of ECLAC, so P^0 is shown rising from 6 percent in 1980 to 11 percent in 1986 and to 21.5 percent in 1989.
8. The informal sector, defined according to the International Labour Organization's definition of labor market segmentation, is made up of self-employed workers (except professionals), employers and employees of establishments made up of less than five workers, and nonsalaried family workers.
9. No correction was made here for underreporting, since our interest is in changes in the earnings differential, rather than the absolute level of real income.
10. See table 4-2 for the average real wage and table 1-3 for the urban minimum wage.
11. Beccaria does not specify the population share of the high-income group. Unfortunately, he does not have observations for 1980, 1982, and 1986.
12. Beccaria (1991, pp. 323, 327) shows the income share of the bottom 30 percent falling from 9.9 percent in 1985 to 7.9 percent in 1989, while the share of the top group rose from 33.3 percent to 41.6 percent. Over the same period, the labor share of national income fell from 32 percent to 24 percent.
13. This section draws heavily on Morley and Alvarez (1992b).
14. The Marquez series used a food price index rather than the consumer price index. This makes a big difference, particularly in the years 1989 and beyond, because the government eliminated general food subsidies as part of its structural reform. As a result, there was a sharp increase in the relative price of food, which reduces the Marquez poverty line and raises his estimates of the poverty ratio relative to the other estimates.

15. During the 1970s, poverty probably fell further than the ECLAC estimates. In calculating changes in poverty during that period, ECLAC adjusted its poverty line to reflect growing overall living standards. If one uses the national consumer price index, the line appears to rise in real terms by at least 100 percent between 1970 and 1980. That obviously increases the poverty figure for 1980 relative to a line held constant in real terms.

16. We adjusted our 1989 survey data for an apparent increase in underreporting, which is why our results differ from those of the World Bank (1990a) and Marquez (1992).

17. Morley and Alvarez (1992b) confirm this pattern in sectoral breakdowns of poverty, finding only 19 percent of the poor employed in agriculture.

18. We get this figure by adding together the between-, within-, and cross-product terms for the two classes.

19. Population shares in the tables 4-12 through 4-14 refer to households rather than individuals. Thus the informal sector comprised 38 percent of urban families in 1981 and 40.6 percent of the urban labor force.

20. The cross-tabulation also tells us that there was almost no change in the age differential for either university or high school graduates. Apparently, the large supply of well-educated new entrants pulled down the wages of all the well educated, not only those of the young.

Chapter Five   Case Studies: Successful Adjustment in Colombia and Costa Rica

1. The discussion of the Colombia case follows closely the analysis in Morley (1992b); the discussion of Costa Rica follows Morley and Alvarez (1992a).

2. It is impossible to say whether real wages increased because of a conscious policy decision by the government or whether they rose because nominal wage adjustments are based on past inflation rates, which tend to create an inverse relation between the ex post real wage and the inflation rate. For our purposes, the effect of this rise in real wages is more important than the intentions of the government in power when it occurred. See Perry and Arbelaez (1990) for a further discussion of the issues.

3. For a good description of the Colombian program, see Liuksila (1991); and PREALC (1990a), esp. vol. 1, chap. 2.

4. Cardoso and Helwege (1992, pp. 20–22). The true source is Urrutia (1985).

5. World Bank (1990b) and Psacharapoulos et al. (1993) both show the Gini falling by around five percentage points. See table 6-1. Altimir (1993) gives percentage changes in the Gini but no national figures, so it is difficult to compare with the World Bank figures shown in table 6-1.

6. Altimir (1993, table 4) reports more rapid reductions in rural inequality between 1986 and 1990 than between 1980 and 1986, which seems strange given the coffee boom.

7. My estimate differs quite dramatically from that of ECLAC (Altimir, 1993,

table 3). ECLAC found no progress on poverty reduction between 1980 and 1986 in its urban survey, which presumably is the same as mine. This is a rather odd result, given that ECLAC reports a reduction in income inequality in the urban area over those years, when we know there was a significant increase in real income. ECLAC also finds a small reduction in poverty in the period 1986–90, whereas I find a small increase between 1986 and 1989. My pattern is consistent with the World Bank income inequality trends reported in table (6-1).

8. A technical description of each survey has been published in mimeograph form by ECLAC under the general title "[Country name]: Encuesta Nacional de Hogares."

9. The more rapid decline in the indexes weighted with the very poor helps explain why the Psacharopoulos et al. (1993) poverty ratio fell so much faster than mine over the entire period 1980–89, even though both studies use the same data source. The Psacharopoulos (1993) study's poverty line is much lower than mine, so it is counting as the poor only those who show up in my calculation as the *very* poor.

10. Agriculture is an exception to the progressive pattern, but since this is an urban survey, the sample of agricultural workers is probably not representative. For example, a PREALC study shows real wages in the traditional and modern sectors of agriculture rising in real terms by 24 percent and 10 percent, respectively, between 1980 and 1988 (1990a, 1:140).

11. As a check on the narrowing of the skill differential, a standard earnings regression for 1980 and 1989 was run, with education, age, and gender as the main explanatory variables. The regression confirms the large reduction in the educational differential. For example, in 1980 for mean-age males, the average college graduate earned 9 times the wages of the average illiterate. That differential shrank to 5.4 times in 1989 (Morley, 1992b).

12. Technically, that happens if food prices are not highly correlated with the exchange rate, acting in essence like nontraded goods.

13. The exports that expanded after the devaluation were oil, coal, stainless steel, and gold, none of which had a large weight in the consumer price index (PREALC, 1990a).

14. It rose by 2 percent per year between 1980 and 1989. That is faster than the rate of increase of either the urban average or minimum wage (Perry and Arbelaez, 1990, p. 29).

15. Rural poverty fell from 85 percent of the rural population in 1982 to 68 percent in 1988 (PREALC, 1990a, 1:22).

16. ECLAC estimates for 1981 and 1988, which show poverty rising, seem to contradict the pattern of declining poverty incidence found by the other sources. Evidence from wage series, distribution statistics, and other poverty estimates all are consistent with a substantial decline in poverty between 1986

and 1989. Furthermore, 1987 presents a particular problem because of the use of too low a poverty line. Trejos (1994) made an adjustment to the poverty figure for 1987 in the Programa Ruta Social series, raising it from 18.5 percent of households to 21 percent.

17. See also Gindling and Berry (1992), who, while casting doubt on the comparability of the household surveys before and after 1986, assert that by 1987–88, the poverty ratio was lower than in 1980.

18. Altimir (1992a) shows Gini estimates for urban and rural sectors separately for 1981 and 1988. They both rose, consistent with his finding on what happened to poverty. However, it is not possible to guess what might have happened to the aggregate Gini from these sector Ginis.

19. This positive association of P^0 with age differs sharply from patterns in other countries, where there was a widening of the age-wage differential during recession (see Morley and Alvarez, 1992c, table 5).

20. The rise in the share of the poor in female households resulted from a rise in the share of women in the labor force, not from a lower rate of reduction in the incidence of poverty in these households.

21. Disaggregating the change in the indexes by occupation was not possible because of a change in the treatment of the agricultural sector. In 1981 there was no generic class for agriculture, and its labor was therefore classified either as operatives or as administrators. Since all agricultural wages are systematically lower that those in other sectors, this change would distort any direct comparisons.

22. This evidence is consistent with the findings of Altimir (1984), who analyzes surveys of households of employees in the private formal sector for 1979 and 1982 and finds that both high- and middle-income workers lost out relative to the bottom 40 percent.

Chapter Six   Determinants of Changes in Poverty

1. The same complaint can be made about the ECLAC household surveys, which, generally speaking, cover the period from 1980 to 1986.

2. To take Costa Rica as an example (see Morley and Alvarez, 1992a), if one raises the poverty line by 20 percent or reduces the income estimate by the same amount, the poverty estimate jumps about 25 percent. However, if one applies the same change to both endpoints of the period, it has almost no effect on the estimated of the change in poverty over the period.

3. Altimir (1993) also estimates that poverty overall stayed constant between 1986 and 1989, but since he shows constant rural poverty and declining urban poverty, that has to be an error.

4. The seven cases were the metropolitan areas of Colombia, 1980–86; Argentina, 1985–88; Chile 1984–86; the urban sector of Colombia, 1986–89; and three observations for Costa Rica, 1981–88 (these last three estimates being

outliers; all other estimates for the same period show poverty declining in Costa Rica).

5. Unfortunately, there is little hard evidence on the size of money balances held by the poor. But in any case, since none of the household surveys asked information on asset holdings, the measured changes in distribution of income and poverty are unaffected by this factor.

6. In Argentina, 1986–89, poverty rose from 10.9 to 21.5 percent; in Brazil, 1986–89, from 12 to 19 percent; in Mexico, 1984–89, from 16.6 to 17.7 percent; in Peru, 1985–90, from 31 to 40.5 percent; and in Venezuela, 1985–89, from 28.4 to 41.3 percent. The average rise was 47 percent.

7. Between 1987 and 1990, GDP per capita fell 12 percent in Argentina, 7 percent in Brazil, and an astonishing 30 percent in Peru.

8. The Gini is for salaries and covers the years 1984–90. Poverty estimates are from Glewwe and Hall (1991) and are for expenditures.

9. Paes de Barros et al. (1992) do not calculate a Gini for household income per capita for 1989, but they show the Lorenz curve for 1986 and 1989; they call the increase in inequality "severe" (p. 15). IADB (1993a) shows that the Gini for the economically active population rose from 0.589 in 1986 to 0.637 in 1989, one of the most unequal distributions in the entire world.

10. Unfortunately, the only observation of the Gini near the beginning of the period was in 1987. There is some ambiguity about whether inequality rose or fell over the entire period 1986–89. The IADB study (1993b) shows it rising from 0.44 to 0.46 between 1987 and 1989, but Altimir (1993) claims that the Gini fell by 7 percent between 1986 and 1990. We know that inequality did decline in 1990, but Altimir does not give us the raw data to enable us to calculate the change between 1986 and 1989.

11. In Chile unemployment fell from 22 percent to 12 percent between 1983 and 1987, in Brazil employment rose by 17 percent, and in Uruguay unemployment was cut almost in half between 1983 and 1989. Furthermore, in contrast to the minimum wage, the average real wage rose in Brazil and Uruguay and was constant in Chile. See Cox Edwards (1991, table 1) for average real wage data; ECLAC, *Economic Survey 1990*, for unemployment rates; and Fox and Morley (1991) for employment figures for Brazil.

12. In Uruguay urban unemployment fell from 15.5 percent in 1983 to 8.6 percent in 1989, while in Mexico it fell from 6.6 percent to 2.9 percent over the same time period (see ECLAC, *Statistical Yearbook 1992*).

13. The minimum wage series diverges sharply from average wages over this period. Between 1982 and 1987 the average wage fell by 25 percent at the same time that the minimum wage is reported to have risen by 42 percent.

14. Perry and Arbelaez (1990) estimate that the exchange rate affects only 8 percent of the goods in the Colombian consumer price index, either directly or indirectly.

15. Paraguay had the highest rate of growth of quantum indexes of agricultural production in all Latin America. It also had the highest rate of growth of exports, which were led by exports of cotton and soybeans (see ECLAC, *Statistical Yearbook 1991*).

16. Cox Edwards (1991) shows real wages in São Paulo increasing between 1981 and 1985, whereas the World Bank, *World Tables 1989*, shows earnings per worker declining by 4 percent.

17. Panama has been left out of this grouping, partly because it did not start its adjustment until 1986 and partly because its political problems and its impending conflict with the United States undoubtedly distorts the 1989 observation.

Chapter Seven   Emerging from the Crisis: Adjustment and Reform after 1990

1. The countries with severe debt burdens in 1982 were Argentina, Bolivia, Brazil, Costa Rica, Chile, Ecuador, and Mexico. All had interest-to-export ratios of 30 percent or more.

2. Until this poverty assessment is officially accepted by the Colombian government and published by the World Bank, none of its data may be divulged.

3. Between 1985 and 1991–92, average tariffs were reduced from 34 percent to 4 percent in Mexico, from 36 percent to 11 percent in Chile, and from 92 percent to 16 percent in Costa Rica (see World Bank, 1993a).

4. Average exports in 1991–92 were $684 million compared to an average of $735 in the years 1983–84 (IADB, various years, *Economic and Social Progress Report*).

5. The export bias of government policies in 1970 has been estimated as equivalent to a 33 percent tax on exports (Sjastaad, 1981, pp. 263–92).

6. In Psacharopoulos et al. (1993), an estimate was made of what urban poverty in Bolivia must have been based on the difference in per capita income between 1980 and 1986. When the figure for that hypothetical base year was compared with the 1989 figure, the urban poverty ratio seems to have increased from 34 percent to 54 percent over the decade.

7. The shrinkage of the government sector under Salinas was particularly impressive. Between 1989 and 1992 government expenditures fell by 6.6 percent of GDP, while taxes rose by 2.8 percent of GDP, turning a large government deficit into an even larger surplus. See IADB, *Economic and Social Progress Report 1993*, pp. 276–77.

8. There was growth in employment in the *maquiladora* sector, but it was not sufficient to offset declines elsewhere. See ECLAC, *Economic Survey 1992*, table 5-3.

9. The 1992 trade deficit was over $20 billion, an amount much larger than the deficits in the early 1980s. See IADB, *Economic and Social Progress Report 1993*, p. 129.

10. The unemployment rate for sixteen cities in Mexico stayed virtually constant for the entire period 1989–92.
11. Taxes as a share of GDP rose by almost 3 percentage points, while total expenditures fell by one 0.5 percent between 1989 and 1993 (CEFSA, 1994).
12. The percentage of families in poverty fell from 24.4 percent in 1991 to 17.4 percent in 1993, an impressive dividend of the rapid growth of these two years (Trejos, 1994, table 1).

Conclusion

1. In 1993 there was a turnaround in Brazil and Peru, but it was too short and too small to have made much of a dent in the backlog of poverty built up since 1985.
2. Panama is left out of this evaluation, partly because it did not start its adjustment until 1986 and partly because its political problem and impending conflict with the United States undoubtedly distorts the 1989 observation.

References

Almeida Reis, Jose G., Jose S. Rodriguez, and Ricardo Paes de Barros. 1991. "A Desigualdade de Renda no Brasil." In Joao Paulo Velloso, *A Questâo Social no Brasil* (Sao Paulo: Nobel).

Altimir, Oscar. 1982. "The Extent of Poverty in Latin America." Staff Working Paper 522. World Bank, Washington, D.C.

———. 1984. "Poverty, Income Distribution, and Child Welfare in Latin America: A Comparison of Pre- and Post-Recession Data." *World Development* 12:261–82.

———. 1992a. "Cambios en las Desigualdades de Ingreso y en la Pobreza en América Latina." ECLAC, Santiago.

———. 1992b. "Crecimiento, Distribución del Ingreso y Pobreza en América Latina: Algunos Hechos Estilizados." Paper prepared for IADB conference, March, Washington, D.C.

———. 1993. "Income Distribution and Poverty through Crisis and Adjustment." Working paper 15. ECLAC, Santiago.

———. N.d. "Latin American Poverty in the Last Two Decades." ECLAC, Santiago.

Anzola, Libardo Sarmiento. 1993. "Política Social y Gasto Público en los Noventa, que tan significativos son los Cambios?" *Coyuntura Social* (Aug.):47–78.

Atkinson, Anthony B. 1987. "On the Measurement of Poverty." *Econometrica* 55:745–46.

Barros, Ricardo Pães de, Rosane Mendonça, and Sonia Rocha. 1993. "Welfare, Inequality, Social Indicators, and Social Programs in Brazil in 1980s." IPEA, Rio de Janeiro.

211

Beccaria, Luis A. 1991. "Distribución del Ingreso en la Argentina: Explorando lo Sucedido desde Mediados de los Setenta." *Desarrollo Económico* 31:319–38.

Beccaria, Luis, and Ricardo Carciofi. 1992. "Social Policy and Adjustment during the Eighties: An Overview of the Argentine Case." Paper prepared for Brookings conference, July, Washington, D.C.

Behrman, Jere. 1993. "Investing in Human Resources." In *Economic and Social Progress in Latin America: 1993 Report*. Washington, D.C.: Inter-American Development Bank.

Bergsman, Joel. 1980. "Income Distribution and Poverty in Mexico." Staff Working Paper 395. World Bank, Washington, D.C.

Berry, Albert. 1987. "Poverty and Inequality in Latin America." *Latin American Research Review* 22:202–14.

Bonelli, Regis, and Guillerme Sedlacek. 1989. "Distribuição de Renda: Evolução no Ultimo Quarto do Século." In Guillerme Sedlacek and Ricardo Pães de Barros, eds., *Mercado de Trabalho e Distribuicao de Renda: uma Coletânea*. Monograph 35. Rio de Janeiro: IPEA.

Bourgignon, Francois, Jaime de Melo, and Akiko Suwa. 1991. "Distributional Effects of Adjustment Policies: Simulations for Archetype Economies in Africa and Latin America." *World Bank Economic Review* (May):339–67.

Cardoso, Eliana. 1992a. "The Macroeconomics of Poverty in Latin America." NBER, Cambridge, Mass.

———. 1992b. "Minimum Wage Legislation and Earnings Inequality in Brazil." NBER, Cambridge, Mass.

Cardoso, Eliana, and Ann Helwege. 1992. "Below the Line: Poverty in Latin America." *World Development* 20:19–39.

Castaneda, Tarsicio. 1992. *Combating Poverty: Innovative Social Reforms in Chile during the 1980s*. San Francisco: ICS Press.

CEFSA. 1994. *Costa Rica: Situación de la Economía en 1993 y Pronóstico Económico CEFSA 1994*. San José: Consejeros Económicos y Financieros S.A.

Chenery, Hollis, et al. 1974. *Redistribution with Growth*. London: Oxford University Press.

Chile. 1970. 1992. *Censo de Población y Vivienda*. Santiago: Instituto Nacional de Estadistica.

Chile. 1970. 1992. *Censo de Población y Vivienda*. Santiago: Instituto Nacional de Estadística.

Cline, William R. 1991. "Venezuela: Economic Strategy and Prospects." Draft Socioeconomic Report. IADB, Washington, D.C.

Costa Rica. 1993. *Encuesta de Hogares de Propósitos Múltiples Módulo Empleo*. San José: Ministry of the Economy, Industry, and Commerce.

Cox Edwards, Alexandra. 1991. "Wage Trends in Latin America." LATHR 18. World Bank, Washington, D.C.

ECLAC (Economic Commission for Latin America and the Caribbean). 1988. "Antecedentes Estadísticos de la Distribución del Ingreso. México, 1950–1977." Serie Distribución del Ingreso 7. Santiago.

———. 1990a. "Magnitud de la Pobreza en América Latina en los Años Ochenta." Santiago.

———. 1990b. "La Pobreza en Chile en 1990." Santiago.

———. 1993a. "Evolución Reciente de la Pobreza en el Gran Buenos Aires, 1988–1992." Working Paper 2. Santiago.

———. 1993b. *Panorama Social de América Latina: Edición 1993.* LC/G 1768, Santiago.

———. Various years. *Economic Survey of Latin America and the Caribbean.* Santiago.

———. Various years. *Statistical Yearbook for Latin America and the Caribbean.* Santiago.

Escobal, Javier, Arturo Briceno, Alberto P. Font, and Jose Rodriguez. 1992. "Gestión Pública y Distribución de Ingresas: Tres Estudios de Caso para la Economía Peruana." Paper prepared by GRADE (Grupo de Análisis para el Desarrollo) for IADB seminar, January, Washington, D.C.

Feres, Juan C., and Arturo Leon. 1990. "The Magnitude of Poverty in Latin America, *CEPAL Review,* no. 41, pp. 133–151.

FIEL. 1994. "Estrategias para Combatir la Pobreza en América Latina: Programas, Instituciones y Recursos." Paper prepared for Third Round, IADB Red de Centros, Buenos Aires.

Fields, Gary S. 1989. "Changes in Poverty and Inequality in Developing Countries." *World Bank Research Observer* 4:167–85.

———. 1991. "Growth and Income Distribution." In George Psacharopoulos, ed., *Essays on Poverty, Equity and Growth.* New York: Pergamon.

Fiszbein, Ariel. 1989. "An Analysis of the Size Distribution of Income in Argentina, 1974–1988." Ph.D. diss., University of California—Berkeley.

Foster, James. 1984. "On Economic Poverty: A Survey of Aggregate Measures." *Advances in Econometrics* 3:215–51.

Foster, James, J. Greer, and E. Thorbecke. 1984. "A Class of Decomposable Poverty Measures." *Econometrica* 52:761–65.

Foster, James, and A. F. Shorrocks. 1988. "Poverty Orderings." *Econometrica* 56:173–77.

———. 1991. "Who Paid the Bill? Adjustment and Poverty in Brazil 1980–95." Staff Working Paper 648. World Bank, Washington, D.C.

Fox, M. Louise, and Samuel A. Morley. 1993. "Poverty and Adjustment in Brazil: Past, Present, and Future." In Michael Lipton and Jacques van der Gaag, eds., *Including the Poor.* Washington, D.C.: World Bank.

Foxley, Alejandro. 1976. *Income Distribution in Latin America.* New York: Cambridge University Press.

Friedman, Santiago, Nora Lustig, and Arianna Legovini. 1992. "Social Spending and Food Subsidies during Adjustment in Mexico." Brookings, Washington, D.C.

Gindling, T. H., and A. Berry. 1992. "The Performance of the Labor Market during Recession and Structural Adjustment: Costa Rica in the 1980s." *World Development* 20:1599–1617.

Glewwe, Paul, and Dennis de Tray. 1989. "The Poor in Latin America during Adjustment: A Case Study of Peru." LSMS 56. World Bank, Washington, D.C.

Glewwe, Paul, and Gillette Hall. 1991. "The Social Costs of Avoiding Structural Adjustment: Inequality and Poverty in Lima, Peru, from 1985–6 to 1990." LSMS 86. World Bank, Washington, D.C.

Graham, Carol. 1991a. *From Emergency Employment to Social Investment: Alleviating Poverty in Chile.* Occasional paper. Washington, D.C.: Brookings.

———. 1991b. "The APRA Government and the Urban poor: The PAIT Programme in Lima's *Pueblos Jovenes.*" *Journal of Latin American Studies* 23:91–130.

———. 1992. "The Politics of Protecting the Poor during Adjustment: Bolivia's Emergency Social Fund." *World Development* 20:1233–51.

———. 1994. *Safety Nets, Politics, and the Poor: Transitions to Market Economies.* Washington, D.C.: Brookings.

Grosh, Margaret E. 1990. "Social Spending in Latin America: The Story of the 1980s." Discussion paper 106. World Bank, Washington, D.C.

———. 1994. *Administering Targeted Social Programs in Latin America: From Platitudes to Practice.* Washington, D.C.: World Bank.

Hanson, James A. 1987. "Growth and Distribution in Colombia: Some Recent Analysis." *Latin American Research Review* 22:255–64.

Hicks, Norman. 1992. "Trends in Government Expenditures and Revenues in Latin America, 1975–88." LAC Discussion Paper. World Bank, Washington, D.C.

IADB (Inter-American Development Bank). 1992a. *Socioeconomic Report: Costa Rica.* GN-1777. Washington, D.C.

———. 1992b. *Socioeconomic Report: México.* GN-1778. Washington, D.C.

———. 1993a. *Socioeconomic Report: Brazil.* GN-1801. Washington, D.C.

———. 1993b. "Toward Effective Social Policy in Venezuela." Social Action Policy Group. Washington, D.C.

———. 1994a. "A la Búsqueda del Siglo XXI: Nuevos Caminos de Desarrollo en Costa Rica." Social Action Policy Group. Washington, D.C.

———. 1993b. "Modernizar con Todos: Hacia la Integración de lo Social y lo Económico en Chile." Social Action Policy Group. Washington, D.C.

———. Various years. *Economic and Social Progress Report: Latin America.* Washington, D.C.

INDEC (Instituto Nacional de Estadísticas y Censos). 1990. *La Pobreza Humana en Argentina.* Buenos Aires.

Jorgensen, Steen, Margaret Grosh, and Mark Schacter. 1992. *Bolivia's Answer to Poverty, Economic Crisis, and Adjustment: The Emergency Social Fund.* Washington, D.C.: World Bank.

Kanbur, Ravi. 1987. "Measurement and Alleviation of Poverty." Staff paper. IMF, Washington, D.C.

Kuczynski, Pedro-Pablo. 1988. *Latin American Debt.* Baltimore: Johns Hopkins University Press.

Levy, Santiago. 1991. "Poverty Alleviation in Mexico." WPS 679. World Bank, Washington, D.C.

Liuksila, Claire. 1991. "Colombia: Economic Adjustment and the Poor." Staff Working Paper 91–81. IMF, Washington, D.C.

Lopez, Cecilia. 1990. "Deuda Social en Colombia: Equidad en los 80 y Perspectivas para los 90." *Coyuntura Social* 2:9–25.

Londoño de la Cuesta, Juan Luis. 1990. "Income Distribution during the Structural Transformation: Colombia 1938–99." Ph.D. diss., Harvard University.

Lustig, Nora. 1990. "Economic Crisis, Adjustment and Living Standards in Mexico: 1982–1985." *World Development* 18:1325–42.

———. 1992. *Mexico: The Remaking of an Economy.* Washington, D.C.: Brookings.

McKinley, Terry, and Diana Alarcon. 1994. "Widening Wage Dispersion under Structural Adjustment in Mexico." Paper prepared for conference in San José, Costa Rica.

Marquez, Gustavo. 1992. "Poverty and Social Policies in Venezuela." Paper prepared for conference at Brookings, July, Washington, D.C.

Marquez, Gustavo, Joyita Mukherjee, Juan Carlos Navarro, Rosa A. Gonzalez, Roberto Palacios, and Roberto Rigobon. 1993. "Fiscal Policy and Income Distribution in Venezuela." In Ricardo Hausmann and Roberto Rigobon, eds. *Government Spending and Income Distribution in Latin America.* Washington, D.C.: IADB.

Meller, Patricio. 1991. "Adjustment and Social Costs in Chile during the 1980s." *World Development* 19:1545–61.

———. 1992. "Review of the Successful Chilean Export Growth." CIEPLAN, Santiago.

———. 1992b. "La Apertura Comercial Chilena: Lecciones de Política." CIEPLAN, Santiago.

Morley, Samuel A. 1992a. "Macroconditions and Poverty in Latin America." IADB, Washington, D.C.

———. 1992b. "Policy, Structure and the Reduction of Poverty in Colombia: 1980–89." Working Paper 126. IADB, Washington, D.C.

———. 1992c. "Poverty and Distribution during Latin American Adjustment in the 1980s." World Bank, Washington, D.C.

———. 1992d. "Structural adjustment and the Determinants of Poverty in Latin America." Paper prepared for Brookings conference, July, Washington, D.C.

————. 1994. *Poverty and Inequality in Latin America: Past Evidence, Future Prospects.* Washington, D.C.: Overseas Development Council.

Morley, Samuel A., and C. Alvarez. 1992a. "Poverty and Adjustment in Costa Rica." Working Paper 123. IADB, Washington, D.C.

————. 1992b. "Poverty and Adjustment in Venezuela." Working Paper 124. IADB, Washington, D.C.

————. 1992c. "Recession and the Growth of Poverty in Argentina." Working Paper 125. IADB, Washington, D.C.

Mujica, Patricio, and Osvaldo Larranaga. 1993. "Social Policies and Income Distribution in Chile." In Ricardo Hausmann and Roberto Rigobon, eds., *Government Spending and Income Distribution in Latin America.* Washington, D.C.: IADB.

Navarro, Juan Carlos. 1994. "Reforming Social Policy in Venezuela: Implementing Targeted Programs in the Context of a Traditional Pattern of Public Intervention." Paper prepared for visiting scholars program. IADB, Washington, D.C.

Newman, John, Steen Jorgenson, and M. Pradhan. 1991. "How Did Workers Benefit from Bolivia's Emergency Social Fund?" *World Bank Economic Review* 5:367–93.

Pães de Barros, Ricardo, Rosane Mendonca, Lauro Ramos, and Sonia Rocha. 1992. "Welfare, Inequality, Poverty, and Social Conditions in Brazil over the Last Three Decades." Paper prepared for a Brookings conference, July, Washington, D.C.

PAHO (Pan American Health Organization). 1992. *Fondos y Programas de Compensación Social: Experiencias en América Latina y el Caribe.* Washington, D.C.

Pardo, Lucia V., Felipe Balmaceda M., and Ignacio Ibarrazaval. 1993. "Pobreza, Crecimiento y Políticas Sociales." In *Comentarios sobre la Situación Económica 1992, Taller de Coyuntura.* Santiago: University of Chile.

Perry, Guillermo, and M. A. Arbelaez. 1990. "Comentarios." *Coyuntura Social* 2:25–33.

Pinera, Sebastían. 1979. *Medición, Análisis y Descripción de la Pobreza en Costa Rica.* Santiago: ECLAC.

Pollack, Molly. 1985. "Household Behavior and Economic Crisis: Costa Rica 1979–1982." Working Paper 270. Santiago: PREALC.

————. 1990. "Poverty and the Labour Market in Costa Rica." In Gerry Rogers, ed., *Poverty and the Labour Market: Access to Jobs and Incomes in Asian and Latin American Cities.* Geneva: International Labour Office.

PREALC (Programa Regional del Empleo para América Latina y el Caribe). 1987. "Pobreza y Mercado de Trabajo en Cuatro Países: Costa Rica, Venezuela, Chile y Perú." Santiago: PREALC, Working Paper 309. Santiago.

————. 1990a. *Colombia: La Deuda Social en los 80.* Geneva: International Labour Office.

————. 1990b. "Pobreza y empleo: un análisis del período 1986–1987 en el Gran Santiago." Working Paper 348. Santiago.

Programa Ruta Social. 1994. "Perfil de la Pobreza en Costa Rica, 1987–1993: Tendencias-Dimensiones-Estadisticas." San Jose: Mideplan.

Psacharopoulos, George, ed. 1991. *Essays on Poverty, Equity and Growth.* New York: Pergamon.

Psacharopoulos, George, Samuel Morley, Ariel Fiszbein, Haeduck Lee, and Bill Wood. 1993. *Poverty and Income Distribution in Latin America: The Story of the 1980s.* Human Resources Division Report 27. Washington, D.C.: World Bank.

Queisser, Monika, Osvaldo Larranga, and Monica Panadeiros. 1993. *Adjustment and Social Development in Latin America during the 1980s: Education, Health Care, and Social Security.* Munich: IFO Institute for Economic Research.

Raczynski, Dagmar van O. 1993. "Pobreza: Avances y Focalización." *CIEPLAN Perspectivas* (Dec):1–4.

Raczynski, Dagmar, and Pilar Romaguera. 1992. "Chile: Poverty Adjustment and Social Policies in the Eighties." Paper prepared for Brookings conference, July, Washington, D.C.

Ravallion, Martin. 1992. "Poverty Comparisons: A Guide to Concepts and Methods." LSMS Paper 88. World Bank, Washington, D.C.

———. 1993. "Growth, Inequality and Poverty." World Bank, Washington, D.C.

Ravallion, Martin, and M. Huppi. 1991. "Measuring Changes in Poverty: A Methodological Case Study of Indonesia during an Adjustment Period." *World Bank Economic Review* 5:57–84.

Sahota, Gian S. 1991. "A Review of Mexico's National Solidarity Program." Preliminary report to UNDP.

Sauma, Fait, and J. D. Trejos. 1990. "Evolución Reciente de la Distribución del Ingreso en Costa Rica: 1977–1986." Working Paper 132. IICE, San José.

Sedlacek, Guillerme L., and Ricardo Paes de Barros. 1989. *Mercado de Trabalho e Distribuição da Renda: Uma Coletânea.* Rio de Janeiro: IPEA.

Selowsky, Marcelo. 1979. "Balancing Trickle Down and Basic Needs Strategies: Income Distribution Issues in Large Middle-Income Countries with special Reference to Latin America." SWP 335. World Bank, Washington, D.C.

Sen, Amartya. 1976. "Poverty: An Ordinal Approach to Measurement." *Econometrica* 44:437–46.

Sjastaad, L. 1981. "La Protección y el Volumen del Comercio en Chile: La Evidencia." *Cuadernos de Economía* 54–55:263–92.

Squire, Lyn. 1991. "Introduction: Poverty and Adjustment in the 1980s." *World Bank Economic Review* 5:177–87.

Tanzi, Vito. 1978. "Inflation, Real Tax Revenue, and the Case for Inflationary Finance: Theory with an Application to Argentina." *IMF Staff Papers,* 25:417–451.

Tolosa, H. C. 1991. "Pobreza no Brasil: Uma Avaliação dos Anos 80." In J. P. dos Reis Velloso, ed., *A Questão Social no Brasil.* Sao Paulo: Nobel.

Trejos, Juan Diego. 1994. "Evolución reciente de la pobreza en Costa Rica, 1987–1992." University of Costa Rica.

UNESCO (UN Economic, Social and Cultural Organization). Various years. *Statistical Yearbook.*

UNDP (United Nations Development Program). 1993. *Human Development Report 1993.* New York: Oxford University Press.

UNICAMP. 1994. "Estrategias para Combatir la Pobreza en América Latina: Programas, Instituciones y Recursos." Paper prepared for Third Round, IADB, Red de Centros, Buenos Aires.

UNICEF. 1985. *State of the World's Children.* New York.

Urrutia, Miguel. 1985. *Winners and Losers in Colombia's Economic Growth of the 1970s.* New York: Oxford University Press.

Weisskoff, Richard. 1992. "Income Distribution and Economic Change in Paraguay, 1972–88." *Review of Income and Wealth* 38:165–83.

World Bank. Various years, *World Tables.* Washington, D.C.

———. 1988. *Costa Rica: Country Economic Memorandum.* Washington, D.C.

———. 1990a. "Venezuela Poverty Study: From Generalized Subsidies to Targeted Programs." Report 9114-VE. Washington, D.C.

———. 1990b. *World Development Report: Poverty.* Oxford: Oxford University Press.

———. 1991. *Guatemala: Country Economic Memorandum.* Report 9378-GU. Washington, D.C.

———. 1993a. *Implementing the World Bank's Strategy to Reduce Poverty: Progress and Challenges.* Washington, D.C.

———. 1993b. *Latin America and the Caribbean: A Decade after the Debt Crisis.* Washington, D.C.

Index

Library of Congress Cataloging-in-Publication Data

Morley, Samuel A.
  Poverty and inequality in Latin America : the impact of adjustment and recovery in the
1980s / Samuel A. Morley.
     p.   cm.
  Includes bibliographical references and index.
  ISBN 0-8018-5064-9 (alk. paper)
     1. Poverty—Latin America.   2. Equality—Latin America.   3. Latin America—
Economic conditions—1982–   4. Structural adjustment (Economic policy)—Latin
America.   I. Title.
HC130.P6M673   1995
339.4′6′098—dc20   95-19147   CIP

Morley, Samuel A.

Poverty and inequality in
Latin America